A Designer's Guide to
Adobe® InDesign® and XML

Harness the Power of XML
to Automate your Print and Web Workflows

James J. Maivald with Cathy Palmer

ADOBE
PRESS

Adobe

A Designer's Guide to Adobe InDesign and XML:
Harness the Power of XML to Automate your Print and Web Workflows
Jim Maivald with Cathy Palmer
Copyright © 2008 by Jim Maivald

This Adobe Press book is published by Peachpit

Peachpit
1249 Eighth Street
Berkeley, CA 94710
510/524-2178
510/524-2221 (fax)

For the latest on Adobe Press books, go to www.adobepress.com

To report errors, please send a note to errata@peachpit.com
Peachpit is a division of Pearson Education

Project Editor: Susan Rimerman
Production Editor: Connie Jeung-Mills
Developmental Editor: Corbin Collins
Tech Editor: Lynn Grillo
Compositor: WolfsonDesign
Indexer: Rebecca Plunkett
Interior & Cover Design: Mimi Heft

ISBN–13 978-0-321-50355-8
ISBN–10 0-321-50355-4

9 8 7 6 5 4 3 2 1

Printed and bound in the United States of America

Dedication

Jim dedicates this book to Christian and Maggie for their unlimited patience through all the days and weeks and months that dad was working on "his book." To Susan, who performed above and beyond the duties of a wife and mom, and to his friends and neighbors for all their support and encouragement.

Cathy dedicates this book to Doug Birkholz for his patience through the late nights of research and editing. Also to her dogs Satchel and Tanner who have been trained to bark at anyone caught using the spacebar instead of setting tabs.

Acknowledgments

This book has been a process of discovery, not only about the technology of XML and InDesign, but also of the creative community of artists, designers, publishers, and graphic production staff who do their best to output great work every day. We could never have learned as much about XML or completed this task without their assistance. So, we would like to thank Jori Curry of Ascend Training & Consulting who gave us our start down this road; David Blatner author and speaker extraordinaire from whom we've learned so much; Barry Anderson of MOGO Media who gave us our first XML forum; Jim Heffron of Farm Progress and Bob Hofner of MagnetStreet who gave us our first glimpse at what cool things XML could do; Katja DeHaney of Cramer-Krasselt Agency and Michael Lemberger who provided data and graphic ingredients for us to test; Joe Grossman and Ty Cooper from Jell Creative who provided needed help with CSS; Anne-Marie Concepción of Seneca Design for words of support and encouragement; Tom Petrillo, Adam Pratt, and Kiyomasa Toma from Adobe Systems who answered our endless questions about XML and InDesign at all hours; and of course our hard-working and ever-patient editorial and production team: Susan Rimerman, Corbin Collins, Lynn Grillo (Adobe), Connie Jeung-Mills, Owen Wolfson, and Mimi Heft. They caught all those pesky typos and made our words look so beautiful on paper. And special thanks to Pam Pfiffner at Peachpit Press for recognizing that we had something significant to say and fought hard to get this book in print. Thanks to all of you.

Contents

CHAPTER 2   **InDesign's XML Features**   **23**

CHAPTER 9   Exporting XML   **235**

CHAPTER 10   XML, HTML & CSS   **269**

CHAPTER 11   Ajax and XSLT   **281**

CHAPTER 12   What's up, DocBook (and Other DTDs)   **297**

Index   **311**

Know the Rules and Don't Break Them!   **324**

Introduction

We don't know why you picked up this book. You may have a deep abiding interest in all things XML. You may be intrigued by the mysterious three-letter combination and wonder what it means. Or you may just have ten minutes to kill before the bus arrives, and the "X" shelf in the bookstore is the one closest to the door. In any case, we've got your attention now.

If you're a programmer, this book may not be for you. But if you are a visual creative person, and long passages of code make your head spontaneously burst into flames, then this book *is* for you.

The two of us writing this book are *not* programmers. We are *not* coders. We are *designers*. Designers who, from time to time, have to dabble under the hood, get our hands dirty in the code, and mess with the gears and cogs that make the magic happen. That's why this is called *A Designer's Guide to Adobe InDesign and XML*—we wrote this book for people like us. We want to make XML easily accessible to the average designer, so you can tap into the power but don't have to go through the pain and anguish we did learning it in the first place. In fact, we firmly believe that anyone who can follow our step-by-step directions can achieve amazing results.

How would you like to create 1, 100, or 1,000 business cards or company IDs by simply pressing a button? How would you like to import text for a book, catalog, or brochure and have it instantly be formatted based on its structure or data type— for example, headings, body text, prices, product descriptions, and so on? Would you like to export all the stories from a daily newspaper or weekly magazine fully formatted for the Web with a single click of the mouse? Or import and manage hundreds or thousands of text or graphical elements with the import of a single file?

Do we have your attention yet? No? You need more? Maybe an example will help. Consider the following true story. This is Jim talking now.

I started on the path of discovering the power of XML in InDesign quite by accident one day when my office phone rang. On the line was a potential customer who needed a 52-page, 4/C product catalog designed in 10 days in InDesign CS. The product information was stored in a Microsoft Access database. Could I handle the project?

"Sure," I replied. I didn't have a clue. But the first rule of every freelance designer, of course, is: You always say yes.

The customer emailed me the database, messengered over the previous version of the catalog, and told me to get started. At that moment—as I sat studying their old design, wondering how I would ever finish a 52-page, 4/C catalog in less than 10 days—I had never heard of XML.

The first task was obvious: I needed to get the data out of Access and into InDesign. I think it humorous now that I wasn't very worried then about how all this would happen, especially since I knew going into it that InDesign could not import directly from Access.

At first I tried to use InDesign's Data Merge feature. One of my favorite Pagemaker tools, it had been brought over as an aftermarket plug-in. But no matter what I tried, each time I clicked the Data Merge button I ended up with 65,000 records! Considering that the database had only 200 products total, that was a problem. It took me three days to determine that Data Merge wasn't going to work.

As it turned out, the problem lay within the database itself. Whoever had created the file had broken one of the cardinal rules of database design: Somehow they had inserted hundreds of tabs, commas, and hard returns throughout the data. Data Merge was simply doing its job. As it merged the data into the layout, each time it encountered an errant tab, comma, or hard return it treated it as a new record and generated another page or text frame as necessary—64,800 times more than necessary. I needed to look elsewhere for a solution.

So I tried to solve the issue with a third-party plug-in. For prices ranging from $600 to $1,200, these products promised miracle solutions—instant documents with automatic formatting. I quickly realized that I had neither the budget nor the time to pursue this course. That's when I stumbled across XML while poking around in Access, desperately looking for an alternative, for some beacon of hope.

I knew only that XML was somehow related to HTML. When I searched for more information, there was almost nothing written about how XML worked in InDesign. Regardless, I plunged ahead. I read everything I could find: two white papers on the Adobe Web site and 51 pages split between two books—*Real World Adobe InDesign CS* (Peachpit Press) and *Adobe InDesign CS: One-on-One* (O'Reilly Media).

Somehow I managed to export XML from the database and import it into InDesign. It worked. While Data Merge had failed miserably with the poorly formatted data, XML and InDesign succeeded in a remarkable way. With a couple clicks of the mouse I had imported the entire catalog and completely formatted the text. Thus began my two-year love affair with InDesign's support of XML.

I looked for every scrap of information on XML and InDesign and spent endless hours testing various XML solutions. I suddenly became an expert in my community. People began to ask me more frequently about XML and InDesign. So I started to give seminars and participate in workshops and conferences. (That's how I met Cathy.) But the most important thing I discovered in those two years was how important it was for designers to learn XML from another designer, someone who held a common perspective, someone who could speak the same language.

This book is intended to guide you on your own personal journey of discovery of the powers of XML and InDesign. The following chapters are written with the sensibilities of the average *IN*designer in mind, using plain English and plenty of screen shots and illustrations. Each project teaches you how to use XML in real-world activities, often using actual projects that we have done ourselves. The projects and lessons are designed for CS3, but work just as well in CS2, with only minor exceptions as noted.

We advise you to refrain from skipping around through the book, no matter how tempting it may seem at first. We know some people like to sample a section of a book here and there and see what strikes their fancy (we confess). To get the most out of this book, though, it's important that you complete the projects in sequence. The reason is simple: We start off with the basics and then build on this foundation with each new lesson to bring you a rich understanding of how XML works with InDesign. Make sure to register your book and download all the support files you'll need for the projects at www.peachpit.com/indesignxmlguide.

Above all, we've tried to make the lessons as fun as they are informative. *We* read all the boring tomes on XML so you don't have to. This book won't teach you everything there is to know about XML, but just enough for you to exploit its full power right out of the box.

1

What Is XML?

If you want to use XML with InDesign, you really can't get around at least a basic discussion of what XML is and where it came from. We promised the book would not feature endless lines of code and such, and we make things here as fun and painless as possible—but yes, you will see a bit of code in this chapter.

XML Basics for Designers

XML stands for *eXtensible Markup Language*. A *markup language* is a technique for marking, or tagging, content—text, graphics, or other elements—with codes to identify it for some secondary purpose or application. The *tag* is a piece of text contained within left and right angle brackets (< >). The markup is completed by placing, or opening, a tag at the beginning of the content and then closing the tag at the end of it (**Figure 1.1**).

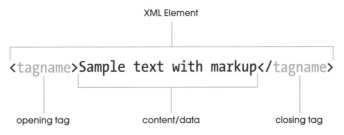

XML Element

`<tagname>Sample text with markup</tagname>`

opening tag   content/data   closing tag

Figure 1.1 Here is a sample XML element, dissected and diagrammed.

eXtensible means that the language is flexible and not restricted to a predetermined set of tags or commands. With XML, you can invent whatever tags you want to describe your own content (as long as they abide by the XML naming rules described here in this chapter).

HTML is an example of a *display* markup language. The purpose of HTML is to format text for display in a Web browser, to make the text pleasing to look at and easier to read. In contrast, XML is a *data* markup language, which means it is not concerned about the *look*, but about the *meaning* of the content (**Figure 1.2**).

XML is both a young and a mature language. It's *young* in the sense that it's been in existence only since 1998; it's *mature* in the sense that, in the computer industry, a decade is a veritable lifetime. Conceived as a Web-based meta language, XML has grown and spread through many different technologies, finding a home in an expanding array of industries, including publishing, science, health care, and manu-facturing, from government agencies to Fortune 500 companies. XML is the glue that binds these disparate entities together and makes a whole world of data-intensive applications possible. (Basically, a *meta language* is a set of rules, syntax, and context that can be used to define other languages.)

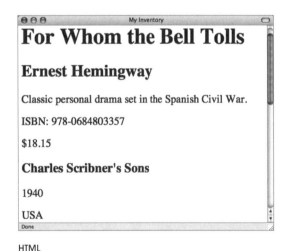
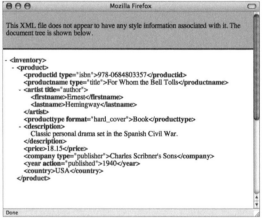

HTML   XML

Figure 1.2 Here's a side-by-side browser window comparison of the HTML and XML code displayed in Table 1.1. As you can see, XML is designed to identify the data, not to make it look good.

The concept of markup languages harks back to the 1960s, to IBM's invention of the Generalized Markup Language (GML). In those pre-PC days, powerful main-frame and mini-computers ruled the landscape. IBM, Univac, Burroughs, and others manufactured and supplied these multimillion-dollar behemoths to governments and corporations alike. Software was usually written or adapted specifically for each customer's unique needs and workflow. The concept of off-the-shelf hardware and software was still more than ten years off.

In those heady days, mainframe computers from competing companies rarely talked to each other, and data transfer was difficult if not impossible between these highly proprietary systems. In fact, incompatibility was often a corporate goal that forced customers into brand loyalty—a company that bought an IBM mainframe would be locked in as an IBM shop from top to bottom.

Eventually, market forces, as well as government regulation, pushed the computer manufacturers to develop methods for sharing and transferring data between disparate systems. GML was IBM's attempt at providing users a means for exchanging data without losing its structure. It was so successful that it germinated the Standard Generalized Markup Language (SGML), which became a standard method for sharing data that was adopted by the federal government and the computer industry.

In the early 1990s, Tim Berners-Lee, a research fellow at the CERN laboratory in Switzerland, created HTML, basing it on a subset of the SGML language. His goal was to provide a better means of accessing and exchanging information over the Internet. As HTML developed and started to gain popularity, some people could see that the language, while flexible, had great limitations when it came to identifying and structuring *data*. Basically designed to be a *display* language, HTML provides no means to handle data-intensive applications.

So a group of researchers began the development of an alternative language. By the end of 1996 the specifications of this language were taking shape, but it took more than a year for version 1.0 of XML to make its debut on February 10, 1998.

HTML vs. XML

As first cousins, HTML and XML have only a slight family resemblance. For example, HTML has built-in codes to format text and create simple structures (tables, layers, and so on) for screen display, but no means for identifying, or differentiating between, *text* and *data* elements. To HTML, text and data are the same thing.

On the other hand, XML is totally data-centric and has no built-in functionality for formatting text at all; in fact, graphical treatment has to be handled outside of XML altogether. XML has very few built-in commands. Instead, it provides a set of guidelines and syntax that allows users to create their own languages, for their own purposes—hence the word *extensible*. The tags and structure that *you* create in XML actually define the kind of information or data *you* want to store and manipulate.

Because most designers have at least some exposure to Web design, one way to learn about XML is to compare and contrast it to HTML. You can clearly see some of the differences in **Table 1.1**, in which two listings describe items in a store. One is a book, the other a video. The HTML markup below gives you few clues that would help you decipher which is which.

Table 1.1   *Comparing HTML to XML*

SAMPLE HTML CODE

```
<HTML>
<Head>
 <Title>My Inventory</Title>
</Head>
<Body>

  <h1>For Whom the Bell Tolls</h1>
  <h2>Ernest Hemingway</h2>
  <p>Classic personal drama set in the Spanish Civil War.
  <p>ISBN: 978-0684803357
  <p>$18.15
  <h3>Charles Scribner's Sons</h3>
  <p>1940
  <p>USA

  <h1>For Whom the Bell Tolls</h1>
  <h2>Ernest Hemingway</h2>
  <h2>Sam Wood</h2>
  <p>Film adaptation of the classic personal drama set in the Spanish Civil War.
  <p>ASIN: 6303560040
  <p>$14.98
  <h3>Universal Studios</h3>
  <p>1943
  <p>USA
</Body>
</HTML>
```

continues on next page

SAMPLE XML CODE

```xml
<?xml version="1.0" encoding="ISO-8859-1"?>
<inventory>
  <product>
    <productid type="isbn">978-0684803357</productid>
    <productname type="title">For Whom the Bell Tolls</productname>
    <artist title="author"><firstname>Ernest</firstname> <lastname>Hemingway</lastname></<artist>
    <description>Classic personal drama set in the Spanish Civil War.</description>
    <price>18.15</price>
    <producttype format="hard_cover">Book</producttype>

    <company type="publisher">Charles Scribner's Sons</company>
    <year action="published">1940</year>
    <country>USA</country>
  </product>


  <product>
    <productid type="sku">6303560040</productid>
    <productname type="title">For Whom the Bell Tolls</productname>
    <artist title="author"><firstname>Ernest</firstname> <lastname>Hemingway</lastname></<artist>
    <artist title="director"><firstname>Sam</firstname> <lastname>Wood</lastname></artist>
    <producttype format="VHS">Movie</producttype>
    <description>Film adaptation of the classic personal drama set in the Spanish Civil
War.</description>
    <price>14.98</price>
    <company type="studio">Universal Studios</company>
    <year action="released">1943</year>
    <country>USA</country>
  </product>
</inventory>
```

As a human being with some basic experience in the real world, you probably know that *ISBN* refers to a book number and *Universal Studios* refers to a movie company. But can you tell whether the book is a hardcover or paperback, or the movie VHS or DVD? Your guess is as good as ours. There's plainly not enough data to be certain, and that's the dilemma with HTML. Although the code, as you see it, is perfectly valid and may look good in the browser, you can see how it takes *human* experience and intuition to make any sense out of it, and that means it's practically useless to machine-based applications. By comparing HTML and XML side by side you can see how they differ. Although the information is identical in both examples, it's difficult for even a human to tell that the two HTML listings for *For Whom the Bell Tolls* refer to a book and a VHS tape. In the XML sample, the tags and the attributes make the distinctions obvious.

On the other hand, by using a combination of tags and attributes, the sample XML code on the right-hand side of **Table 1.1** provides a wealth of information that spells out clearly what you're looking at—take the elements `<producttype format="hard_cover">Book</producttype>` and `<producttype format="VHS">Movie</producttype>`, for example. Notice how they each have a distinct attribute called **format** that specifies what kind of product it actually is. Well-designed XML content leaves nothing to chance and has no room for guesswork.

The simplest way to explain the difference between the two languages is that HTML tags refer to *how* the text should be displayed, whereas XML tags refer to *what* is being displayed. An XML file is like a plain-text database.

Terms and Definitions

As a graphic designer, you're probably a visual communicator. We understand that you're not a code freak and are probably not a fan of acronyms, initials, or abbreviations, either. However, it's important to learn a few key terms and phrases central to the language of XML so that you can understand the markup as well as communicate intelligently with IT personnel, Web developers, database managers, and even other designers working with XML. The following is a very basic list of essential XML terms to learn and understand (arranged alphabetically, except for the first one, Element, which is so important it must come first).

Element

Elements are the basic building blocks of XML. They are the tags with which you create the structure of an XML file. You can name an element anything you like as long as it conforms to the rules described later in this chapter. Elements can be empty or can consist of single or multiple pieces of data, or other elements. Note how each element, to be properly constructed, consists of both an opening and a closing tag. The closing tag uses the same text as in the opening, only with a slash inserted just inside the less than character, such as: `</tag>`.

Examples of properly formed XML elements that could be used to describe the contents of a book:

```
<book>
  <title>Paul Clifford</title>
  <byline type="author">Edward Bulwer-Lytton</byline>
  <toc>
    <toc_entry page="10">Chapter 1</toc_entry>
  </toc>
```

```
<chapter number="1">
    <para>It was a dark and stormy night...</para>
</chapter>
</book>
```

Attribute

Attributes provide values that help describe, or modify, tagged data. For example, an XML-based card catalog at a library can store the names of artists and keep track of whether the person is an author, composer, or director. Attributes must follow XML naming rules, but the value can be almost anything you want it to be. Values must be contained within single [' '] or double [" "] quotes.

Sample attributes:

```
<artist title="author">Ernest Hemingway</artist>
<artist title="composer">Ludwig van Beethoven</composer>
<artist title="director">Alfred Hitchcock</artist>
```

CDATA

CDATA means *character data*. It is text or part of an element that is parsed (interpreter, covered later in this list) as plain, or literal, text. For example, the characters "&", "<", " >" and ";" are also part of the XML markup. By declaring an element as CDATA you are telling the parser to *display* them and not treat them as markup.

Child Element

A *child element* is an element contained, or nested, within another element. In XML, elements can be empty, contain data, or contain one or more other elements or groups of elements. There's really no limit except your imagination and the needs of your application.

Sample child elements:

```
<root>
        <title>Breakfast of Champions</title>
</root>
<author><firstname>Kurt</firstname><lastname>Vonnegut</lastname></author>
```

DTD

DTD stands for *Document Type Definition*. A DTD is a separate file or inline element that declares what elements, entities, and attributes can legally appear in a specific XML file. A DTD can be used to validate the structure of the XML, and an XML file that conforms to the DTD is considered *valid*. DTDs were originally developed for SGML and then adapted to the XML language. A newer method for describing

XML structure is the XML schema language (coming up later in this list). DTDs are favored for *text*-intensive applications, whereas schemas are better for *data*-intensive ones. Because InDesign only supports DTDs, we cover them in more detail at the end of the chapter.

Sample DTD (partial):

```
<!ELEMENT employees (Efirstname, Elastname, Etitle, Ephone, Eemail)+>
    <!ELEMENT Efirstname (#PCDATA)>
    <!ELEMENT Elastname (#PCDATA)>
    <!ELEMENT Etitle (#PCDATA)>
    <!ELEMENT Ephone (#PCDATA)>
    <!ELEMENT Eemail (#PCDATA)>
```

Entity

Like a stand-in on a movie set, an *entity* temporarily holds the place of another piece of data that's dropped in when the XML is displayed in a browser, imported into InDesign, or otherwise parsed. One of the coolest tricks of XML, you can use entities to insert names, special typesetting characters or symbols, or long passages of text and data stored in separate files. Some entities are standard (those for bullets and special type characters) and can be used without restriction; all others first must be defined within a DTD or schema.

Entities were developed because the plain-text files in which XML is stored didn't support font formatting and some special characters. **Table 1.2** contains a handful of the standard entities. User-defined entities must be specifically declared in a DTD or schema.

Table 1.2 *Sample Standard Entities*

DESCRIPTION	TYPE THIS	GET THIS
Ampersand	&amp;	&
Bullet	&#x2022;	•
Copyright	&#xA9;	©
Registered Trademark	&#xAE;	®
Trademark	&#x2122;	™
Greater than	&gt;	>
Less than	&lt;	<

HTML

HTML is short for *Hypertext Markup Language.* HTML is the basic language of the Web. Derived from SGML, HTML favors design and display over content.

Parent Element

A *parent element* is any element that contains other elements. For example, all XML files have at least one parent element represented by the root element itself.

Sample parent elements:

```
<root>
        <title>Breakfast of Champions</title>
</root>
<author><firstname>Kurt</firstname><lastname>Vonnegut</lastname></author>
```

Parser

Also sometimes called an *interpreter,* a *parser* is a program, or portion of a program, that can interpret XML markup to produce a defined result. Some programs, such as Web browsers, have limited parsing capabilities and are mainly geared to *displaying* text or data. Other applications, such as Adobe FrameMaker and InDesign CS3, have more robust interpreters that can generate wholly new XML, text, and even PDF files from XML markup.

Parsing

The act of interpreting raw markup, or code, to produce a defined result. In plain English, if the code tells the browser to draw a circle, the browser draws a circle.

PCDATA

PCDATA stands for *Parsed Character Data.* PCDATA refers to raw text contained within elements and/or entities that appear between opening and closing tags within an XML file that is interpreted to produce a defined result. The resulting text that appears on the page or in the browser is PCDATA.

Schema

Developed in 2001, *schemas* are similar to DTDs (covered earlier in this list) in that they declare what elements, attributes, and structure may permissibly appear in an XML file. An XML file that conforms to the schema is considered *valid.* Schemas are favored for *data*-intensive XML applications; DTDs work better for *text*-intensive ones. Schemas are typically saved with the extension .XSD (XML Schema Definition).

Sample schema (partial):

```
<xsd:element name="dataroot">
  <xsd:complexType>
    <xsd:sequence>
        <xsd:element ref="employees" minOccurs="0" maxOccurs="unbounded"/>
    </xsd:sequence>
   <xsd:attribute name="generated" type="xsd:dateTime"/>
  </xsd:complexType>
</xsd:element>
```

SGML

SGML stands for *Standard Generalized Markup Language.* The mother of all markup languages, it was developed during the 1970s and '80s as a standard to facilitate the transfer of structured data between dissimilar computer systems.

Valid XML

Valid XML refers to XML data that conforms to the structure as defined by a DTD or schema.

Well-Formed XML

Well-formed XML is XML data that conforms to the basic rules of XML construction as described later in this chapter.

XHTML

XHTML is short for *eXtensible Hypertext Markup Language*, a combination of HTML and XML that provides the user with the formatting capabilities of HTML and the extensibility of XML in one language. XHTML is an attempt to merge content *and* design. XHTML is supported by most popular Web browsers.

XML

As you know, this stands for *eXtensible Markup Language*, a markup language derived from SGML that stresses content over design.

XSD

XSD stands for *XML Schema Definition* (see Schema, earlier in this list).

XSL

Means *eXtensible Stylesheet Language*. This is a language used to style XML data for display in Web browsers.

XSLT

This is short for *eXtensible Stylesheet Language Transformation*. XSLT is a method that combines the use of a style sheet (XSL) and a processing application (a parser) that can *transform* a source XML file into a wholly different document, file format or structure, such as HTML, XHTML, plain text or even a PDF. The use of XSLTs within InDesign CS3 is covered in **Chapter 11**.

XML Rules

HTML is a forgiving language. It tolerates a host of sins, from imprecise markup to altogether missing elements, and can still generate a Web page in the browser. XML, on the other hand, is basically a tyrant. Violate even the most trivial rule, and the browser or your application will crash. Some find comfort in the uncompromising nature of XML because it won't work unless you build it correctly! It's great to get instant feedback when you do something wrong.

Nine Rules for Creating Good XML

Keep this list in a handy spot:

1 All XML must have a root element.

2 All tags must be closed.

3 All tags must be properly nested.

4 A tag name can't start with "xml", a number, or punctuation, except for "_".

5 Tag names are case sensitive.

6 Tag names cannot contain spaces.

7 Attributes must appear within quotes (" ")

8 White space is preserved.

9 HTML tags should be avoided (optional).

There are nine basic rules for building good XML. XML that follows these rules is called *well formed*. Don't confuse *well-formed XML* with *valid* XML, which we discussed earlier in the chapter.

1: All XML Must Have a Root Element

A root element is simply a set of tags that contains your XML content.

```
<root>

        <author>Ernest Hemingway</author>
        <author>John Steinbeck</author>
        <author>James Joyce</author>

</root>
```

NOTE   *It doesn't have to be called* root.

2: All Tags Must Be Closed

When a tag is *declared*, or opened, it must also be closed. Any unclosed tags will break the code. Even tags that do not need to be closed in HTML must be closed in XML or XHTML. To open a tag, type the name of the element between less than "<" and greater than ">" characters, such as: <author>. To close a tag, repeat the opening tag exactly but insert a slash in front of the tag name, such as: </author> Even empty tags, such as **<hr>** and **
,** must be closed.

Right:

```
<author>Ernest Hemingway</author>
<p>Roses are Red</p>
<hr></>
<hr />
```

Wrong:

```
<author>Ernest Hemingway
<p>Roses are Red
<hr>
```

3: All Tags Must Be Properly Nested

When you insert, or nest, one tag within another, pay attention to the order in which you open each tag, and then close them in the reverse order. If you open element A and then element B, you must first close B before closing A. Even HTML tags that usually will work without a strict structure must follow the stricter XML rules when they are used within an XML file.

Right:

```
<A><B>Text</B></A>
<b><i>Text</i></b>
```

Wrong:

```
<A><B>Text</A></B>
<b><i>Text</b></i>
```

4: Tag Names Can't Start with "xml," Numbers, or Punctuation, Except for "_"

The group of letters *XML* is used in various commands and can't start your tag name. Numbers and punctuation are also not allowed in the beginning of the tag name.

Right:

```
<author>
<_author>
```

Wrong:

```
<01_author>
<"author">
```

5: Tag Names are Case Sensitive

Uppercase and lowercase matter in XML. Opening and closing tags must match exactly: For example, <ROOT>, <Root>, and <root> are three different tags.

Right:

```
<author>Hemingway</author>
<AUTHOR>Hemingway</AUTHOR>
```

Wrong:

```
<author>Hemingway</AUTHOR>
<Author>Hemingway</aUTHOR>
```

Note   Although XML doesn't care whether your tag names and other structural elements are uppercase or lowercase, some applications that use XML do care. A good rule of thumb is to check the naming conventions used by the intended application before you begin a project, or to use all lowercase as the safest and most universally acceptible format.

6: Tag Names Cannot Contain Spaces

Spaces in tag names can cause all sorts of problems with data-intensive applications, so they are prohibited in XML.

7: Attribute Values Must Appear within Quotes

Attribute values modify a tag or help identify the type of information being tagged. If you are a Web designer, you may be used to the flexibility in HTML, where some attributes don't require quotes. In XML, all attribute values must appear within quotes.

Example:

```
<chapter number="1">
<artist title="author" nationality="USA">
```

8: White Space Is Preserved

If you're in the habit of adding extra spaces and hard returns in your HTML code, watch out! Such spacing is honored by XML and can play havoc with your applications. Use extra spacing judiciously.

9: Avoid HTML Tags (Optional)

Because you can name tags anything you want, you could use tags reserved for HTML markup, such as `<h1>`, `<p>`, `<li>`, and so on. Although permissible in XML, avoid using such tag names unless you wish the data formatted thusly when it's viewed in a browser window. (We experiment with this concept in **Chapters 9** and **10**.)

The ABCs of DTDs

Before we leave the topic of what XML is, we need to describe the role of DTDs in an XML workflow. The reason is simple: DTD support is built into InDesign.

However, one point must be made clear up front: A DTD is *not* a requirement in an XML workflow inside, or outside, of InDesign. In fact, there's no real advantage in using a DTD in small or custom one-off projects. On the other hand, in large or complex projects a well-written DTD can be a life (job) saver. Here are at least two reasons for taking a closer look at DTDs:

- DTDs help you conform to internal or external standards.

- DTDs help you validate and maintain proper structure as you work.

Remember, the main purpose of XML in the first place is to facilitate the use and exchange of information. To do this, your XML structure must be compatible with whomever you are exchanging data. Because very few constraints are placed on how an XML structure can be designed and built, how can two people working independently achieve compatibility? It can come down to the most mundane topics such as what tag names are used, what order the elements are in, and what type of data is captured.

These are the questions a good DTD can answer. It provides the guidelines, or blueprint, for constructing compatible XML structures. Then it helps you maintain the structure and data integrity over time. It may help to think of a DTD as a meticulous proofreader who never tires, never needs a break, never takes a vacation and, most importantly, never misses even the smallest mistake!

The ability to scan and interpret the structure specified in a DTD is an invaluable asset in an XML workflow. Don't worry, it's a lot easier than it sounds.

Target XML Structure

A properly constructed DTD will define the structure of an XML file and prevent a whole host of errors, unintentional or otherwise. Below is the target XML structure that needs to be defined. The XML describes two product listings: a book and a movie version of *For Whom the Bell Tolls.*

The following code in **Table 1.3** breaks down the XML elements and structure in plain English. The XML in the table describes product data from a book/video store. The structure needs to be flexible enough to accommodate a variety of items—including books, DVDs, CDs, and other products.

Table 1.3 XML in Plain English

RAW XML	DESCRIPTION
`<inventory>`	The `<inventory>` tag encloses the entire XML content, making it the root element. It is the parent of all other elements.

`<product>`
`  <productid type="isbn">978-0684803357</productid>`
`  <productname type="title">For Whom the Bell Tolls`
`    </productname>`
`  <artist title="author">`
`   <firstname>Ernest</firstname>`
`   <lastname>Hemingway</lastname>`
`  </artist>`
`  <producttype format="hard_cover">Book</producttype>`
`  <description>Classic personal drama set in the Spanish`
`    Civil War.</description>`
`  <price>18.15</price>`
`  <company type="publisher">Charles Scribner's Sons`
`    </publisher>`
`  <year action="published">1940</year>`
`  <country>USA</country>`
`</product>`
	The `<product>` tag is the first *child* element within the root. It is also a parent element, enclosing 11 other elements but no *untagged* data. In other words, `<product>` consists only of other elements.
	
	The `<artist>` tag is the only child element of the `<product>` tag that contains other elements. The remaining elements consist of text or numeric data.
	
	Note how the element `<producttype>` and several others contain *extra* information within the tag name. Such additions of information to a tag are called *attributes*. As described earlier in the chapter, attributes provide further information to help describe or clarify an element or its contents.

continues on next page

Table 1.3 XML in Plain English *(continued)*

RAW XML	DESCRIPTION

```<product>```
 `<productid type="sku">6303560040</productid>`
 `<productname type="title">For Whom the Bell Tolls</productname>`
 `<artist title="author">`
 `<firstname>Ernest</firstname>`
 `<lastname>Hemingway</lastname>`
 `</artist>`
 `<artist title="director">`
 `<firstname>Sam</firstname>`
 `<lastname>Wood</lastname>`
 `</artist>`
 `<producttype format="VHS">Movie</producttype>`
 `<description>Film adaptation of the classic personal drama set in the Spanish Civil War.</description>`
 `<price>14.98</price>`
 `<company type="studio">Universal Studios</publisher>`
 `<year action="released">1943</year>`
 `<country>USA</country>`
 `</product>`
 `</inventory>`
	The second `<product>` element follows the first, duplicating almost exactly its order and structure. Other than the expected differences in the data, the second element differs from the first in that it contains *two* `<artist>` elements. Is that legal?
	
	 Sure. The order and number of individual elements within a file is not a problem for XML—remember, the language is *extensible*. As long as you conform to XML rules—as described earlier in this chapter—you can name and assemble the pieces any way you like.
	
	 Specifying the number and/or arrangement of elements within any particular data structure is where the DTD comes in.

DTD Grammar

DTDs have a grammar and syntax all their own. Because they descended directly from SGML, the DTD language predates XML and doesn't follow the same rules. The DTD language consists of order indicators, qualifiers, data and content types, and attribute types. The keys given in this section can be helpful in deciphering the XML structure as defined by the DTD. In the next section, we show you how to use these items to define the XML structure in **Table 1.3**.

DTD Order Indicators and Qualifiers Key

The following punctuation marks are used within the DTD to define or modify the target XML structure:

( ) Groups elements together or indicates a child element.

| Indicates a choice among two or more elements.

, Indicates that elements must occur exactly in the order specified.

* Indicates that an element may occur zero or multiple times.

? Indicates an optional element that may occur once or not at all.

+ Indicates a required element that must occur one or multiple times.

Data Content Types Key

XML elements can contain several different types of data. By declaring what type of data is allowable, or legal, within an element, it enables the DTD to flag items that don't belong. In other words, the DTD is acting like a bouncer at an exclusive night-club: If your name's not on the list, you don't get in.

Here are the four possible data types:

- ANY: A catchall term, meaning literally that the element can contain any *type* of data. Use this data type sparingly, if at all. Because the purpose of the DTD is to define the *type* of elements and data that can legally be used, what's the point in using a term that's so vague?

- EMPTY: The element contains no data, such as `<!ELEMENT br EMPTY>`, which is the code for a line break in HTML. Okay, you are probably wondering: Why declare an element that's *empty*? Empty simply refers to the fact that the element doesn't contain text or other character data. Empty elements are used to define images, document structure (such as horizontal rules), and contain attributes.

- (*Element?*): Elements can contain one or more other elements. Put the desired element name, or names, within parentheses ( ), as in `<!ELEMENT product (productid, productname, artist+, producttype, description, price, company, year, country)>`. Multiple element names can be separated either by commas [,] or pipes [|]. Comma separation [,] indicates that each element is required and must follow the exact order specified within the DTD, whereas the pipe [|] is used to indicate that you must choose among the listed items.

- (#PCDATA): Parsed Character Data. In other words, the elements contain text or parsible entities.

Attribute Types Key

Attributes modify elements to provide additional information, the same way adjectives modify nouns. In this section is a complete list of the 11 different attributes available in XML. However, most InDesign users will ever only encounter a fraction of these attribute types. In the next section, we take a closer look at the ones most commonly used.

CDATA	Value is any character data.
(A? | B? | C? |...)	Value is from a list of given values.
ENTITY	Value is an unparsed entity.
ENTITIES	Value is a list of unparsed entities.
ID	Value is a unique ID.
IDREF	Value is the id of another element.
IDREFS	Value is a list of other IDs.
NMTOKEN	Value is a valid XML name.
NMTOKENS	Value is a list of valid XML names.
NOTATION	Value is a name of a notation declared in the DTD.
xml:attribute?	Value is a predefined, or reserved, XML value, such as xml:lang or xml:space.

Reading DTD

As a designer you may never have to write your own DTD (which is okay, because you probably have that code phobia we've been talking about). But if you're going to work with XML, you absolutely need to know how to read DTDs and be able to decipher what they say.

Table 1.4 is a DTD that describes our target XML from **Table 1.3**. It shows one possible way to define the target XML using a DTD. We dissect it for you line by line to give you some valuable insight into how the validating structure is defined by a DTD. The DTD can be contained within the XML file itself—this is referred to as *inline*. Or you can save it in an external file using the extension .DTD—this is referred to as *linked*. We cover the use of DTDs in InDesign in **Chapter 12**.

Sample DTD

The following is one possible way a DTD could define the structure of the XML in **Table 1.3**. This code can be inserted as an inline element in the XML itself or simply referenced as an external DTD file.

```
<!ELEMENT inventory (product)*>
<!ELEMENT product (productid, productname, artist+, producttype, description,
    price, company, year, country)>
<!ELEMENT productid (#PCDATA)>
<!ELEMENT productname (#PCDATA)>
<!ELEMENT firstname (#PCDATA)>
<!ELEMENT lastname (#PCDATA)>
<!ELEMENT producttype (#PCDATA)>
<!ELEMENT description (#PCDATA)>
<!ELEMENT price (#PCDATA)>
<!ELEMENT company (#PCDATA)>
<!ELEMENT year (#PCDATA)>
<!ELEMENT country (#PCDATA)>
<!ELEMENT artist (firstname?, lastname?)>
<!ATTLIST productid type (isbn | sku) #REQUIRED>
<!ATTLIST productname type CDATA "title">
<!ATTLIST artist title (author | director | singer | performer) #REQUIRED>
<!ATTLIST producttype format (hard_cover | paperback | CD | DVD | VHS)
    #REQUIRED>
<!ATTLIST company type (publisher | studio | label) #IMPLIED>
<!ATTLIST year action (published | released) #REQUIRED>
```

Table 1.4 *DTD in Plain English*

DTD BASED ON THE XML IN TABLE 1.3	DESCRIPTION
`<!ELEMENT inventory (product)*>`	This line declares the root element `<inventory>` and specifies that it contains only the child element `<product>`. The `*` indicates that the root can contain zero or more products—which means the root can be empty. While the other element definitions can occur in any order within a DTD, the root must be the first element declared. Note how the word `ELEMENT` is typed in all caps preceded by an exclamation (`!`) point.
`<!ELEMENT product (productid, productname, artist+, producttype, description, price, company, year, country)>`	This line defines the `<product>` element. Like the root, `<product>` consists only of child elements. There are 11 total child elements each separated by commas. Commas specify that each child is required and must appear in the order indicated. The `+` after `<artist>` allows `<product>` to contain one or more artists. If even one child is missing or out of order, the DTD will invalidate the XML code.

continues on next page

Table 1.4 *DTD in Plain English (continued)*

DTD BASED ON THE XML IN TABLE 1.3	DESCRIPTION

`<!ELEMENT productid (#PCDATA)>`
`<!ELEMENT productname (#PCDATA)>`
`<!ELEMENT firstname (#PCDATA)>`
`<!ELEMENT lastname (#PCDATA)>`
`<!ELEMENT producttype (#PCDATA)>`
`<!ELEMENT description (#PCDATA)>`
`<!ELEMENT price (#PCDATA)>`
`<!ELEMENT company (#PCDATA)>`
`<!ELEMENT year (#PCDATA)>`
`<!ELEMENT country (#PCDATA)>`
	If an element is used within the XML, it must be declared, or defined, in the DTD. Elements can be empty, contain text, other elements, or combinations of all the above. If its content is plain text or parsible entities, the data type is declared as #PCDATA.

`<!ELEMENT artist (firstname?, lastname?)>`	Here <artist> is defined as containing both child elements <firstname> and <lastname>. Since some artists may not use a first name and a last name (such as Madonna, Michelangelo, Plato, and others), the ? allows either element to be missing but not break the structure.
`<!ATTLIST productid type (isbn | sku) #REQUIRED>`	Attributes modify, or help describe, the content of XML elements. This attribute indicates that <productid> must contain either ISBN or SKU data.
`<!ATTLIST productname type CDATA "title">`	This line defines "title" as the *default* attribute for <productname>. If you don't add a value of your own, "title" is assigned automatically.
`<!ATTLIST artist title (author | director | singer | performer) #REQUIRED>`	Here the pipes indicate that the attribute for <artist> must be selected from the choices of author, director, singer, or performer.
`<!ATTLIST producttype format (hard_ cover | paperback | CD | DVD | VHS) #REQUIRED>`	Here the attribute value must be selected from the choices of: hard_cover, paperback, CD, DVD, or VHS.
`<!ATTLIST company type (publisher | studio | label) #IMPLIED>`	The data type #IMPLIED indicates that the attribute for <company> is a choice between, publisher, studio, or label, but is *not* required.
`<!ATTLIST year action (published | released) #REQUIRED>`	The attribute for <year> must be selected from the choices: published or released.

Congratulations, you've survived a quick lesson in reading DTD code. If you've made it this far without falling asleep or bursting into flames, you have a good foundation toward understanding XML and how it's constructed. Although it's a good start, there's plenty more to learn about this powerful language that can't be covered completely between the covers of this book.

Where to Get More Information

In **Table 1.5** we list some books that we recommend for further study of XML. We have all of them on our own bookshelves. Check them all out at your local library or bookstore. You should be able to tell in a few pages whether the book connects to you and your sensibilities. Just don't expect any one book to answer all your questions or teach you *everything* you want or need to know about XML.

Table 1.5 *Books for Further Study of XML*

TITLE	AUTHOR(S)	PUBLISHER	ISBN	COVER PRICE
DocBook XML Publishing	Joe Brockmeier & Kara Pritchard	Prima Tech	0761533311	$39.99
Learn XML In a Weekend	Erik Westermann	Premier Press	159200010X	$24.99
XML for the World Wide Web: Visual QuickStart Guide	Elizabeth Castro	Peachpit Press	0201710986	$19.99
No Nonsense XML Web Development With PHP	Thomas Myer	Sitepoint	097524020X	$39.99
XML, HTML, XHTML Magic	Molly Holzschlag	New Riders	0735711399	$34.99
XML: A Beginner's Guide	Dave Mercer	Osbourne	0072127406	$29.99
XML: A Primer	Simon St. Laurent	Hungry Minds	0764547771	$19.99
XML Pocket Consultant	William Stanek	Microsoft Press	0735611831	$29.99

2

InDesign's XML Features

In this chapter we take you on a whirlwind tour of InDesign's XML features, menus, panels, and commands. Having all this information in one place is handy for you any time you need to jog your memory concerning any of these items. It also reduces the need for repetitive instructions throughout the book. Remember, this is just a surface look at these features; we cover them all in depth in later chapters.

InDesign has a clean, straightforward implementation of XML that encompasses several aspects of the interface from the Layout view and Structure pane, to the Story Editor and InCopy. Believe it or not, the program has provided some support for XML all the way back to version 2—but it's so well hidden that you may never stumble across the features unless you're specifically looking for them. Let's take a closer look.

Layout View

We're going to start off where most designers work, in Layout view. We check out the XML features in the Story Editor and InCopy later in this chapter.

Importing XML

InDesign's XML import interface is your first stop in an XML workflow, but before anything can be imported you have to have an open document. Download the sample files for Chapter 2 from the book's support site: www.peachpit.com/indesignxmlguide/. Open the file **xml_interface_1.indt** (**Figure 2.1**).

Figures 2.2 and **2.3** show how to import XML.

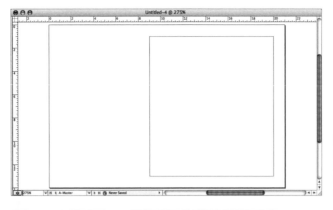

Figure 2.1
xml_interface_1.indt
is a typical InDesign
document with no XML
structure whatsoever.

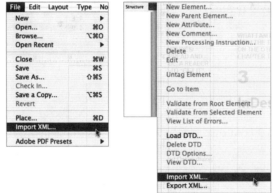

Figure 2.2 You can import XML
from the File menu or from the
Structure pane menu.

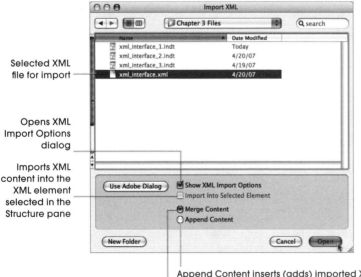

Selected XML
file for import

Opens XML
Import Options
dialog

Imports XML
content into the
XML element
selected in the
Structure pane

Figure 2.3 Select the target XML file.
Select Show XML Import Options
checkbox. Choose Merge Content
or Append Content.

Append Content inserts (adds) imported XML content into the existing file

Merge Content replaces all existing XML content in your layout

The XML Import Options dialog (**Figure 2.4**) is responsible for most of the XML magic. Take a minute to familiarize yourself with the possible settings (**Table 2.1**). We demonstrate what they do in detail in upcoming chapters.

For the purposes of this lesson, leave all checkboxes unchecked and click OK.

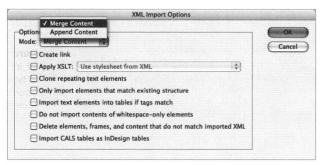

Figure 2.4 The XML Import Options dialog usually starts the ball rolling. In this dialog you specify how you want to import the XML content. If no checkboxes are selected, the entire XML file imports into the Structure pane.

Table 2.1 XML Import Options

OPTION	DESCRIPTION
Merge Content	Replaces all existing XML content in your layout.
Append Content	Inserts (adds) imported XML content into the existing file.
Create Link	Creates a live link to the XML file stored on your hard drive. When the XML is changed, the Links panel indicates the file is out of date.
Apply XSLT	Uses an XSLT to manipulate the XML during import (InDesign CS3 only). XSLTs can be used to sort or filter the XML, or completely transform it into another data structure.
Clone repeating text elements	Automatically replicates tagged and untagged text and inline objects within your workflow. Use this option to create repetitive layouts, such as phone directories, price lists, business cards, catalogs, and so on.
Only import elements that match existing structure	Filters incoming XML elements against the existing document structure, preventing elements not already represented in the structure from entering the layout.
Import text elements into tables if tags match	Filters incoming XML elements against the existing structure of a table, placing them into table cells that are similarly tagged.
Do not import contents of whitespace-only elements	Causes InDesign to ignore white space (extra spaces, hard returns, and so on) stored within the XML file between the tagged elements. Instead, InDesign uses the spacing and alignments as depicted in your structured layout.

continues on next page

Table 2.1 XML Import Options (continued)

OPTION	DESCRIPTION
Delete elements, frames, and content that do not match imported XML	Deletes tagged page elements when the imported XML does not contain a similarly tagged item. This option prevents the inclusion of empty text and picture frames in your final layout.
Import CALS tables as InDesign tables (InDesign CS3 only)	CALS stands for Continuous Acquisition and Lifecycle Support, an initiative by the Department of Defense for the specification of standards for electronic documents. Technically speaking, XML can't create objects, like tables. The CALS specifications were created so that the inclusion of tabular information could be compatible with the data-centric nature of XML. Choose this option to convert CALS-based tables into InDesign-supported tables.

When an XML file is imported into InDesign it does not automatically appear in your layout the way regular text and graphics do. Instead, InDesign loads it into an interface called the Structure pane and then populates the Tags panel with the names of the available elements.

The key word here is *structure*. Mention the word "structure" in a crowded room and you can instantly tell who works with XML because their eyes light up. Structure is at the heart of the technology. XML is all about *how* the pieces are put together. The Structure pane and the Tags panel work hand in hand to reveal the *how*. The Structure pane gives you the big picture—the view from 20,000 feet. The Tags panel brings you up close and personal.

Can we use any more clichés? Okay, two more: The Structure pane is the yin balancing the Tags panel's yang. They are the one-two punch of InDesign's XML interface. Let's take a closer look at each one.

Structure Pane Close-up

Although it's pretty well hidden, we've heard many humorous tales from perplexed designers who revealed the Structure pane *accidentally* and thought that they had broken the program.

The Structure pane (**Figure 2.5**) is available only in Layout view. There are four ways to reveal (on *purpose*) the Structure pane. You can:

A. Select View > Structure > Show Structure.

B. Click anywhere on the left border of the Layout view window.

C. Click the Show Structure button at the lower-left edge of the Layout view window.

D. Press Option-Cmd-1 (Ctrl-Alt-1).

Showing Text Snippets, Attributes, Comments, and Processing Instructions

When the XML content first appears in the Structure pane, it's hard to make heads or tails of the icon display. So InDesign provides snippets of text to help you identify the contents of each element.

Figure 2.6 shows you how to turn on Text Snippets.

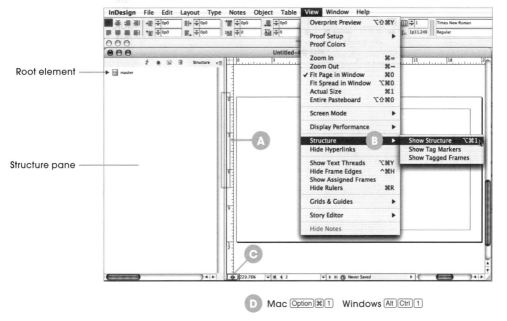

Root element

Structure pane

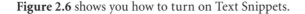

Mac Option ⌘ 1   Windows Alt Ctrl 1

Figure 2.5 The Structure pane opens automatically when you import the XML file. InDesign gives you four more methods to open the pane.

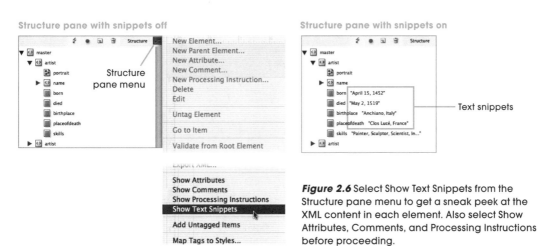

Structure pane with snippets off

Structure pane menu

Structure pane with snippets on

Text snippets

Figure 2.6 Select Show Text Snippets from the Structure pane menu to get a sneak peek at the XML content in each element. Also select Show Attributes, Comments, and Processing Instructions before proceeding.

Expanding the Structure

By default, the XML structure schematic starts off fully closed. It may be empty or contain one or multiple elements, attributes, and/or comments. To reveal, or expand, the structure, click on the triangle in front of each element, as shown in **Figures 2.7** through **2.9**. To expand an entire parent element at once, see **Figure 2.10**.

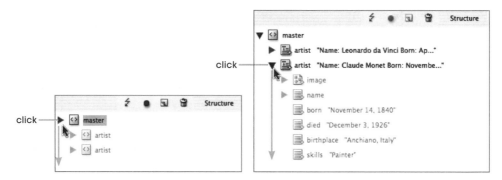

Figure 2.7 Click on the triangle in front of the **master** element to reveal that it contains two **artist** elements.

Figure 2.8 Click on an **artist** element to reveal seven child elements contained within.

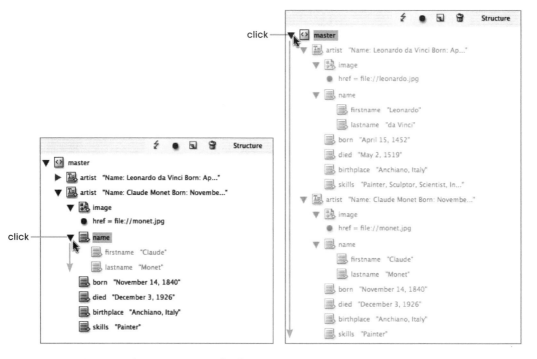

Figure 2.9 Click on **image** to reveal the **href** attribute; click on **name** to show the **firstname** and **lastname** child elements.

Figure 2.10 Option-click (Alt-click) on the **master** element to expand the entire structure at once.

Collapsing the Structure

To collapse the structure, click on each open triangle until the elements are all closed, or to close the entire structure at once, see **Figure 2.11**.

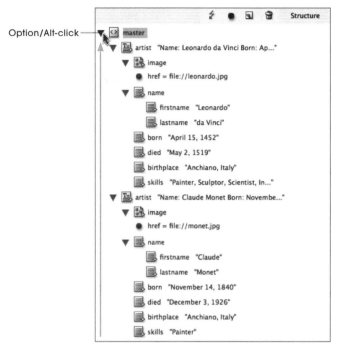

Option/Alt-click

Figure 2.11 Option-click (Alt-click) on the **master element** to collapse all levels of the structure at once.

Structure Pane Anatomy

The Structure pane provides a graphical overview of your XML structure that displays all elements, attributes, comments and processing instructions contained within the XML (**Figure 2.12**).

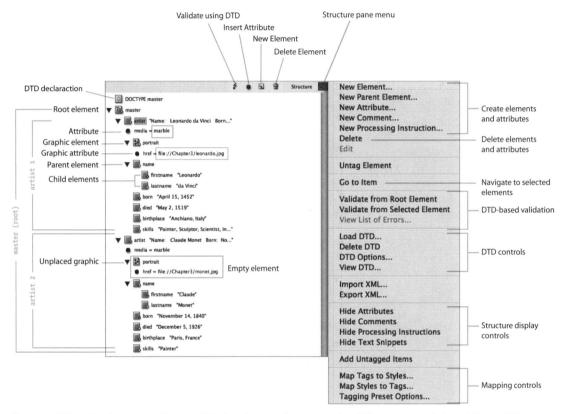

Figure 2.12 The Structure pane also provides handy, one-stop access to all the commands for adding, editing, and deleting these components.

Within the Structure pane you may see as many as 17 different icons. **Table 2.2** helps you familiarize yourself with their names and descriptions.

Table 2.2 Structure Pane Icons

ICON	NAME	DESCRIPTION
▶	Closed triangle or "twirlie"	Represents a closed element that contains one, or more, child element(s) or attribute(s). Click the triangle to open, or expand, the element and reveal its contents.
▼	Open triangle or "twirlie"	Represents an open element. Click the triangle to close, or collapse, the element to hide its contents.
●	Attribute	Represents an XML attribute or other metadata. Attributes do not appear in the layout, nor do they print, but they may be accessed by an XML application.
	Comment	Represents a comment. Comments are non-printing notes stored within the XML. Comments are imported with the XML content and can be added and edited within InDesign. All comments visible within the Structure pane are included whenever XML is exported from InDesign.
	DOCTYPE element	Indicates that a DTD has been loaded.
	Empty element	Represents a graphic or unassigned frame that is empty.
	Graphic element	Represents a tagged frame that contains a graphic. Graphic elements automatically include an href attribute that defines the path or URL to the graphic file.
	Graphic element–unplaced	Represents an XML reference to an image that has not been placed within the document.
	Processing instruction	Represents an instruction that will trigger an action in applications that can read such instructions, such as an XML parser.
	Root element	The first XML element that automatically contains all other elements. All XML files will have one root element. Note: Although Root is the default name in InDesign, most XML applications will probably call it something else.
	Story element	Represents a story in a single frame or several linked frames. One such icon is displayed on the parent element of each story flow.
	Table element	Represents a tagged table.
	Table–body cell element	Represents a tagged cell within the body of a table.
	Table–footer cell element	Represents a tagged cell in the footer row of a table.
	Table–header cell element	Represents a tagged cell in the header row of a table.
	Text element	Represents tagged text within a frame.
	Text element–unplaced	Unplaced text element not yet associated with a page item.

Placing Unformatted Elements from the Structure Pane

We said earlier that the XML content is actually stored within the Structure pane. You can place text and graphics stored in the Structure pane by dragging the elements to your layout.

Figure 2.13 shows how to place a graphic element from the Structure pane.

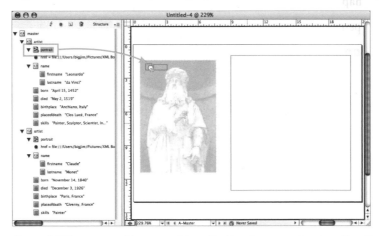

Figure 2.13 Drag a graphic element from the Structure pane to place it on the page.

Figure 2.14 shows how to place a text element from the Structure pane.

Figure 2.14 Drag a text element from the Structure pane to place it in the layout.

NOTE A placed text element will fill an existing text frame or automatically create its own frame that conforms to the page margins. If you place a text element into a frame occupied by another similarly tagged element, the new element will completely replace the existing one.

The Tags Panel Close-up

The Tags panel has second billing in your XML extravaganza, just under the Structure pane. Tags are used to identify every XML element in a structured layout. They can be applied to frames—both graphic and text—paragraphs, sentences, words, and even down to individual characters. Tags can also be empty or wrapped around other elements, as when a child element is nested within a parent element (described in **Chapter 1**).

Open **xml_interface2.indt** from the Chapter 2 folder (**Figure 2.15**).

Figure 2.15 This file features a fully structured layout, can you tell? If your XML interface is turned off, it will look like any other InDesign document—a page with a graphic and a bunch of text. Don't let that fool you. A structured InDesign document is just like the ocean: Most of the action is happening under the surface.

Let's dive in and see what you've been missing. **Figure 2.16** shows how to open the Tags panel, and **Figure 2.17** shows the Tags panel.

Figure 2.16 Access the Tags panel from the Window menu.

Figure 2.17 The Tags panel is used to create, edit, import, or delete tags; to identify currently tagged elements within your layout; or to assign tags to your content or XML placeholders. The Tags panel displays all the available XML elements. Notice the color chip associated with each tag name.

Figure 2.18 shows how to expose the remaining parts of InDesign's XML interface, and **Figure 2.19** displays how the InDesign layout should look when the XML structure is all turned on. The tag markers appear as colored brackets at the beginning and end of each element. Tagged frames appear as if they are filled with the tag color. All this color is intended as a visual cue to help identify the XML elements. Don't worry, the brackets and colored frames do not print or appear in exported files, such as JPEGs or PDFs.

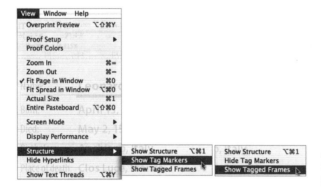

Figure 2.18 Select Show Tag Markers and Show Tagged Frames from the View menu.

Figure 2.19 InDesign uses brackets and color as visual cues to the structure of your XML.

Identifying Tagged Elements

Use the Tags panel to identify currently tagged elements (see **Figures 2.20** through **2.23**)

Figure 2.20 Using the Selection tool, when you select the picture frame, the **image** tag highlights in the Tags palette.

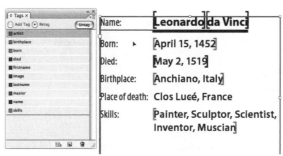

Figure 2.21 Using the Selection tool, when you select the text frame, the **artist** tag highlights.

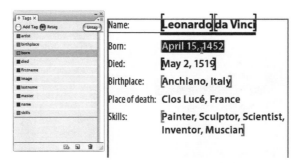

Figure 2.22 Using the Text tool, select the text April 15, 1452. Note how the **born** tag highlights.

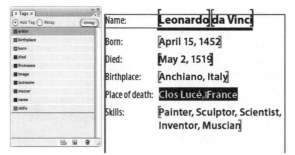

Figure 2.23 You may notice the text Clos Lucé, France has no brackets. This text is technically *untagged*—there is no element for *Place of death*. Because the text has no tags of its own, it automatically assumes the tag of the parent element or the frame in which it resides.

Creating Tags

Figures 2.24 and **2.25** show you how to create a tag.

New Tag button

Figure 2.24 To create a tag, select New Tag from the Tags panel menu or click the New Tag button at the bottom of the panel.

Figure 2.25 Type Portrait in the New Tag dialog. The tag name typed here must match the element name from the XML file exactly, as we explain in Chapter 1. Click OK.

Editing Tags

Whoops! We just made a mistake. Notice how all the other XML tags in the panel shown in Figure 2.25 are typed in lowercase? You should open the actual XML file to be certain, but assume for this exercise that `Portrait` should be lowercase, too. Let's edit the tag we just created to conform with all the other element names (**Figures 2.26** and **2.27**).

Figure 2.26 Select the **Portrait** tag in the Tags panel and then double-click it or select Tag Options from the Tags panel menu.

Figure 2.27 Edit the tag name so that **portrait** is entirely lowercase. Click OK.

Loading Tags

Tag names are added to the panel automatically whenever you import an XML file. But this method imports the XML data contained in the file as well. If there is no need for the data, InDesign provides a method for importing only the tag names from XML files and even from other InDesign or InCopy documents (**Figures 2.28** through **2.30**).

Figure 2.28 Select Load Tags from the Tags panel menu.

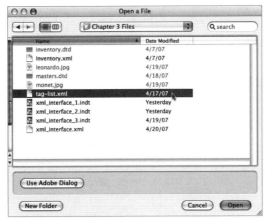

Figure 2.29 Select **tag-list.xml** from the Chapter 2 folder. You can load tags from any XML, InDesign, or InCopy file. Click Open.

Figure 2.30 The tags **placeofdeath** and **media** appear in the Tags panel.

Deleting Unused Tags

You can delete tags at any time within your document, whether they are used or unused. **Figure 2.31** illustrates how to delete unused tags.

Figure 2.31 Select **media** in the Tags panel. Select Delete Tag from the Tags panel menu or click the Delete Tag button at the bottom of the Tags panel.

Delete Tag button

Deleting Used Tags

Deleting a tag that is currently assigned to one or more elements within your document could damage your XML structure, so InDesign adds an extra step to the process to prevent any trouble (**Figure 2.32**).

Figure 2.32 Select and delete the **image** tag. This tag is assigned to the graphic frame on page 1. When an assigned tag is deleted, InDesign requires that you retag tagged elements with another tag from the panel. Select **portrait** as the replacement tag. Click OK.

Saving Tags

After editing, renaming, and deleting tags, you may want to share your new list of tags with coworkers or use them in other workflows. InDesign provides an easy way to save the tag list to a separate file (**Figure 2.33**).

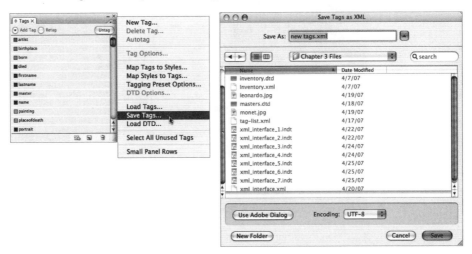

Figure 2.33 Select Save Tags from the Tags panel menu. The tag names are saved into an XML file. The file includes only the names themselves; no XML data from the layout is included.

Applying Tags to Text

Tags can be applied to both text and graphics. Open **xml_interface_3.indt**. **Figure 2.34** shows how to apply a tag to text.

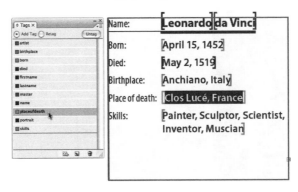

Figure 2.34 Using the Text tool, select the text Clos Lucé, France. Click the tag **placeofdeath** in the Tags panel. You can also right-click on the selected text and choose **placeofdeath** from the Tag Text context submenu.

Applying Tags to Graphics

To apply tags to graphics, follow **Figure 2.35**.

Figure 2.35
Using the Selection tool, select the picture frame. Click **painting** in the Tags panel.

NOTE *The tag color can be difficult to see when the frame contains a graphic.*

NOTE *With graphics, tags are applied to the frames not the contents.*

Changing Tag Assignments

Figure 2.36 shows how to change tag assignments.

Figure 2.36
Using the Selection tool, select the picture frame. Click **portrait** in the Tags panel.

Untagging Graphics and Text

At some point in your workflow, the XML tags and structure may no longer be needed. While tags can sit in graphic or text frames for years without causing you a whit of trouble, InDesign provides an easy way to remove all traces of the XML structure. **Figures 2.37** through **2.40** show you how to untag graphics, text, an entire text frame, and everything on a spread, in that order.

Figure 2.37 Go to page 2. Using the Selection tool, select the picture frame. Click the Untag button in the Tags panel.

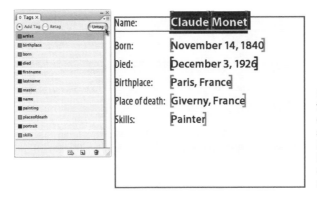

Figure 2.38 Using the Text tool, select the entire text of or simply insert the cursor somewhere within Claude Monet. Click the Untag button in the Tags panel or right-click on the selection and choose Untag Text.

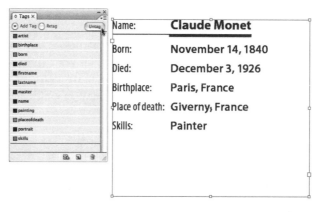

Figure 2.39 Using the Selection tool, select the text frame on page 2. Click the Untag button in the Tags panel.

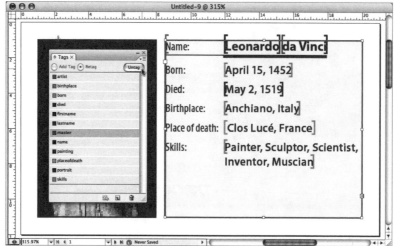

Figure 2.40 Using the Selection tool, press Cmd-A (Ctrl-A) to select all objects on the spread. Click the Untag button in the Tags panel.

WARNING *When an object is untagged, tags are removed not only from the frame and its contents but also from all linked frames on whatever page(s) they reside on.*

Tags vs. Structure

So far you've learned how to access and use both the Structure pane and the Tags panel. You've seen how the Tags panel works like a grocery list, showing you all the essential parts of your XML workflow. You've seen how the Structure pane works like an X-ray device, revealing *how* the elements are put together. Although they serve completely different purposes, their features overlap in some important and helpful ways.

Identifying Elements from the Structure Pane

Open **xml_interface_4.indd** from the Chapter 2 folder (**Figure 2.41**).

Figure 2.41 xml_interface_4.indt features a fully structured layout.

In **Figure 2.42**, we matched up the XML content to its display in the Structure pane. Even if you knew nothing about XML it's easy to see the similarities. Can you see how each line in the Structure pane relates directly to the structure of the XML file? Can you figure out the element names? Can you identify the attributes?

Click the first **artist** icon in the Structure pane (**Figure 2.43**). See the tag name highlight in the Tags panel. Also notice that the icon for this element indicates that it has been placed in the layout. Because the icon and the actual content on the page are the same thing, you can use the Structure pane to identify these elements in the layout. Double-click the first **artist** icon in the Structure pane (**Figure 2.44**).

Target XML code

Structure pane

```xml
<?xml version="1.0" encoding="UTF-8" standalone="yes"?>
<master>
    <artist>
        <portrait href="file://leonardo.jpg" />
        <name>
            <firstname>Leonardo</firstname>
            <lastname>da Vinci</lastname>
        </name>
        <born>April 15, 1452</born>
        <died>May 2, 1519</died>
        <birthplace>Anchiano, Italy</birthplace>
        <placeofdeath>Clos Lucé, France</placeofdeath>
        <skills>Painter, Sculptor, Scientist, Inventor, Muscian</skills>
    </artist>
    <artist>
        <portrait href="file://monet.jpg" />
        <name>
            <firstname>Claude</firstname>
            <lastname>Monet</lastname>
        </name>
        <born>November 14, 1840</born>
        <died>December 3, 1926</died>
        <birthplace>Paris, France</birthplace>
        <placeofdeath>Giverny, France</placeofdeath>
        <skills>Painter</skills>
    </artist>
</master>
```

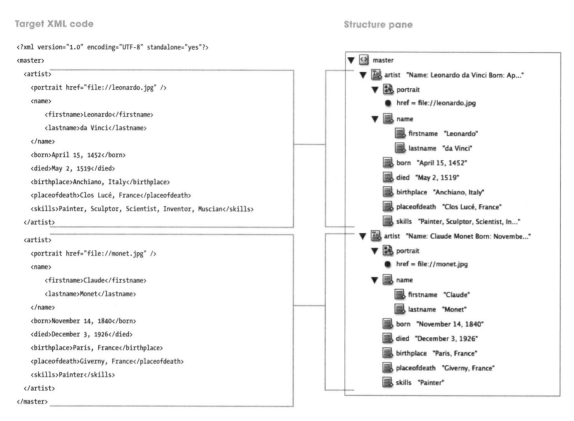

Figure 2.42 If you can find these elements in the Structure pane, you can use it to find them in your layout, too.

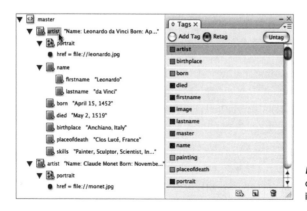

Figure 2.43 The icon and the actual element in the layout are, in effect, the same thing.

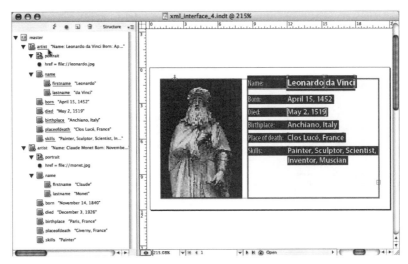

Figure 2.44 Notice in what ways the elements in the Structure pane and the content in the layout each indicate they are selected.

To identify XML graphic elements in your layout using the Structure pane, double-click on the first **portrait** element in the Structure pane (**Figure 2.45**).

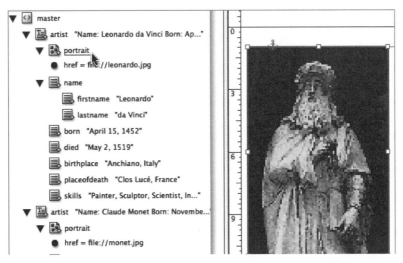

Figure 2.45 See how the image of Leonardo da Vinci is highlighted in the layout and in the Structure pane.

Observe the other child elements within the first **artist** element. You can use the Structure pane to select them individually, too. **Figure 2.46** shows how to select a single element using the Structure pane. See how each icon relates to the placed content in the layout? This connection between the Structure pane and the layout will come in very handy in our upcoming lessons as well as in your own XML workflow.

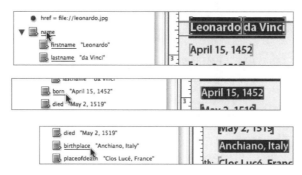

Figure 2.46 In turn, double-click the **name** icon, the **born** icon, and then the **birthplace** icon.

Identifying Structure from the Layout

An important aspect of the relationship between the Structure pane and the layout is that it is a two-way street. Just as you used the Structure pane to identify elements in the layout, you can use layout elements to help identify the structure (**Figure 2.47**).

Figure 2.47 Using the Text tool, click in the text Anchiano. See how the **artist** and **birthplace** icons highlight in the Structure pane and Tag panel? Click in some other text elements and see how they are tagged and where in the XML structure they exist.

Untagging Elements from the Structure Pane

Earlier you learned how to untag elements using the Tags panel. The Structure pane can be used to untag elements, too. **Figures 2.48** through **2.50** show you how to untag a placed graphic element, untag a text element, and untag multiple elements at once, in that order.

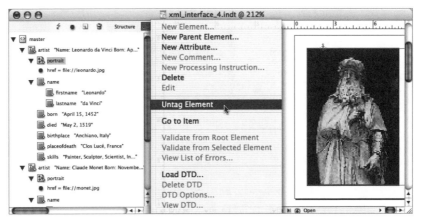

Figure 2.48 Click once on the **portrait** icon in the Structure pane. Select Untag Element from the Structure pane menu. Note how the element is removed from the Structure pane altogether but the picture remains in the layout.

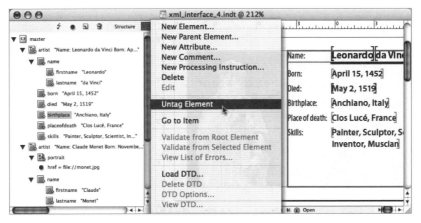

Figure 2.49 Click once on the **birthplace** icon in the Structure pane. Select Untag Element from the Structure pane menu. Note how the element and the text snippet are removed from the Structure pane. However, the text remains in the layout although the tag brackets are no longer displayed.

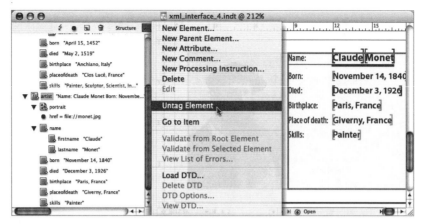

Figure 2.50 Click the second **artist** element in the Structure pane. Select Untag Element from the Structure pane menu. Note how all the child elements and their text snippets are removed from the Structure pane. The content remains in the layout, but no longer displays any tag brackets.

NOTE *Sometimes when you press the Untag button it removes the entire XML structure from the element (**Figure 2.51**).*

Figure 2.51 In these situations, InDesign displays a warning dialog to confirm your action.

Deleting Elements Using the Structure Pane

Placed (and/or unplaced) elements can be deleted using the Structure pane. **Figure 2.52** shows how to delete a placed object, and **Figure 2.53** shows how to delete multiple elements at once.

Figure 2.52 Click once on the **portrait** element in the Structure pane. To delete it completely, click the trash can icon at the top, select Delete from the Structure pane menu, or press the Delete key. When the Delete XML Element dialog appears, it gives you the option to delete or simply untag the element. Click the Delete button.

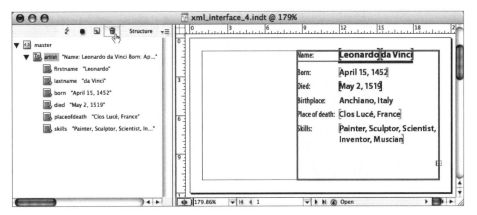

Figure 2.53 Click once on the **artist** icon in the Structure pane. Click the trash can icon at the top of the Structure pane. Click the Delete button.

NOTE *The root element can't be deleted.*

Formatting XML Content Automatically

One of the most powerful features of InDesign's XML tools (and one of our favorites) is the ability to apply Paragraph, Character, and Table (CS3 only) styles to imported content automatically. It means that, potentially, with the right template, you could create instant documents completely formatted from scratch with a few clicks of the mouse.

Open **xml_interface_5.indt** and have a look at **Figure 2.54**.

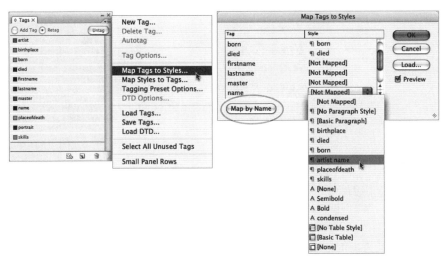

Figure 2.54 Select Map Tags to Styles from the Tags panel menu or from the Structure pane menu. Click Map by Name if your tag names match your style names exactly—or map them manually, one by one, to the desired styles. Click OK.

Tagging Text Elements Automatically

If we can style text that's already tagged, wouldn't it be nice if you could tag text that was already styled? 'Nuff said. InDesign can do that, too! Open **xml_interface_6.indt** and check out **Figures 2.55** and **2.56**. For a detailed description on how to do this properly see **Chapters 9** and **10**.

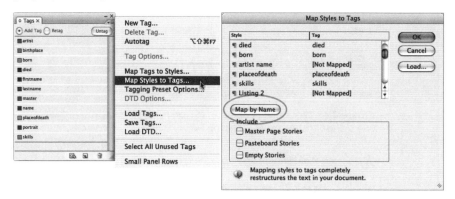

Figure 2.55 Select Map Styles to Tags from the Tags panel menu or from the Structure pane menu. Click Map by Name if your style names match your tag names exactly, or map them manually, one by one, to the desired XML elements. Click OK.

NOTE   *Not all styles or tags can be mapped automatically. For example, you won't always have style and tag names that match. Some elements will have to be tagged manually.*

Name:	⌊Leonardo⌉⌊da Vinci⌉
Born:	⌊April 15, 1452⌉
Died:	⌊May 2, 1519⌉
Birthplace:	⌊Anchiano, Italy⌉
Place of death:	⌊Clos Lucé, France⌉
Skills:	⌊Painter, Sculptor, Scientist, Inventor, Muscian⌉

Figure 2.56 XML tag brackets appear automatically around some of the text in the layout. A good start, but the job isn't done. Note how the picture and the text frames are still untagged. This layout still requires some manual tagging.

Exporting XML

InDesign's XML export interface may be your last stop in an XML workflow. To export your structured layout to XML, select File > Export. Give the file a name, choose XML from the Format pull-down menu, and click Save.

The Export XML dialog (**Figure 2.57**) is responsible for creating the exact type and structure of XML file you want. Take a minute to familiarize yourself with the possible settings (**Table 2.2**). We demonstrate what they do in detail in upcoming chapters.

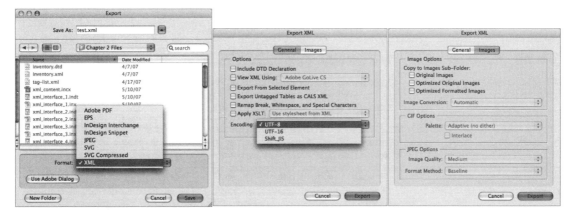

Figure 2.57 The Export XML dialog provides options for creating a usable XML file from the tagged text and images within your document. InDesign can even convert print images into GIFs or JPEGs for Web use, if necessary.

> **NOTE** *This point is important enough that we mention it several times within the book. When InDesign exports XML, it includes everything within a tagged story, including any untagged text as well as the text from any linked text frames. Be aware that while untagged content may not cause trouble in InDesign, it may give other XML applications fits.*

Here are some brief descriptions of the XML export options:

Table 2.2 *XML Export Options*

GENERAL

OPTION	DESCRIPTION
Include DTD Declaration	Includes the name and path of the DTD used within your structure. This option is only selectable when a DTD has been loaded by you or referenced by your imported XML content.
View XML Using	Select the program in which you wish to view your XML after export. You can choose any program capable of viewing XML, including compatible browsers and HTML editors, such as Adobe Dreamweaver. Deselect if you do not want to view the file.
Export from Selected Element	Allows you to export XML starting from a specific point within your structure. To use this option, you must first select the element you want to export using the Structure pane. Then choose this option within the dialog.
Export Untagged Tables as CALS XML (CS3 only)	Converts untagged tables into CALS-compatible markup. For this option to apply in InDesign, the table must sit in a tagged frame but contain no tagged elements itself.

continues on next page

Table 2.2 *XML Export Options (continued)*

OPTION	DESCRIPTION
Remap Break, Whitespace, and Special Characters (CS3 only)	Exports breaks, whitespace, and special characters as code entities, which we describe in **Chapter 1**. See "Wasting Spacing" in **Chapter 3** for additional information.
Apply XSLT (CS3 only)	Applies an XSL stylesheet transformation to the XML upon export. As described in **Chapter 1**, an XSLT can reformat, filter, sort or perform some other desired transformation to the data.
Encoding	Choose among UTF-8, UTF-16, or Shift_JIS encodings for the exported data. Check what type of encoding your desired application requires before exporting. For most applications, UTF-8 or UTF-16 is fine.

OPTION	DESCRIPTION
Copy to Images Subfolder:	InDesign can export tagged images within the document for use in an XML workflow. The images will be exported along with the XML markup into an Images Subfolder.
Original Images	Exports tagged images in their original formats.
Optimized Original Images	Exports and converts tagged images within the layout to JPEG or GIF formats.
Optimized Formatted Images	Exports images to JPEG or GIF formats that have been transformed within InDesign. Among the transformations supported are cropping, rotation, and skewing.
Image Conversion	Select the image format you want, GIF or JPEG. Automatic allows InDesign to select the type of format itself based on the image properties, such as color, quality, and so on.

OPTION	DESCRIPTION
Palette	Select from the available GIF color palettes.
Interlace	Prepares images to download in alternating rows of pixels, which allows images to appear in a browser more quickly at slower connection speeds.

OPTION	DESCRIPTION
Image Quality	Choose between high-quality, large file sizes and low-quality, small file sizes.

Using DTDs

The last XML feature we look at in Layout view is the use of Document Type Definitions, known as DTDs, to validate XML structure. This topic is covered in detail in **Chapter 11**, but here's the dime tour.

Open **xml_interface_7.indt**.

Loading a DTD

If a DTD is not included as an inline element within the XML file itself, you must load it manually (**Figure 2.58**).

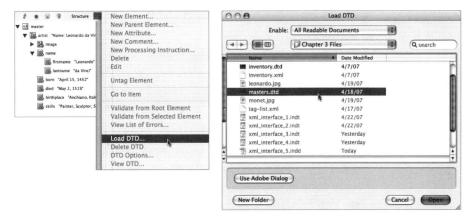

Figure 2.58 The DTD can be loaded from either the Structure pane menu or the Tags panel menu. The controls for DTD validation are located at the top of the Structure pane. Select masters.dtd in the Load DTD dialog. Click Open.

Validating Structure with a DTD

As we explain in **Chapter 1**, a DTD can be used to test an XML structure to make sure it follows the rules. By validating your structure against the DTD, InDesign identifies parts that don't conform and gives you tips on how the problem may be fixed. **Figure 2.59** shows how to validate an existing XML structure. Click the lightning bolt icon at the top of the Structure pane to validate the current document structure. Errors are indicated within the structure schematic and suggested fixes appear in their own section of the pane.

Click to validate
to DTD

DTD reference

Validation errors

Suggested fixes

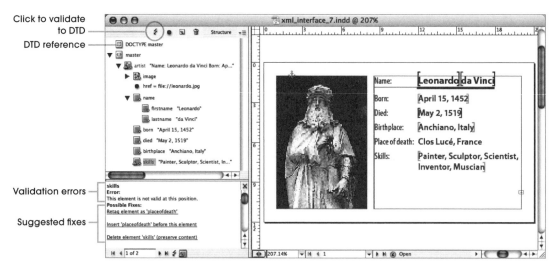

Figure 2.59 In this file the DTD found at least one error. But don't make any changes yet. The suggested fix is actually incorrect!

Viewing the DTD

The error messages in the Structure pane can be somewhat cryptic and often inaccurate. This is a case where knowing how to read DTD comes in handy, and InDesign provides a simple way to get a first-hand look at the DTD that you loaded (**Figure 2.60**). Select View DTD from the Structure pane menu.

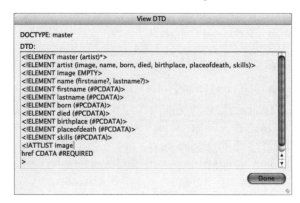

Figure 2.60 From our coverage of DTD syntax and grammar in Chapter 1, you should be able to parse out the proper XML structure. If so, you'll see that the real problem with our structure is that no text is tagged with the element **placeofdeath**.

Fixing XML Structure

Let's put your newly acquired knowledge to the test. To fix the structure you must select the text **Clos Lucé, France**, tag it with the element `placeofdeath`, and then revalidate the layout (**Figure 2.61**).

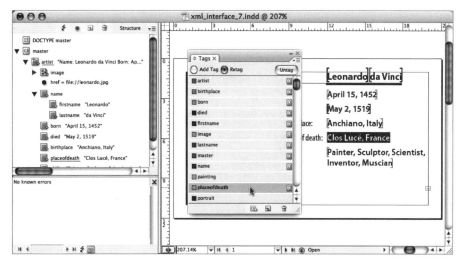

Figure 2.61 Here you see the properly structured layout. Once the tag is applied to Clos Lucé, France the layout validates with no errors.

InDesign's Story Editor

The Story Editor often gets overlooked or regarded by many as an afterthought by Adobe, but Story Editor is a fully functional word processor and a handy tool. We love it. We use it frequently for a host of tasks, especially when stories span multiple pages or when we're working in a complex XML workflow. In this section, we look at the XML features provided by Story Editor.

Accessing Story Editor

Open **xml_interface_8.indt**. Using the Selection or Text tool, click on or in the main text frame. Select Edit in Story Editor from the Edit menu or press Cmd-Y (Ctrl-Y). If you're used to the hubbub and clutter of Layout view, Story Editor will appear Spartan, almost severe. The interface is geared for writers and editors, not designers (**Figure 2.62**).

Anchored or inline graphics

Paragraph styles

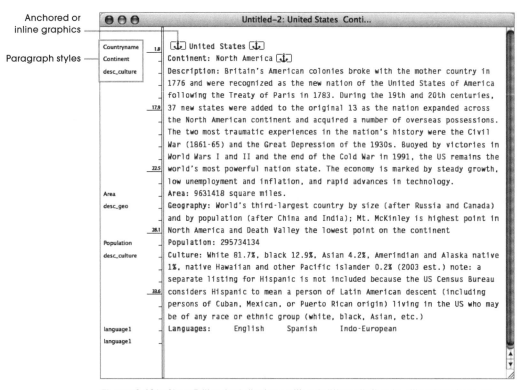

Figure 2.62 In Story Editor, text displays without differentiation in either typeface or font size, and the only graphics that appear are the icons representing *inline* or anchored graphics and XML tags.

Showing the XML Interface

Because Story Editor is designed to work only with text, its XML functionality is basically limited to assisting in tagging and structuring text.

To show the XML interface, see **Figures 2.63** and **2.64**. Select View > Structure > Show Tag Markers to display the tag markers. Select Window > Tags to display the Tags panel, if it's not visible. Story Editor has no access to the Structure pane, so the only XML tools you have to work with are the Tags panel and the tag markers, which appear as colorful five-sided polygons.

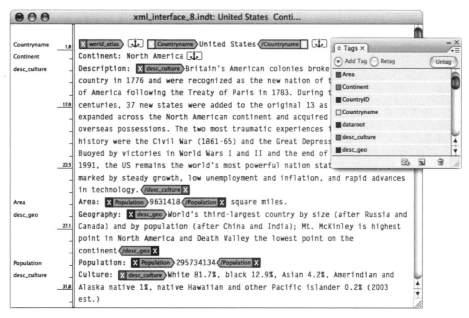

Figure 2.63 Note how the polygons appear at the beginning and end of each element.

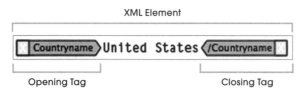

Figure 2.64 Tag markers in Story Editor appear as colorful, 5-sided polygons at the beginning and end of tagged text. You don't need to look at the Tags panel to identify this element as **Countryname**.

Identifying Text Elements Using the Tags Panel

To identify text elements in the Story Editor, see **Figure 2.65**. Identifying XML elements within Story Editor is pretty straightforward compared to Layout view.

Figure 2.65 You can also identify elements using the Tags panel. Click in the text **United States**, and the **Countryname** tag highlights in the Tags panel.

Identifying Inline/Anchored Elements in Story Editor

Although it's true that you can't see or edit the content of a graphic within Story Editor, we discovered a way to at least check what element is supposed to be represented in an inline/anchored object. This trick only works with objects inline or anchored within the frame being edited. We assume for the purpose of this lesson that the inline/anchored object (**Figure 2.66**) is a graphic, but it could just as easily be an anchored text frame instead. Select the Anchor icon that appears after the text **North America** by dragging your Text cursor across it.

Figure 2.66 Be sure to select only the icon and none of the text or spaces that appear on either side of it. The **map** tag highlights in the Tags panel.

Tagging Text in Story Editor

Figure 2.67 shows how to tag *untagged* text in the Story Editor.

Figure 2.67 Select the text **North America**. Click the tag name **Continent** in the Tags panel.

Retagging Text in Story Editor

Figure 2.68 shows how to retag text in the Story Editor. Select the number **9631418**, which is tagged incorrectly as Population.

Figure 2.68 Make sure that the radio button Retag is selected in the Tags panel. Click the tag name **Area** to retag the number properly.

Adding Tags to Text in Story Editor

At times, you need to nest one XML element within another, or wrap an element around another. By default, InDesign wants to retag the text when you click on a different tag name in the panel. To facilitate *nesting* and *wrapping*, the Tags panel provides the Add Tag radio button. By selecting this button before you tag an element, InDesign leaves any existing tag(s) in place and then *adds* the new tag in the manner you designate (**Figure 2.69**). To add, or insert, one element within another, first select the number **9631418.**

Figure 2.69 Select the Add Tag radio button in the Tags panel and click the **land** tag in the Tags panel. This inserts, or nests, the **land** element inside the **Area** element.

To wrap a tag around an existing element, see **Figure 2.70**. To add a tag outside, or wrap, another element, select the number **295734134** *and* the opening and closing `Population` tags surrounding it.

Figure 2.70 Note how the Add Tag button is selected by default. Click the AD2007 tag in the Tags panel. This wraps, or nests 295734134 and the **Population** tags within the AD2007 element.

NOTE The Retag and Add tag functionality works identically in Layout view as it does in Story Editor. We prefer to use Story Editor when we need to nest multiple elements, because the element tag icons are so much easier to identify, as you can see in **Figure 2.71**. Note how easy it is to identify the elements and how they are nested in Story Editor.

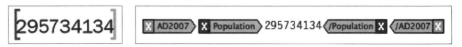

Figure 2.71 Compare the display of the identically tagged elements in Layout view (left) and Story Editor (right). Which display would you prefer to work with?

InCopy

Adobe InCopy is a standalone application, purchased separately, that provides robust text-editing tools for non-designers. Like Story Editor, InCopy focuses almost entirely on the words and is intended to be used by the editors and writers who work side by side with designers. At less than half the price of InDesign, it's more cost effective to give editors and writers InCopy instead of InDesign. Although InCopy has nearly all the features of a normal word processor, such as Microsoft Word, it also provides some important advantages.

First, it's fully integrated with InDesign—for example, the menus and commands for editing and formatting text are identical. When you open an InDesign file or assignment within InCopy, you have direct access to all the Paragraph and Character styles and color swatches stored in the document. Second, InCopy provides a direct connection to the other people involved in your workflow—keeping track of who is currently working on it, what changes have been made, and then updating the layout or text as necessary. Finally, nothing beats InCopy's advantage of working in the actual layout, especially when you need an accurate visual to fit text into a tight space, wrapping it around graphics and other stories.

The XML features in InCopy are almost the same as those in InDesign. For example, InCopy has both a Structure pane and a Tags panel. And tags and elements can be created, edited, imported, and applied exactly the same way you do as in InDesign and Story Editor.

So, in this section, we don't waste time repeating the ways these programs are similar; instead, we briefly describe the ways these applications differ. If you need a refresher course in tagging or XML structure, turn back to the earlier descriptions of the XML features in InDesign and Story Editor.

Basically, the program has four methods of working with XML. InCopy can:

- Open an InDesign document to edit or add XML structure.

- Open an InDesign assignment or InCopy .INCX file to edit or add XML structure.

- Open an XML file directly.

- Create an XML file from scratch.

Installing InCopy Plug-Ins in InDesign

The capability of creating, editing, and opening InCopy assignments and files is an add-on feature to InDesign enabled through plug-ins. These features are installed automatically in CS3, but you have to add the plug-ins manually for CS2. The plug-ins are stored on the Resources and Extras disc in the CS2 disc set or on Disc One in the stand-alone version of InDesign CS2, as seen in **Figure 2.72**.

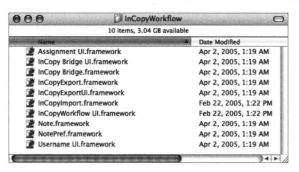

Figure 2.72 Look in the folder Technical Information > InCopy CS2 Plug-ins. To install the InCopy features, copy all the plug-ins into the InDesign CS2 > Plug-Ins > InCopyWorkflow folder as shown here and restart InDesign.

Opening an InDesign Document with InCopy

Open **xml_interface_9.indd** using InCopy. Here you see the Layout view of InCopy. Can you see the similarities between InCopy and InDesign, such as the Structure pane and Tags panel and their respective menus? Although InCopy users can't create or modify the layout, they can open the actual InDesign file itself and work on the text either on the page or within Story or Galley view. However, there's one catch: Before the InCopy user can make any changes, the InDesign user must first create an assignment or export the layout content to InCopy .INCX files. In **Figure 2.73** you can see the InCopy Assignment Available icon above the main text frame.

Structure pane   Structure pane menu   InCopy Assignment Available   Tags panel   Tags panel menu

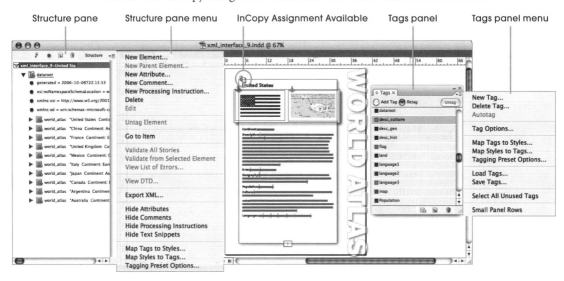

Figure 2.73 The Assignment Available icon indicates that this story can be checked out in InCopy to edit the text or work on its XML structure.

Opening an InCopy Assignment

InCopy provides three working spaces: Layout view, Story view, and Galley view. Layout view shows the actual page layout of the InDesign document, including text, pictures, graphics, margins, and column geometry, as seen in Figure 2.73. The exact amount of detail is determined by the InDesign user, who controls access by making the assignments. In **Figure 2.74** you see Story view, which is similar to Story Editor in InDesign. It provides access only to the words within a story, whether it's in a single frame or a set of linked text frames. InCopy's Galley view also provides access to the words with the added benefit that it depicts the line breaks or line count as they appear in the actual InDesign layout. Once in an InCopy workflow, you can't modify anything in the document until you check it out for editing as shown in Figure 2.74.

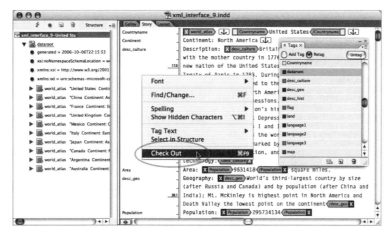

Figure 2.74 Right-click in the content to access the Check Out command. The right to check out content can be granted only by the InDesign user.

Opening an XML File

We don't know or understand why, but InCopy has no ability to import XML. (It probably has something to do with the fact that InCopy cannot create text frames or pages in the InDesign layout). If you want XML in your layout, you first have to import it using InDesign. However, unlike InDesign, InCopy can *open* XML files directly (**Figure 2.75**). In a pinch, InCopy can be used as an XML editor, allowing you to assign, create, or delete tags, edit and restructure content, and do whatever else you need to do to prepare the file for use in your workflow.

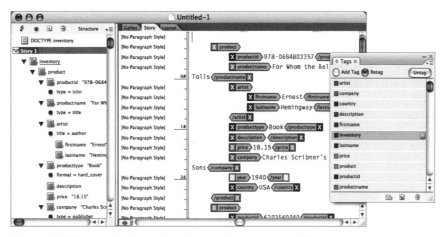

Figure 2.75 When you're done, simply export the content as XML.

Creating XML in InCopy

In **Figure 2.76** you see the Export dialog (File > Export) showing XML as one of the possible file formats the program can create. In **Chapter 3** we'll show you how to create XML content in InCopy as well as several other programs. To get a full appreciation of the features and utility of InCopy, check out *The Adobe InCopy CS2 Book* (Adobe Press) or the DVD and online training available from Lynda.com and Totaltraining.com.

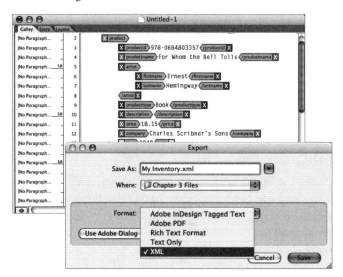

Figure 2.76 InCopy is not a replacement for an XML editor, but it can pinch hit if you don't have one available. It offers robust features for creating as well as editing XML files.

3

Making XML

"Where does the XML come from?"

The question was simple and straightforward, but frustrating nonetheless. It came in the Q&A period after three detailed XML demonstrations at the Chicago InDesign User Group. And it wasn't the substance of the query that surprised us, but the tenor. It was the same tone usually reserved for questions like: "Where does the Easter Bunny come from?" and "How does Santa fit down the chimney?"

By the blank expressions on the faces of all the other users assembled for the meeting it was clear that the questioner was not alone. It seemed that the three hours of demonstrations had been wasted. We had lost them at "Hello." Instead of concentrating on the dazzling XML magic taking place up on the projector screen, the users were focusing on those three mysterious letters at the end of the file name. It was our own fault: We had assumed that everyone understood what XML was. But we were wrong. We vowed not to make that mistake again. So that's the purpose of this chapter.

XML is neither manna from heaven nor an Easter egg; it is simply a type of computer file that stores marked-up text that can be created by a number of means. In this chapter we explore a handful of methods for creating your own XML. As a designer you probably won't have to do this yourself. But over the years we've found that even when we didn't need to create our own content, we did need to know *how* it was created and be able to tell the editors, writers, or IT personnel *what* we needed.

There are no magic seeds, no *Jack and the Beanstalk* moments needed with XML. You don't have to spend a fortune or hire an expensive consultant to create it. If you have a (working) computer you probably have the means to create all the XML you will ever need already at your disposal. XML is simply *plain text*. It is non-proprietary and requires no special program or expertise to create it, as we'll now demonstrate.

Feel free to try each of the programs we describe in this chapter or skip to the ones you want to learn more about. Save all the resulting XML files into the same location on your hard drive. In our final lesson we compare the files to see what differences there are between them, if any.

NOTE Download all applicable files for Chapter 3 from the www.peachpit.com/ indesignxmlguide and copy them to a folder on your hard drive (approximately 5K).

TextEdit and Notepad

Pros: Simple, easy to use, and built into the operating system (Mac and Windows, respectively) and therefore free. They don't add unwanted or invisible characters and coding.

Cons: No features for automatic tagging or validating XML structure. No efficiency or labor-saving features for creating XML.

Macs and Windows machines each come with programs that can create and edit plain text files. Usually, these files are saved with the extension .TXT, but this is not the only extension used by plain text files. Other popular extensions include .COM, .BAT, .PLIST, .STRINGS, .HTML, and, of course, .XML. Although TextEdit and Notepad don't have any fancy XML tagging or structure tools, they can get the job done in a pinch.

To create XML in these programs, do this:

1. Launch TextEdit in OSX or Notepad in Windows (**Figure 3.1**).

NOTE (Mac only) TextEdit can produce both plain and rich format text files. Select Format > Make Plain Text before proceeding. If the option Make Rich Text appears in the menu instead, the file is already plain text and you are ready to start typing.

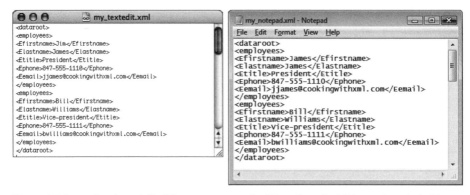

Figure 3.1 One advantage is that these programs don't insert any invisible, and undesirable, elements into the code the way InDesign, InCopy and other programs do.

2. Type the following text:

```
<dataroot>
<employees>
<Efirstname>James</Efirstname>
<Elastname>James</Elastname>
<Etitle>President</Etitle>
<Ephone>847-555-1110</Ephone>
<Eemail>jjames@cookingwithxml.com</Eemail>
</employees>
<employees>
<Efirstname>Bill</Efirstname>
<Elastname>Williams</Elastname>
<Etitle>Vice-president</Etitle>
<Ephone>847-555-1111</Ephone>
<Eemail>bwilliams@cookingwithxml.com</Eemail>
</employees>
</dataroot>
```

3. Select File > Save.

The Save As dialog appears.

4. Name the file **my_textedit.xml** or **my_notepad.xml**, as appropriate, in the Save As field.

5. Click the Save button.

TextEdit may open a dialog to confirm whether you want to use the extension .TXT or .XML. Click the "Use .xml" button.

Congratulations! You have just created your first XML file. Here are several important reminders:

■ As explained in **Chapter 1**, the tag names must follow all the XML rules and be typed exactly as they appear, including case and spelling.

■ Include at least one root element at the beginning and end of your code. (Remember, it doesn't have to be called *root*.)

■ Spacing, tabs, and hard returns inserted between the XML tags can be used or ignored by your applications. See the sidebar "Wasting Spacing" for a detailed description.

■ The XML code as typed is perfectly usable in InDesign, but some applications may require a processing declaration on the first line of the file, such as `<?xml version="1.0" encoding="UTF-8"?>`. This line declares the version, encoding, and mode for the XML document. Before creating the XML code, check the specific needs of your application.

Wasting Spacing

Adding white space (extra spaces and hard returns) between code elements is a common practice in Web design. White space in HTML—and XML—makes the code easier to read but doesn't affect the placement, formatting, or meaning of the elements. The concept of spacing being ignored by a computer application is hard to understand unless you've had extensive experience in HTML.

Here we demonstrate the concept by writing the same piece of code three times. **Important:** Note that all the white space differences occur *between* elements and not *within* the data.

The first line represents the basic code:

```
<data><alphabet><letter>A</letter><letter>B</letter></alphabet></data>
```

In the second example we add spaces between the elements:

```
<data>   <alphabet>   <letter>A</letter>   <letter>B</letter>   </alphabet>   </data>
```

In the third example we insert hard returns between the elements:

```
<data>
<alphabet>
<letter>A</letter>
<letter>B</letter>
</alphabet>
</data>
```

Very simply, the data depicted in each of these three examples is identical: AB.

There is one caveat: In HTML, white space is ignored by default; in XML, whether white space will be ignored is up to the specific application, and the user.

For example, in InDesign's XML Import Options dialog you must choose whether to ignore the white space in the imported code (**Figure 3.2**).

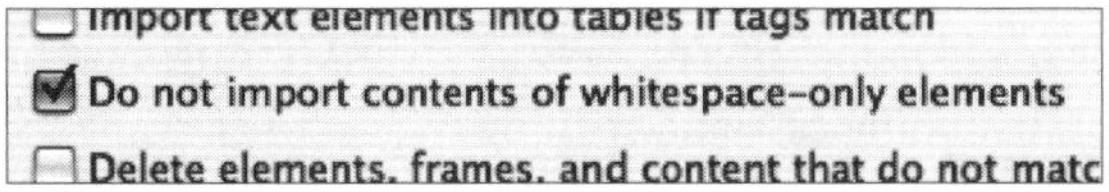

Figure 3.2

When the box is checked, InDesign ignores the white space between the elements and imports *only* the data. Leaving the option unchecked brings in the data *and* the white space. Be careful, though. Importing white space can open a Pandora's Box of trouble, playing havoc with your layouts. Luckily, InDesign's powerful Undo feature can save you. If only Pandora had had Undo.

InDesign, Story Editor, and InCopy

Pros: Feature powerful WYSIWYG capabilities for creating, editing, and applying XML tags. Enable you to view and modify XML structure, add attributes, comments, and processing instructions. Provide support for DTD validation. Available for Mac and Windows computers.

Cons: No support for XML Schema validation. Insert extraneous code elements and invisible characters in the XML, which can cause trouble when using the XML for applications outside of InDesign or repurposing within InDesign.

In a pinch, TextEdit and Notepad can serve your XML creation needs but, if you have a lot of code to write, typing all the tag names manually can get really tedious really fast. Additionally, the chances of making a typo multiply with each line of code you have to create. Using a program that can reduce or eliminate the need for manual tagging would be a great advantage, right? Luckily, the chances are good that you, as a reader of this book, already own at least one of these programs.

You may have gathered from **Chapter 2** that InDesign, Story Editor, and InCopy have exceptional XML tagging capabilities (see **Figure 3.3** for an example of Story Editor's features). These programs offer serious advantages over your operating system's text editor.

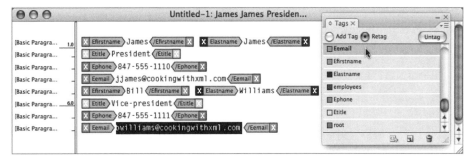

Figure 3.3 The large, colorful tag icons in InDesign's Story Editor make the job of adding XML structure simple and nearly foolproof.

To create XML in InDesign, Story Editor, or InCopy, do this:

1. Launch InDesign or InCopy.

2. Create a new document. Any size will do.

3. Show the Structure pane, tag markers, and tagged frames (see "Revealing XML Structure" in **Chapter 2**).

4. Select and rename the default **Root** element as dataroot (see "Editing Tags" in **Chapter 2**).

5. Create the following tag names in the Tags panel (see "Creating Tags" in **Chapter 2**):

- `<employees>`
- `<Efirstname>`
- `<Elastname>`
- `<Etitle>`
- `<Ephone>`
- `<Eemail>`

6. Create a new text frame in InDesign's Layout view or insert your cursor in an existing frame in InCopy.

In InDesign you first have to create a text frame before typing in Layout view or Story Editor. Make the frame big. The frame size and text size do not have an impact on the code—they only make it more convenient for you. If you are working with multiple pages, you'll find the continuous scrolling view of Story Editor or InCopy's Story and Galley views more manageable.

7. Type the following text:

```
James James
President
847-555-1110
jjames@cookingwithxml.com
Bill Williams
Vice-president
847-555-1111
bwilliams@cookingwithxml.com
```

8. In Layout view in InDesign and InCopy, select the text frame using the Selection tool and tag it with `<employees>`. In InDesign's Story Editor, or InCopy's Galley or Story view, insert the cursor in the text without selecting any content; click the `<employees>` tag.

9. Using the Text tool, select the first *James* and tag it with `<Efirstname>` (see "Applying Tags to Text" in **Chapter 2**).

10. Select and tag the second *James* with `<Elastname>`.

11. Select and tag *President* with `<Etitle>`.

12. Select and tag *847-555-1110* with `<Ephone>`.

13. Select and tag *jjames@cookingwithxml.com* with `<Eemail>`.

14. Select and tag the second employee data the same way as in the first. The structure is completely tagged.

Exporting XML from InDesign and InCopy

Once all the text is tagged, the structure is complete and ready for exporting to XML.

To export your content to XML, do this:

1. Select the text frame or insert your text cursor into the story.

2. Select File > Export.

3. Select XML in the Format pull-down menu.

4. Name the file **my_indesign.xml**. In InCopy save it as **my_incopy.xml**.

5. Click the Save button.

The Export XML dialog appears (see "Exporting XML" in **Chapter 2**).

6. Deselect all checkboxes.

7. Click Export.

The XML file is exported to the folder specified.

NOTE *All the text within a story is exported to XML, even text that isn't tagged. Tagged text in non-linked frames is exported, too.*

Microsoft Word

Pros: Provides enhanced WYSIWYG features for XML tagging and validation, Windows version only. Provides support for validation using XML Schema (*See* "Schema" in **Chapter 1**).

Cons: No XML features in Mac version (Word 2004). Windows version requires Schema file to enable automated tagging and validation features. No support for DTD validation.

Microsoft Word is a popular word-processing application that provides varying levels of XML support, depending on whether you are on the Mac or Windows platform. For example, it can edit plain text files, and you can use it like Notepad or TextEdit: Just type the code manually and save it as XML.

NOTE *You can create XML in any version of Word if you type the XML code manually. But remember to save the file as Text Only—any other format is incompatible with an XML workflow.*

Creating XML in Word

To create XML code in either the Mac or Windows version of Word, do this:

1. Launch Microsoft Word on Mac or Windows.

For this method almost any version of Word will work.

2. Type the following code:

```
<dataroot>
<employees>
<Efirstname>James</Efirstname>
<Elastname>James</Elastname>
<Etitle>President</Etitle>
<Ephone>847-555-1110</Ephone>
<Eemail>jjames@cookingwithxml.com</Eemail>
</employees>
<employees>
<Efirstname>Bill</Efirstname>
<Elastname>Williams</Elastname>
<Etitle>Vice-president</Etitle>
<Ephone>847-555-1111</Ephone>
<Eemail>bwilliams@cookingwithxml.com</Eemail>
</employees>
</dataroot>
```

3. Select File > Save As.

4. Select Plain Text (*.txt) from the Save As Type pull-down menu.

5. Name the file **my_word.xml** (**Figure 3.4**).

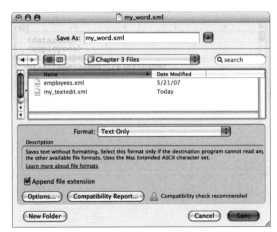

Figure 3.4 Save the file as Text Only. Any other format will not be compatible with our XML workflow.

Notice the name of the file after you save it. Word sometimes adds extensions such as .TXT automatically to the end of a filename when it's saved. So it may look like this: **my_word.xml.txt**. If so, just delete the extra .TXT extension.

How Plain Is Plain Enough?

In the good old 8-bit ASCII text days, *plain text* was exactly that, plain. Plain text files stored the basic ASCII character set, hard returns, spaces, sometimes tabs, but little else. Fonts, color, graphics, margins, and everything else were tossed out.

The .TXT file you stumble across on your hard drive today, though, may not be yesterday's humble text file. Open it and you might get a big surprise—say bullets, dingbats, even Chinese characters!

A brave new text world has arrived, bringing with it a panoply of different encodings and character support. Unicode, UTF-8, UTF-16, and other encodings have opened up the simple text file format to thousands of characters that were simply not supported in the past. And, of course, the new expanded capabilities have also brought with them some new problems.

We've said several times that XML is a plain text format and that's true. But what you'll discover is that some programs (such as InDesign and InCopy) insert characters into the code that aren't supported by some Internet browsers or older XML applications. And, as if that's not bad enough, sometimes these characters are *invisible*!

That's right, you can't see them. They're infesting the entire text file waiting for the most inopportune moment to suddenly become visible and wreak havoc on some poor unsuspecting Web designer or, worse, you yourself (**Figure 3.5**)!

Figure 3.5 On the left you see some odd characters that sometimes appear in a browser when XML is exported from certain programs. On the right is the correct view.

There are several methods for correcting the odd character problem. We tackle these invisible demons again in **Chapter 11**. For now, here's a quick and easy way to deal with them:

1. Open the text (XML) file in TextEdit or Notepad.

2. In TextEdit select Format > Make Plain Text. In Notepad, select File > Save As. In the Encoding pull-down menu of the Save As dialog, experiment with the settings: Unicode, Unicode big endian, or UTF-8. Do not use ANSI: This will turn all the invisibles into question marks "?".

3. Save the file.

This procedure should create a file that eliminates the undesirable characters.

Accessing Word's Advanced XML Support

For Windows users, Word 2003 and later versions offer additional features for tagging and validation that aren't available to users of any Mac version to date. To access these features you must first create and load a Schema file. This is a drawback for designers because InDesign and InCopy support only DTDs. Lucky for you, we have a sample Schema already prepared.

To access the advanced XML features in Word for Windows, do this:

1. Launch Word 2003 or later.

Word appears with a new, empty document.

NOTE *The XML features in Word 2007 are accessed through the options available in the Developer tab (**Figure 3.6**). If this tab is not visible, select Office Button > Word Options > Popular > Show Developer Tab in the Ribbon.*

Office Button   Structure Pane   Load Schema   Developer Tab

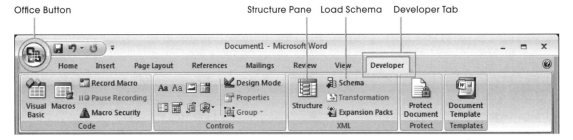

Figure 3.6 In Word 2007 you have to activate the Developer tab to access the advanced XML support.

2. Type the following text:

```
James James
President
847-555-1110
jjames@cookingwithxml.com
Bill Williams
Vice-president
847-555-1111
bwilliams@cookingwithxml.com
```

3. Select Developer > Schema.

The Templates and Add-Ins dialog appears and should display the XML Schema tab automatically. If you have never used these features before, the Schema library will probably be empty.

4. Click the Add Schema button (see "Schema" in **Chapter 1**).

5. Open the Chapter 3 Files folder downloaded from the book's Web site. Select **employees.xsd**. Click Open.

The Schema Settings dialog appears (**Figure 3.7**). Here we're loading the Schema file (*.XSD) to take advantage of Word for Windows' advanced tagging and validation features.

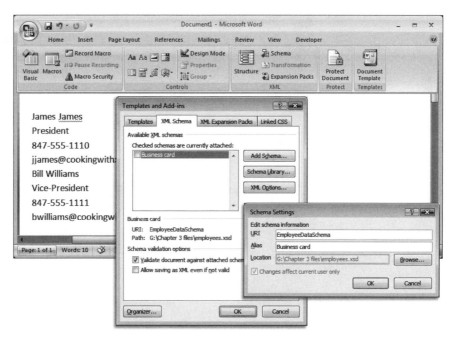

Figure 3.7 Because Word requires the use of a Schema instead of a DTD, its usefulness is limited to a support role for our XML workflow.

6. Type **EmployeeDataSchema** in the URI text field of the Schema Settings dialog.

The URI is the schema's formal name, which can also incorporate a URL to enable access to it on the Internet. The URI reference is appended to the top of the XML file when it's saved from Word.

7. Type **Business Cards** in the Alias text field.

The Alias is a name used only by Word to help you more quickly identify and differentiate between the schemas in your library.

8. Click OK.

The dataroot and employees elements appear in Word's XML Structure pane.

9. Press Ctrl-A to select all the text.

10. Click the dataroot element in the XML Structure pane.

The "Apply to entire document?" dialog appears (**Figure 3.8**). Click the Apply to Entire Document button. Tag markers for the dataroot element appear at the beginning and end of the text.

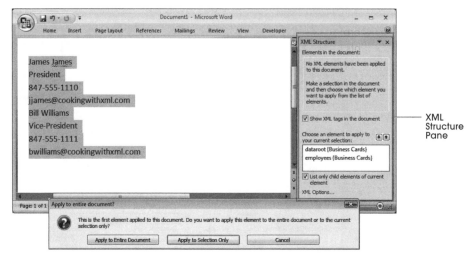

Figure 3.8 The XML structure in Word begins by adding a root element from the XML Structure menu in the Task Pane.

11. Select the name, title, phone number, and email address for James James.

12. Click the employees element.

The employees tags appear at the beginning and end of the selection. Element names for **Efirstname**, **Elastname**, **Etitle**, **Ephone**, and **Eemail** appear in the XML Structure pane.

13. Select and assign the appropriate XML element to each piece of data.

14. Repeat steps 11–13 as necessary for the next employee: Bill Williams.

The text is completely tagged.

"V" Is for Validation

You will notice that the existing structure doesn't validate according to the schema we're using (**Figure 3.9**) because it's missing text tagged with the element `EmployeeID`. We don't use the `EmployeeID` element in our sample workflow in **Chapter 4**, so missing the element here is not a problem. However, in some XML workflows a missing or out-of-place element can bring the roof crashing in (proverbial, that is). In this case the fix is easy: Insert a unique ID number in front of both `Efirstname` elements and tag them as `EmployeeID`. The structure should now validate according to the schema.

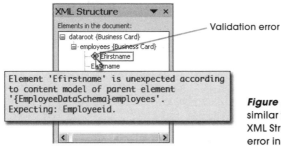

Figure 3.9 Word provides validation features similar to InDesign and InCopy. Notice how the XML Structure pane indicates that there is an error in the structure.

To save the file as XML, do this:

1. Select File > Save As.

2. In Word 2003 choose XML Document from the "Save as type" pull-down menu. In Word 2007, choose Word 2003 XML Document from the "Save as type" pull-down menu.

3. Choose the "Save data only" checkbox (**Figure 3.10**).

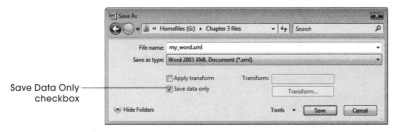

Figure 3.10 STOP! It's easy to miss it, but you'll be sorry. Make sure you choose the "Save data only" checkbox or your XML will be pretty useless. Word 2007 offers two XML formats; only the Word 2003 XML Document is usable in our XML workflow.

NOTE *If the "Save data only" checkbox is not checked, Word creates a bloated and largely unusable XML file.*

4. Name the file **my_word2.xml**.

5. Click the Save button.

Voila, the XML file is created. Word offers editors and writers many of the same advantages as InDesign and InCopy for tagging text. The main advantage of using Word is saving the cost of buying and learning another program. Since most editors and writers already have Word, but may not own InDesign or InCopy, this can be a significant savings of cost in large work groups.

Microsoft Excel

Pros: Provides enhanced features for creating data-driven XML files, Windows version only. Provides support for validation using XML Schema (see "Schema" in **Chapter 1**).

Cons: Virtually nonexistent XML support in Mac version. No support for DTD validation.

Another popular program and a natural candidate for creating XML files—especially ones that emphasize data over text—is Microsoft Excel. Unfortunately, as we learned with Word, Excel's XML features are entirely on the Windows side of the family. Excel 2004 for the Mac allows you to save a spreadsheet as XML, but don't bother. For our purposes, the Mac-Excel file is practically worthless in an XML workflow.

Creating XML in Excel

To create a usable XML file from Excel for Windows, do this:

1. Launch Excel 2003 or later.

2. In Excel 2003 select View > Task Pane. Then, choose XML Source from the Task Pane pull-down menu. In Excel 2007, select Source from the Developer tab.

> NOTE *If the Developer tab is not visible in Excel you can display it (as in Word 2007) by accessing the Popular tab of the Excel Options dialog and clicking the checkbox: Show Developer tab in the Ribbon.*

3. Click the XML Maps button in the Task Pane.

The XML Maps dialog appears. If you have never used this feature, the dialog should be empty.

4. Click the Add button.

The Select XML Source dialog appears. You may select any XML or XSD (Schema) file to structure your data.

5. Open the Chapter 3 Files folder and select **employees.xml**. Click Open.

The dataroot_Map appears in the XML maps dialog.

6. Click OK.

The dataroot_Map appears in the XML Structure Pane with a list of XML elements beneath it.

Tagging Spreadsheet Cells with XML Elements

At this moment the spreadsheet is not structured. To create an XML structure you have to tag cells with the elements from the XML Structure pane. There are two ways to tag the cells.

To tag cells one at a time in Excel, do this:

1. Click on cell A1.

Which cell you start in doesn't matter, but remember that the new data is inserted vertically in columns. It makes sense to allow space for the data to expand.

2. Double-click Employeeid in the XML Structure pane.

The XML structure appears in cell A1.

3. Click on cell A2. Double-click the Efirstname element.

The XML structure appears in cell A2.

You can continue to assign the elements one at a time, but there's a faster way if you have multiple elements to map.

To map multiple elements at once, do this:

1. Press Ctrl-A to select all.

2. Select Edit > Clear > Contents.

This method requires a fresh start. You must clear the existing structure because an XML element cannot be assigned twice in the same spreadsheet.

3. Drag the employees parent element from the XML Structure pane to cell A1 (**Figure 3.11**).

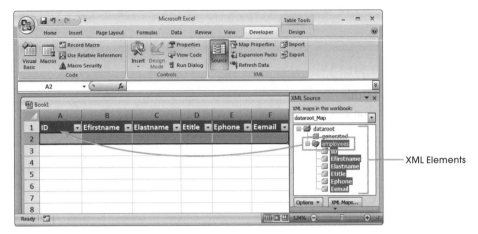

Figure 3.11 Excel 2003 for Windows and later makes an excellent source for data-intensive XML.

The entire employees structure appears in the spreadsheet, starting in cell A1. The exact cell you start in is not important as long as you allow the structure enough space to expand as data is added.

Entering Data into an XML Structure

The structure is now ready to accept data for your XML project. For data-intensive workflows, Excel makes a handy tool.

To enter data into the XML structure, do this:

1. Click in cell A2.

2. Type **1**. Press the Tab key.

    Cell B2 is automatically selected.

3. In cell B2, type **James**. Press the Tab key.

4. In cell C2, type **James**. Press the Tab key.

5. In cell D2, type **President**. Press the Tab key.

6. In cell E2, type **847-555-1110**. Press the Tab key.

7. In cell F2, type **jjames@cookingwithxml.com**. Press the Tab key.

8. In row 3, enter the following data into consecutive cells: **2, Bill, Williams, Vice-president, 847-555-1111, bwilliams@cookingwithxml.com**.

Exporting XML from Excel

When you are finished entering data and ready to create XML, there's an important trick that you need to know about creating usable XML from Excel. Although Excel provides a Save As "XML Spreadsheet" (Excel 2003) or "XML Spreadsheet 2003" (Excel 2007) command, don't touch it. The resulting file is really not usable for our XML workflow.

Although there's one way you *shouldn't* use to create XML, Excel offers several ways that can create XML properly, do this:

1. In either version choose XML Data (*.xml) from the "Save as type" pull-down menu in the Save As dialog or right-click in the tagged data itself and select XML > Export from the context menu. In Excel 2003 select Data > XML > Export. In Excel 2007 select Export from the Developer tab.

The Export XML dialog appears.

2. Name the file **my_excel.xml** (**Figure 3.12**).

Figure 3.12 The "Save as type" pull-down menu offers two choices for XML. Choose XML Data (*.xml) or look in the Data menu for the XML Export command.

3. Click Export.

The XML file is complete.

FileMaker Pro

Pros: Provides an easy method for creating data-driven XML files. Available for Mac and Windows platforms.

Cons: Difficult procedure for importing XML data into database.

As XML is basically a method of storing and transferring data, the use of a database program to create XML seems natural. Apple's cross-platform FileMaker Pro and Microsoft Access are popular database programs that both offer XML support in their latest versions. The nice thing about using a database over other methods is that you can take advantage of the abilities of the program to produce a variety of calculations, including sums, averages, and products. Databases are also good at sorting, grouping, and filtering. For example, before you create an XML file for a direct mail piece, it's a simple task to filter your clients' records by their interest and/or income and then sort them by ZIP code for bulk mailing.

FileMaker Pro is one of the few database programs available to Mac users, but it also offers an equally usable Windows version. To create XML in FileMaker Pro, do this:

1. Launch FileMaker Pro 8 or later.

The program opens and the New Database dialog appears automatically.

2. Select "Create a new empty file" and click OK.

The "Create a new empty file named:" dialog appears. (Database programs require you to name the file before you can enter any data.)

3. Name the file **my_employees.fp7**. Click Save.

The Define Database for "employees" dialog appears. Use this dialog to create the field names used to identify the data stored within the file. Because the field names will become your XML element names when you export the data, they should conform to the rules described in **Chapter 1**.

4. Type **Efirstname** in the Field Name text field. Select **Text** in the Type field. Click the Create button.

The Efirstname field appears in the field name list.

5. Create the remaining fields with the following specifications:

FIELD NAME	TYPE
Elastname	Text
Etitle	Text
Ephone	Text
Eemail	Text
Ephoto	Text

You may have noticed that the Ephoto field is defined as a text field. FileMaker Pro and Access are both capable of storing images and other objects as well as text and numbers. So you may be wondering: Why are we storing the employee's photo as text?

The simple answer is that we have no choice. Like HTML, XML supports only text-based references to graphics. So we're going to store the "name" of the image and eventually connect it to its location on the hard drive, or to a URL on the Internet, later in the process.

6. Click OK (**Figure 3.13**).

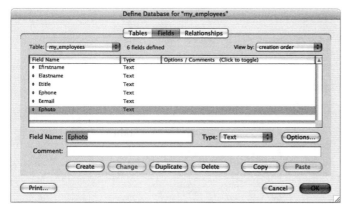

Figure 3.13 In a database program the field names will become our XML elements, so the names should conform to XML rules. Abbreviate whenever possible. For example, we shortened **Employee First Name** to **Efirstname**.

Entering Data into FileMaker Pro

The database is ready to accept data entry. To enter data into FileMaker Pro, do this:

1. Select Records > New Record.

The text cursor appears in the **Efirstname** field.

2. Type **James** in the Efirstname field. Press the Tab key to move to the next field.

3. Type **James** in the Elastname field. Press the Tab key.

4. Type **President** in the Etitle field. Press the Tab key.

5. Type **847-555-1110** in the Ephone field. Press the Tab key.

6. Type **jjames@cookingwithxml.com** in the Eemail field. Press the Tab key.

7. Type **jjames.jpg** in the Ephoto field (**Figure 3.14**).

Figure 3.14 FileMaker Pro's ability to sort, filter, and perform calculations allows you to quickly and easily generate XML files with unlimited variations.

The first record is complete. To start a new record, do this:

8. Press Cmd-N/Ctrl-N.

A blank record layout appears.

9. Repeat steps 2–8 and enter the following records into the database:

Efirstname	Elastname	Etitle	Ephone	Eemail	Ephoto
Bill	Williams	Vice-president	847-555-1111	bwilliams@sf.com	bwilliams.jpg
Martin	Marty	CEO	847-555-1112	mmarty@sf.com	mmarty.jpg
Steve	Stephens	Line Supervisor	847-555-1113	sstephens@sf.com	sstephens.jpg
Lillie	Lilac	CFO	847-555-1114	llilac@sf.com	llilac.jpg
Mildred	Millie	Operations Manager	847-555-1115	mmillie@sf.com	mmillie.jpg

Exporting XML from FileMaker Pro

To export XML from FileMaker Pro, do this:

1. Select File > Export Records.

The Export Records to Files dialog appears.

2. Choose XML from the Type pull-down menu.

3. Name the file **my_filemaker.xml**. Click Save.

The Specify XML and XSL Options dialog appears.

4. Choose **FMPDSORESULT** from the Grammar pull-down menu (**Figure 3.15**). Click Continue.

The Specify Field Order for Export dialog appears.

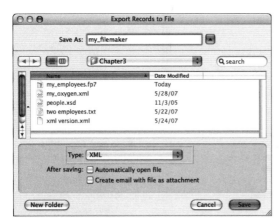
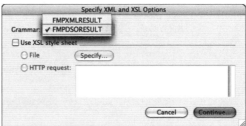

Figure 3.15 FileMaker offers two formats, or grammars, for exporting XML. Choose FMPDSORESULT exclusively for an XML workflow. FMPXMLRESULT creates XML that is virtually unusable in InDesign.

5. Click Move All to export all the fields from the database (**Figure 3.16**).

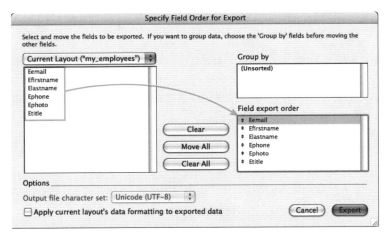

Figure 3.16 Note how FileMaker Pro lists the Field names in alphabetical order. Place them in the desired order before exporting the data to XML.

6. Arrange the fields in the following order: **Efirstname**, **Elastname**, **Etitle**, **Ephone**, **Eemail**, **Ephoto**.

The fields need to be placed in the proper order for use in InDesign.

7. Click Export...

The XML file has been created.

Microsoft Access

Pros: Provides an easy method for creating data-driven XML files. Automatically generates XSD Schema on XML export. Allows XSL Transformation on export.

Cons: Available on Windows platform only. Supports Schemas, but not DTDs.

Microsoft added support for XML in the 2002 version of Access. To create XML, do this:

1. Launch Access 2002 or later.

2. Select File > New. (In Access 2007 skip this step.)

The New File Task Pane appears.

3. Click the Blank database link in the New File Task Pane. In Access 2007 click the Blank Database button in the Getting Started screen.

The File New Database dialog appears.

4. Name the database **my_employees.mdb** (or **my_employees.accdb** in Access 2007). Click Create.

   The Access Database window appears.

5. Select the Database tab of the Database window. Double-click Create Table in Design view. In Access 2007 click the View button to switch to Design View. The program may ask you to name the table before proceeding; name it **employees**.

   The Design view window appears.

6. Type **Efirstname** in the first Field Name position. **Text** appears as the default data type.

7. Create the remaining fields with the following specifications:

FIELD NAME	TYPE
Elastname	Text
Etitle	Text
Ephone	Text
Eemail	Text
Ephoto	Text

   In Access a text field can store up to 255 characters, but 50 characters (pictured in **Figure 3.17**) should be sufficient for any of the fields in our employee database.

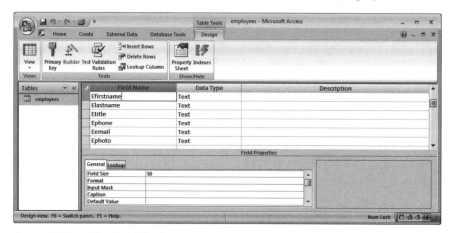

Figure 3.17 Specify a Field Size large enough to accommodate the anticipated data, but to optimize the database, don't make it larger than necessary.

8. Select View > Datasheet View.

The Save As dialog appears. In Access 2007 a dialog appears prompting you to save the table.

9. Name the Table **my_employees**. In Access 2007 click Yes to save the changes to your table.

In Access 2002, a warning dialog appears requesting that you define a primary key. A *primary key* is a unique field that can be used to identify one record from another, like an individual's social security number. If this were an actual employee database, you would add an Employeeid field to serve as the primary key. For the purposes of this lesson, it is unnecessary. No warning dialog appears in Access 2007 because it creates an ID field automatically that becomes the primary key by default.

10. Click No. In Access 2007 no response is necessary.

11. Enter the following data into the **my_employees** table as described in "Entering Data into FileMaker Pro," steps 2–7, earlier in this chapter.

EFIRSTNAME	ELASTNAME	ETITLE	EPHONE	EEMAIL	EPHOTO
James	James	President	847-555-1110	jjames@cookingwithxml.com	jjames.jpg
Bill	Williams	Vice-president	847-555-1111	bwilliams@cookingwithxml.com	bwilliams.jpg
Martin	Marty	CEO	847-555-1112	mmarty@cookingwithxml.com	mmarty.jpg
Steve	Stephens	Line Supervisor	847-555-1113	sstephens@cookingwithxml.com	sstephens.jpg
Lillie	Lilac	CFO	847-555-1114	llilac@cookingwithxml.com	llilac.jpg
Mildred	Millie	Operations Manager	847-555-1115	mmillie@cookingwithxml.com	mmillie.jpg

In Access 2007 each record begins with an ID field that is filled in automatically by the program as each new record is added. When entering data in Access 2007 press the Tab key to bypass the ID field and move to the Efirstname field to start typing.

12. Select File > Export. In Access 2007 select External Data > More > XML File (**Figure 3.18**).

The Export Table 'my_employees' To… dialog appears. In Access 2007 the Export — XML File dialog appears.

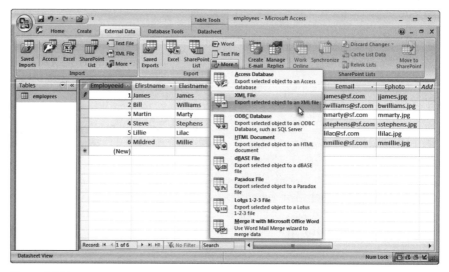

Figure 3.18 Access got a major facelift, like all the Microsoft Office 2007 applications. The XML export command is in the More menu, under the External Data tab.

13. Choose XML (*.xml) from the "Save as type" pull-down menu. In Access 2007 skip to step 14.

14. Name the file **my_access.xml**. Click Export All. In Access 2007 click OK.

The Export XML dialog appears. This dialog allows you specify what XML components you want to export: Data, Schema, and/or XSL. Click the More Options button if you want to apply an XSLT (see "XSLT" in **Chapter 1**) to the data during export.

15. Select only the Data (XML) checkbox. Click OK.

The XML file has been created.

Adobe Dreamweaver

Pros: Provides an easy method for creating, tagging, and editing XML data. Provides method for checking well-formed XML. Powerful tools for creating and applying XSL transformations. Comes in Mac and Windows versions.

Cons: No support for validation to DTD or XSD Schemas.

Adobe Dreamweaver is the most popular of the WYSIWYG Web design programs. In addition to its unmatched HTML capabilities, it also has powerful and handy tools for creating XML, DTD, XSD, and XSL files.

To create XML in Dreamweaver, do this:

1. Launch Dreamweaver MX or later.

Like TextEdit and Notepad, Dreamweaver can create and edit XML data out of the box. But this is no reason to use the program. The real advantage to Dreamweaver is its ability to automatically tag data and a rudimentary ability to check for well-formed XML. To access Dreamweaver's tagging features you first have to load the tag names, like this:

2. Select Edit > Tag Libraries….

The Tag Library Editor dialog appears.

3. Click the Plus (+) sign and select DTD Schema > Import XML DTD or Schema File.

The Import XML DTD or Schema File dialog appears.

4. Click the Browse button. Select **employees.dtd**. Click OK in each dialog to return to the file window (**Figure 3.19**).

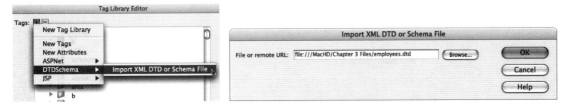

Figure 3.19 To prepare Dreamweaver for creating XML you first have to load a DTD or Schema that defines the desired structure.

The tag names from the DTD are loaded into the Tag Library; however, the DTD is *not* used to validate the XML data or its structure.

5. Select File > New. Select Blank Page > XML. Click Create.

An Untitled document is created and displays in Code view only. Note the XML DOCTYPE declaration in line 1.

6. Insert the cursor at the end of line 1 and press Return/Enter to create a new line.

7. Type **<** in line 2 or press Cmd-Spacebar/Ctrl-Spacebar to open the code hints list.

The code hints list opens, displaying a list of available Tag names (**Figure 3.20**).

Figure 3.20 The code hints list opens automatically when the opening bracket (<) is typed. Note how after the DTD is loaded in step 3 the XML tags appear in the code hints list.

8. Select ‹dataroot› from the list by double-clicking or press Return/Enter to insert the entire element name. You may need to type the > symbol to properly complete the element name.

The element is inserted automatically into the code window.

9. Repeat step 7 and insert the ‹employees› element.

10. Insert ‹Efirstname›. Type **James**.

11. Type **</.**

The closing element ‹/Efirstname› automatically appears.

12. Add the following XML code to the file:

```
<Elastname>James</Elastname>
<Etitle>President</Etitle>
<Ephone>847-555-1110</Ephone>
<Eemail>jjames@cookingwithxml.com</Eemail>
</employees>
<employees>
<Efirstname>Bill</Efirstname>
<Elastname>Williams</Elastname>
<Etitle>Vice-president</Etitle>
<Ephone>847-555-1111</Ephone>
<Eemail>bwilliams@cookingwithxml.com</Eemail>
</employees>
</dataroot>
```

13. Save the file as **my_dreamweaver.xml**.

The XML file has been created. In **Chapter 11**, we return to Dreamweaver to demonstrate how you can use it to quickly format XML data for Web display.

SyncRo Soft

Pros: Provides an easy method for creating, tagging, and editing XML data. Provides method for checking well-formed XML and validation based on both DTD and Schemas. Available in Mac and Windows versions.

Cons: No WYSIWYG display or editing of tags or code elements.

We waited until the end of the chapter to demonstrate dedicated XML editors. Before showing you how these programs worked, we felt it important you understood that XML is simply a way to mark up text, and not some sort of special type of computer file or proprietary technology. We hope you realize that you don't need a dedicated XML editor to create XML—but having one can pay enormous dividends. Several XML editors are available, and we have direct experience with two: SyncRo Soft <oXygen/> and Altova XMLSpy.

Unlike the other programs and methods we've explored in this chapter, XML editors, such as <oXygen/> and XMLSpy, provide a variety of efficiencies, both in code making as well as validation. The advantages are significant enough that we recommend at least one person in every work group have a dedicated XML editor, if not everyone.

Feel free to try them before you buy them; most of the XML editors that we looked at offer free downloads and as many as 30 days to test-drive the programs.

SyncRo Soft <oXygen/> is one of the handful of XML editors available on the Mac platform; most are Windows-based. One nice aspect of <oXygen/> is its cross-platform support. If your company uses both Macs and Windows, it allows you to standardize on one XML editing package to minimize training and support costs.

You can use <oXygen/> to create XML manually, line by line, but then it's no better than TextEdit and Notepad. We prefer to automate the process by throwing a DTD or Schema into the mix. To create XML, do this:

1. Launch <oXygen/>.

2. Select File > New.

   The New dialog appears (**Figure 3.21**).

3. Choose XML Document in the New document file list. Click OK.

   The "Create an XML document" dialog appears.

Figure 3.21 <oXygen/>, like most XML editors, is capable of creating a whole host of file types needed for a comprehensive XML workflow, including .DTD, .XML, .XSD, .XSL, .XHTML, and others.

Because InDesign uses DTDs but not Schemas, let's use a DTD as the foundation of our XML file:

4. Select the DTD tab. Click the folder icon in the SystemID: text field. Locate and select the **employees.dtd** file. Click Open.

The path to the DTD file will appear in the SystemID: text field.

5. Choose dataroot in the Document root: pull-down menu (**Figure 3.22**). Click OK.

An Untitled XML file will appear within the program interface.

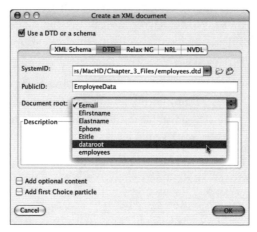

Figure 3.22 Like Dreamweaver, <oXygen/> requires that you load a DTD or Schema to access specific XML features.

6. Insert the cursor in the blank space in line 4 or anywhere after the <dataroot> opening element.

7. Type **<**.

The element list appears.

8. Select employees and press the Return key (**Figure 3.23**).

A complete <employees> element, along with its child elements, appears in the document window.

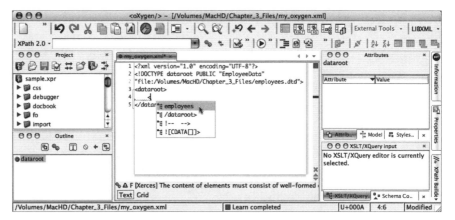

Figure 3.23 When the new document is created based on the DTD, several elements are automatically added to the file including the DOCTYPE declaration and the root element. Note how the element list opens when you type the opening < symbol.

9. Press Cmd-] to insert the cursor within the <Efirstname> element. Type **James**.

10. Press Cmd-] twice to insert the cursor within the <Elastname> element. Type **James**.

11. Repeat step 9 until the following data is added to the file:

<Etitle>President</Etitle>

<Ephone>847-555-1110</Ephone>

<Eemail>jjames@cookingwithxml.com</Eemail>

12. Insert the cursor after the </employees> element. Type **<**.

13. Select <employees> and press the Return key. Type the following data into the new <employees> element.

<Efirstname>Bill</Efirstname>

<Elastname>Williams</Elastname>

<Etitle>Vice-president</Etitle>

<Ephone>847-555-1111</Ephone>

<Eemail>bwilliams@cookingwithxml.com</Eemail>

14. Save the file with the name: **my_oxygen.xml**.

The XML file is created.

Altova XMLSpy

Pros: Provides an easy method for creating, tagging, and editing XML data. Provides method for checking well-formed XML and validation based on both DTD and Schemas. Multiple modules available for complete XML workflow.

Cons: No WYSIWYG display or editing of tags or code elements. No Mac version.

Altova XMLSpy offers one of the easiest-to-use XML editors with a straightforward, clean interface. The procedure for making XML in XMLSpy is similar to that used in <oXygen/>. To create XML, do this:

1. Launch XMLSpy.

2. Select File > New.

The "Create new document" dialog appears.

3. Select XML Document (**Figure 3.24**). Click OK.

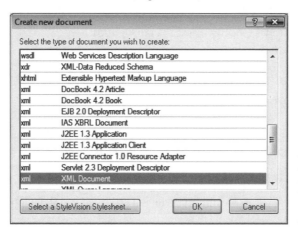

Figure 3.24 XMLSpy can create any type of file necessary for a comprehensive XML workflow, including .DTD, .XML, .XSD, .XSL, and .XHTML among others.

The New File dialog appears asking whether you want to use a DTD or Schema to construct the file. If you click Cancel, you will have to create the file manually as we did with TextEdit and Notepad.

4. Select DTD. Click OK.

The XMLSpy dialog appears, in which you select the DTD or Schema file.

5. Click Browse. Select the **employee.dtd**. Click Open.

Note the "Make path relative to the Untitled.xml" checkbox. Check this box if the DTD is stored in the same folder, or in a subfolder, as the XML file. Leave the box unchecked if the DTD or Schema is located on the Internet or in a public folder on a network accessible by the user (**Figure 3.25**).

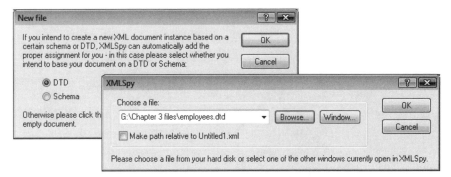

Figure 3.25 Loading a DTD or Schema is not required but is essential for accessing XMLSpy's advanced XML features, including validation.

6. Click OK.

A file window appears automatically with DOCTYPE and DTD declarations and the dataroot element inserted. Note that a dataroot element has been inserted as an empty element (see "Data Content Types Key," **Chapter 1**). You must replace this with a normal <dataroot> element.

7. Select and delete the <dataroot/> element.

8. Type <.

The element list window appears.

9. Select the <dataroot> element. Press the Enter key. Type the closing > symbol.

A complete **<dataroot>** element appears.

10. Type <.

11. Select the <employees> element. Press the Enter key. Type the closing > symbol.

A complete **<employees>** element, along with its child elements, appears in the document window.

12. Type the following data into the appropriate elements:

<Efirstname>James**</Efirstname>**

<Elastname>James**</Elastname>**

<Etitle>President**</Etitle>**

<Ephone>847-555-1110**</Ephone>**

<Eemail>jjames@cookingwithxml.com**</Eemail>**

XMLSpy provides another method for inserting elements into the file window:

13. Insert the cursor after the `</employees>` element. Double-click the `<>` `employees` item in the Elements window (**Figure 3.26**).

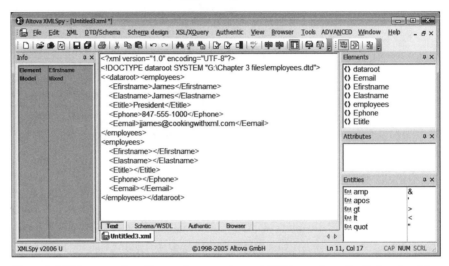

Figure 3.26 When you close the **<employees>** element, XMLSpy automatically inserts all the tags in the order specified by the DTD. Wow! All that's left for you to do is to type in the data and save the file.

14. Type the following data into the appropriate elements:

`<Efirstname>`Bill`</Efirstname>`

`<Elastname>`Williams`</Elastname>`

`<Etitle>`Vice-president`</Etitle>`

`<Ephone>`847-555-1111`</Ephone>`

`<Eemail>`bwilliams@cookingwithxml.com`</Eemail>`

15. Save the file with the name: **my_xmlspy.xml**.

The XML file is created.

Validation

Whereas dedicated XML editors offer incremental advantages over some of the other methods we explored of creating code, the true power of <oXygen/> and XMLSpy is found in their validation features. Both programs check the code against the DTD or Schema each time you save the file, instantly warning you when the code is invalid.

Try this:

1. In <oXygen/> or XMLSpy, delete one of the closing tags in your code.

2. Press Cmd-S or Ctrl-S to save the file.

Both programs warn you that the code is no longer well-formed.

3. Replace the deleted tag.

4. Select the entire `<Ephone>` element and its data. Insert it after the `<Etitle>` element.

5. Press Cmd-S or Ctrl-S to save the file.

Both programs warn you that the code is no longer valid according to the DTD definition, because one of the elements is out of order. <oXygen/> and XMLSpy are able to check for both well-formed and valid XML code, among other things, which can be invaluable under high-pressure deadlines and tight production schedules.

Comparing Code

Side by side, it's easy to see how similar the XML is from file to file and program to program. If you created a sample file for each of the programs we examine in this chapter you should have nearly a dozen XML files in your folder. Go ahead and open all the files in <oXygen/> or XMLSpy, or any other program we describe, and compare them side by side. The first thing you'll notice is that all the programs created nearly identical XML code. With only a stray attribute or comment here and there to differentiate them, each of the files could be used interchangeably in an XML workflow. In fact, the data in these examples is the same used for the business card project in **Chapter 4**. Feel free to substitute one of the XML files you created in place of the data supplied for that project.

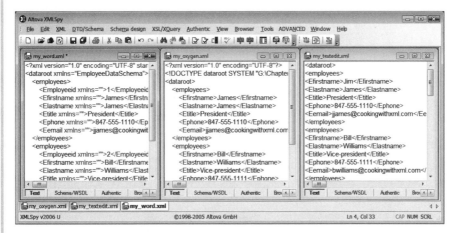

Figure 3.27 Aside from a comment or attribute here and there, the code is identical and, most importantly, interchangeable.

NOTE *Both <oXygen/> and XMLSpy check for well-formed and valid XML each time you save the file. In turn, both programs prevent you from saving badly written or invalid code until the errors have been corrected. If you want to check the code as it's being written, use the following commands:*

- *To check for well-formed XML:*
  In <oXygen/> press Cmd-Shift-W (Ctrl-Shift-W). In XMLSpy press F7.

- *To check for valid XML:*
  In <oXygen/> press Cmd-Shift-V (Ctrl-Shift-V). In XMLSpy press F8.

Review

In addition to InDesign, we strongly recommend that every XML work group includes at least one copy of Dreamweaver as well as a dedicated XML editor. Data-intensive workflows may choose to add Excel and FileMaker or Access to their programmatic options. With these programs at hand, you will be well prepared to handle anything an XML workflow can throw at you.

We covered a lot of ground in this chapter. Things went by so fast you may have missed some important points. Here's a quick recap:

- XML is non-proprietary. You don't have to buy special software or pay any licensing fees.

- XML is XML no matter what program creates it.

- Some programs offer advantages over others when creating or editing XML.

- You will probably need more than one program for an XML workflow.

Structure Basics

In this chapter you will learn how to:

- Create/import XML tags

- Create a structured layout

- Import XML

- Flow XML into a structured layout

- Work with InDesign's Structure pane

This chapter introduces you to InDesign's XML tools and capabilities. We have chosen a simple, real-world project on which to cut your XML teeth, because the best way to learn how to do something is to actually do it. As the ABCs are often the first thing we learn as children, designing business cards is basic to the vocabulary of the average designer.

By its description a *business card* is the very definition of a structured document. First, business cards use a standard design: fonts, color, and placement are identical on each card. Second, each card contains the name, title, and contact information for one employee, as well as the company name, logo, and address. In effect, each business card is a single record in the corporate database.

Let's start by opening a partially finished version of the project that'll jump start your XML education and show you what a completed project looks like.

NOTE   Download all files for Chapter 4 from www.peachpit.com/indesignxmlguide and copy them to a folder on your hard drive (approximately 2 MB).

Sample Project: One-Up Business Card

The following lessons begin your education in how XML works with InDesign by creating a simple data-driven project.

Lesson 4-1: XML Foundation

Scenario: You have just received a job from a new customer. The company hired six new employees and wants you to create a business card for each. An XML-savvy coworker set up an InDesign template and forwarded the layout and XML to you for completion.

1. Open **1card.indt** from the Project 1 folder (**Figure 4.1**).

NOTE All project files have been saved as templates (.INDT files) to prevent you from saving over the master files accidentally.

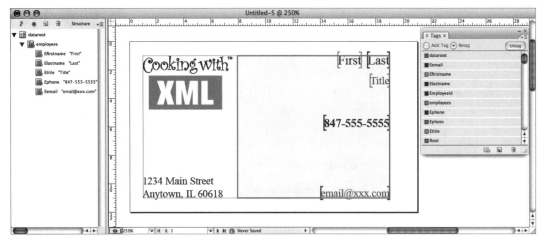

Figure 4.1 The sample business card is already structured and tagged. It is ready for you to import the XML data.

2. Display the Structure pane and the Tags panel.

Select View > Structure > Show Structure.

3. Show Tag Markers and Tagged Frames.

Select View > Structure > Show Tagged Frames.

4. Select Show Text Snippets from the Structure pane menu.

Before we go any further, take a moment to study the layout of the structured business card on the screen. Pay special attention to the colorful brackets and frames around the XML placeholder text. Later in the chapter we take you through the process step by step and explain in detail the ins and outs of constructing a structured layout. For the time being, sit back and enjoy the magic that's about to explode on your screen.

5. Select the **dataroot** element in the Structure pane (**Figure 4.2**).

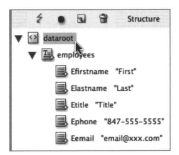

Figure 4.2 Always select the root element before importing the XML.

6. Select File > Import XML.

There are three places in InDesign where you can invoke the import XML command:

■ From the File menu.

■ From the Structure pane menu.

■ By right-clicking on a **Root** or other element within the Structure pane itself.

Don't worry. These commands all perform the same task; pick the one you prefer or use the one most convenient at the time.

7. Select **employees.xml** from the Project 1 folder.

Click the **Show XML Import Options** (**Figure 4.3**) checkbox to select it. After your XML structure is built, this checkbox should be your default selection.

■ **Import Into Selected Element** is also a default selection. If this is checked, InDesign flows the XML content into the selected tree or element—unchecked, the text flows only into the root element of the Structure pane.

■ **Merge Content** replaces any existing XML content that matches the imported XML structure.

■ Use **Append Content** when you want to import additional data into your layout.

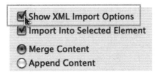

Figure 4.3 In most structured layouts you'll want to access the XML Import Options.

XML Import Woes

Do not rush the task of importing your XML; this is where the most common errors occur (**Figure 4.4**). If something does not look the way you expect it to, or does not look the same as it appears in the screen shots, STOP. Take a breath and check the Structure pane first. You may have inadvertently imported the XML into a child element instead of the root *(see **Chapter 1** if you don't know what that means)*.

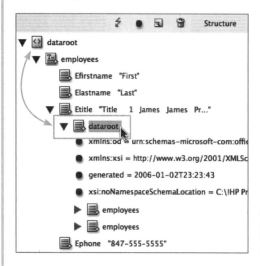

Figure 4.4 Here you can see XML content imported incorrectly into a **child** element. It must be deleted and reimported.

If this happens, and you catch the error immediately, just Undo. Otherwise select the errant content in the XML tree and trash it. In most cases, you cannot use badly imported XML for dynamic content. Just start over and remember to select the root before importing the XML the next time.

8. Click Open.

9. When the XML Import Options dialog (**Figure 4.5**) appears, turn on the following onscreen selections:

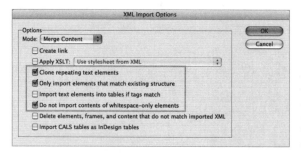

Figure 4.5 It's essential that you understand how the XML Import Option dialog affects the import of the XML content. For a full description of these options, see **Chapter 1**.

Turn off all the rest.

10. Click OK.

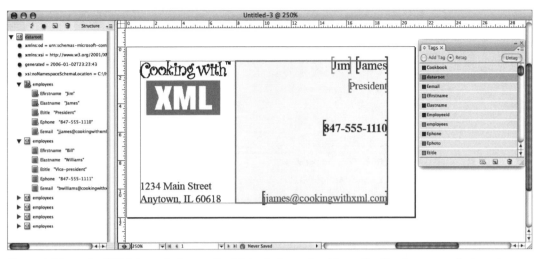

Figure 4.6 Once the XML is imported correctly, this is what you should see. The Structure pane displays six employees elements, and your placeholders have been replaced by the elements of the first record.

If everything went well, the XML placeholders have been replaced by the name, title, phone number, and email address of the first employee listed in the XML file (**Figure 4.6**). In the Structure pane you will see six employees elements. Here are some of things we want you to notice:

■ Each element of the XML data landed in the placeholder tagged for that element. For example: the employee's first name replaced the placeholder tagged as [Efirstname], his last name replaced the placeholder tagged [Elastname], and so on.

■ Only the data from the first employee listed in the XML landed in the text frame.

■ The Structure pane displays six employees elements in total. Note that the first employees icon is different from the others, indicating that this element has been placed into the document (**Figure 4.7**).

■ All elements in the layout are still tagged with the XML structure.

Although the previous example could be mildly entertaining to a jaded designer, the next exercise can knock your socks off.

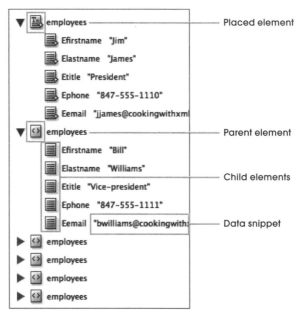

Figure 4.7 The Structure pane is a handy reference during XML workflows. It displays a wealth of information about the imported XML file, such as how many elements have been imported; the names of the elements; and, if snippets are turned on, a glimpse of the XML content as well. It can also tell you which elements may already be in your layout; here we can see by the change in the first element icon that "Jim James" is on page 1.

Lesson 4-2: Fun with the Structure pane

By importing the XML into a structured layout in **Lesson 4-1**, you created a living relationship between imported XML and the structured document. Let's explore some of the powers of this relationship:

1. Open the element for the second employee in the Structure pane.

2. Click and drag the icon for this employee's element and drop it on the tagged text frame on your layout (**Figure 4.8**). Watch out for two potential errors here:

   - You could accidentally select and drag a `child` element to the layout instead of the `parent`.

   - You could drop the element outside of the text frame.

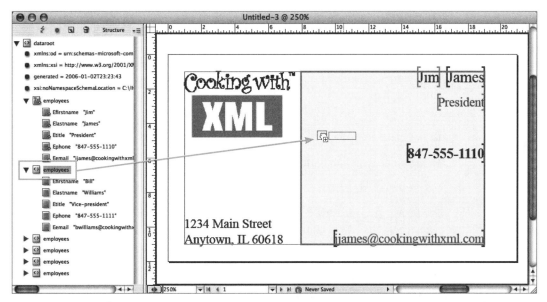

Figure 4.8 Each employees parent element contains five child elements: Efirstname, Elastname, Etitle, and so on. Dragging the parent icon over the structured layout causes InDesign to swap the existing child elements with the one selected.

The information from the second employee has now replaced all the information from the first (**Figure 4.9**). Notice the following:

- The new information completely replaced the old information.

- The new information assumed the exact placement and formatting as the old.

- The icon for the second employee now indicates that it has been placed in the layout, while the icon for the first employee has returned to the default setting.

Figure 4.9 The second record completely replaces the first and adopts the formatting, too. It's like magic.

3. Drag the first **employees** element back to the layout.

So far, we have demonstrated that the relationship between the structured layout and the XML is dynamic. Because the employee information is stored in identically named fields, you can replace any data in the layout with a similar record from the Structure pane.

We're sure you are thinking right about now, "This is great for the first layout, but we need to make six identical business cards!"

Here's where you had better hold onto your hosiery.

4. Create a new page from A-Master (**Figure 4.10**).

Page 2 features the logo, company address, and a text frame all generated by the master page. If you cannot see the edges of this text frame, select View > Show Frame Edges.

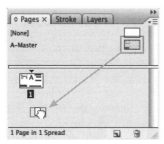

Figure 4.10 Dragging the A-Master icon to the Document pages area of the Pages panel creates a new page with features identical to page 1. The master page contains the company logo, address, and a text frame needed to make the next business card.

5. Drag the second **employees** element from the Structure pane into the empty text frame on page 2.

The information from the second employee should appear in the empty frame on page 2. The layout and formatting should be identical to page 1.

Wow! The structure layout from page 1 has magically transferred itself to page 2. Still have your socks? Well, we are determined to see you barefoot before the end of this lesson.

Lesson 4-3: Data Integrity

It would be a simple matter now to add four more pages to the document, drag in the remaining employee records, and finish the project. But you still have more things to learn about how XML can save you time, money, your job, and create world peace. (Okay, the last one may be reaching a bit.)

In the past, clients passed sheets of paper to designers with the names and contact info for their new employees. This info then had to be reentered into layouts manually by the designer. It is a process that often led to typos, transpositions, and other errors, delays, and costly corrections. On occasion it may have also cost the designer a client or two. The process has been improved since the introduction of email and digital files, which can be supplied by the client. But copying and pasting can lead to errors, too. XML eliminates these types of mistakes altogether.

Today, employee data is stored in databases. Current databases can export the data (names, titles, phones, and so on) directly to XML. In an XML workflow, the data can travel directly from the HR department to your layout without the need for further transcribing. This way, typos now are the responsibility of the HR manager, which certainly makes us designers sleep better at night. The result: time, money, job—all saved!

There are other benefits to using XML. A few years ago, we were laying out sheets of business cards 18-up, three columns of six cards each. The printer ran 500 sheets through the press (18 employees' worth at a time), and each of the 18 employees got 500 cards. In the process of creating cards for over 100 employees, two employees' cards were accidentally printed twice. Not a big deal in the overall scheme of things, but a waste of resources nonetheless. If we had been using an XML workflow at the time, the duplication would never have happened.

Let's see how XML prevents unintentional data duplication:

1. Observe the employee's name on page 2 of your layout, as seen back in Figure 4.6.

2. Drag the element of the first employee from the Structure pane to the text frame on page 2.

   We're sure when you see the first employee's name and info replace the data on page 2, you'll think, "Hey, I just made two cards for the first employee!"

   But you'd be wrong, bucko.

3. Navigate to page 1.

   Page 1 is blank.

4. Drag the first `employee` element to the blank text frame on page 1.

   The first employee's info reappears on page 1.

5. Navigate to page 2.

   Page 2 is blank.

6. Delete page 2.

Designer's XML Rule #1

XML only allows elements to be used once in each layout.

Lesson 4-4: Layout Automation

Up to this point you may already be seeing the value in developing an XML workflow: XML can get the data from the client to your page error-free and prevent unwanted data duplication. This is a win-win proposition in anyone's book. Yet we have barely scratched the surface of what XML can do for you, your company, and your clients. How would you like to add automation to the mix as well?

The first card was created automatically when you imported the XML. But the second card required you to add a page and drag out the next data element manually. For each of the remaining employees, these two steps would have to be repeated. Not a big deal for six business cards, but what if you had to do hundreds or thousands? This is where XML really shines.

Let's see how XML can automate the process:

1. Navigate to page 1.

2. Select the text frame on page 1 with the Selection tool.

3. Observe the text frame's out port.

The out port is empty, indicating that there is no more text to place.

It may be confusing at first to see the empty out port because you know there are six employees and that this card represents only one record. You can obviously see that there are five more elements in the Structure (**Figure 4.11**). So then, where is the rest of the text?

In Chapter 1, you learned that XML is simply plain text. But when InDesign imports it into the Structure pane, it treats it as a wholly different animal. InDesign interprets the XML structure and understands that each `employees` element is a standalone entity, a *single* record in a database. This capability to differentiate one record from another is the reason InDesign knows how to import the XML content into the structured layout and how to replace one record with another.

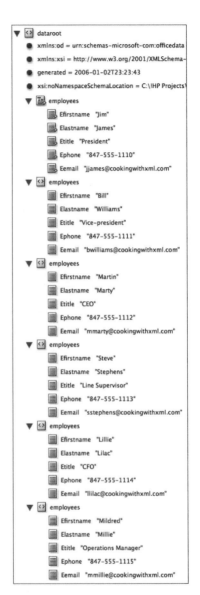

Figure 4.11 By looking at the Structure pane it is easy to assume that all the information displayed should flow into a single text frame.

As we drag the next **employees** element into the text frame, InDesign substitutes each element on the card with a similarly tagged element of the new record. No matter how many **employees** icons you drag onto the frame, you can never get more than one record at a time. So, is it even possible to flow all the records automatically? Yes.

It may help to imagine the **employees** elements as several cul-de-sacs branching off a main road. Each branch of the XML tree represents an intersection at the entrance to a cul-de-sac (one employee's record). **Dataroot**, on the other hand, represents the main road that links them all together.

Did this help you figure out the answer? Try this:

4. Drag **dataroot** to the text frame on page 1.

Did you notice that the color of the main text frame changed?

5. Select the text frame on page 1 with the Selection tool.

- The Tag panel indicates that the frame is now tagged as **dataroot**.

- The out port indicates overset text.

6. Create a new page based on A-Master as we did in Figure 4.10.

7. Click the out port from the text frame on page 1.

8. Display page 2.

9. Shift-click the loaded text icon on the empty text frame on page 2 to autoflow (**Figure 4.12**).

Figure 4.12 Watch for the solid serpentine arrow when you hold the Shift key, indicating that the XML will autoflow into your structured layout.

Designer's XML Rule #2

Use a root element when you want to flow multiple records.

NOTE To autoflow properly, place the ⌐ *over the existing text frame. If you miss the existing frame, InDesign will generate one of its own, which will not be linked to the master text frame. If you experience this error, stop, Undo, go back to page 2, and try again.*

WARNING Autoflow also may not function correctly when text frames are manually overridden from the master. The best solution is to delete and re-create the page from the master on the Pages panel.

As the XML flows from the Structure pane into the layout, each record automatically creates a page for itself (**Figure 4.13**). You should have at least six new cards when it's finished flowing. A blank seventh card may appear because of the hard return inserted at the end of the last record. Extra pages can be deleted without harm.

Figure 4.13 The Pages panel will be your first indication that the autoflow worked properly. Six additional cards should be created by the XML data. The last card is blank thanks to a hard return inserted after the *email* placeholder. The blank card can be deleted.

No matter how many times we demonstrate this task, we end up with these silly grins on our faces thinking about how cool this is. At seminars and workshops, it's usually easy to tell who in the audience are production designers because they are smiling, too.

Review

Here's what you have learned so far:

■ InDesign treats the XML as a standalone database and is able to differentiate one record from another.

■ Each branch (child) element in the Structure pane is an entity separate and distinct from all the others.

- When XML is imported into a structured layout, the imported data assumes the same placement and formatting as in the original placeholder.

- To flow multiple records the layout must target a **root** element.

Sample Project: 6-Up Business Cards

Lessons 4-1–4-4 established the basic concepts you need to go forward in an XML workflow. But we're sure some of you are saying, "Hey, I can't print business cards one at a time! I need a press-ready layout." And you're right.

Lesson 4-5: XML Foundation Part 2

In this project we apply the things you have already learned to create a 6-up, production-ready version of the same job.

1. Open **6cards.indt** from the Project 1 folder.

2. Select View > Show Text Threads.

3. Make sure all the Structure markers are turned on.

4. Select any of the tagged text frames on the layout (**Figure 4.14**).

   - All the text frames are linked together on the layout.

   - All the frames are tagged with the **employees** element.

   - In the first card, text placeholders have already been created, formatted, and tagged for the XML structure.

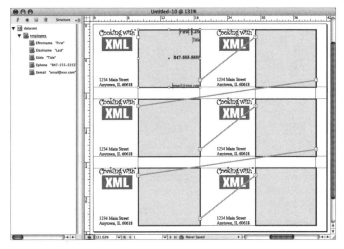

Figure 4.14 This is one of the possible ways to lay out a press-ready structure. The text frames are linked together from left to right and then down. You could also go top to bottom and then across, it's up to you. The XML will work either way.

5. Select the **dataroot** element.

6. Import **employees.xml**.

7. Observe the XML Import Options dialog. The checkboxes used for **Lesson 4-1** should still be selected. If so, click OK.

After the XML import is complete, the first employee's name and information appears in the first card. The data from the remaining five employees appears in the Structure pane but not in your layout. Why?

The color of the tagged frame should give you a hint. Notice how the color of the text frame is the same color as the tag for the **employees** element? Although there are frames ready for each of the six employees, the structure in the layout is tagged to allow only one element into it at a time. Knowing what you know now, have you figured out how to fix the problem? Right, it's the same way you fixed the single-card layout in **Lesson 4-4**.

8. Drag the **dataroot** element from the Structure pane onto the tagged text frame.

- The color of the tagged frames changes to the color of the **dataroot** element.

- Six cards are now filled with the data of the six new employees.

- All the information is properly laid out and formatted (**Figure 4.15**).

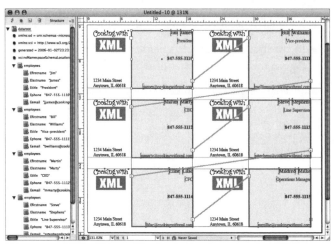

Figure 4.15 More magic. Six cards completely finished and ready for the press.

Quick, look down! Got socks?

No matter how jaded you are as a designer, that will put a smile on your face. In barely the time it took you to blink, six business cards are finished and ready to be printed. Had the XML contained 600 names, all 600 cards could be finished in less than the time it takes you to read this paragraph. Wow!

Now that we've got your attention, it's time to show you how to do this magic trick for yourself. And, unlike David Copperfield, there's no magician's union to prevent us from showing you how all it works.

Creating Structured Layouts

In the following lessons we take you step by step through setting up a structured layout.

Lesson 4-6: Basic Document Setup

Let's start with the basic document setup:

1. Select File > New > Document.

2. Set up the document with the specifications appearing in **Figure 4.16**. Click OK.

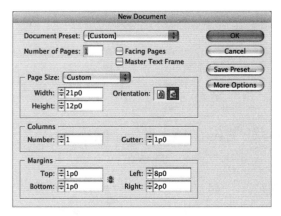

Figure 4.16 Create a new document with these specifications.

We're not going to worry about the company logo and return address; these are elements you can add later if you desire. Instead, let's concentrate on the XML portion of the design.

The first issue we have to address is creating or obtaining the XML structure. There are three methods you can use for populating the Tags panel:

■ Manually, using the Tags panel to create each tag

■ By loading the tags from an existing InDesign document or XML file

■ By loading a DTD

We experiment with the first two options in this exercise, but reserve the DTD for **Chapter 11.**

Lesson 4-7: Creating Your Own Tags

The tags displayed in the Tags panel reflect the underlying structure of an XML file. Some of the names refer to "content" elements (`Efirstname`, `Elastname`, and so on) and some refer to "organizational" elements (**dataroot**, **employees**). If you create these tags manually, don't forget to follow the basic XML rules from **Chapter 11**. Remember, the tag names in the panel must be identical in every way to those from the XML file itself. Any deviation, no matter how trivial, will invalidate the tag.

Here's a complete list of the tags from **employees.xml**:

- dataroot
- employees
- Employeeid
- Efirstname
- Elastname
- Etitle
- Ephone
- Eemail
- Ephoto

Lesson 4-7A: Creating Tags Manually

To create a tag manually, do the following:

1. If the Tags panel is not visible, select Window > Tags to display the panel.

2. Select New Tag from the Tags panel menu (**Figure 4.17**).

   You can also create tags by clicking the New Tag button at the bottom of the Tags panel. Use the button when you want to create tags quickly and you don't care what color is assigned to it. Pressing the button doesn't open the New Tag dialog, so double-click on the tag name to access the Tag Option dialog for editing the tag name and color.

3. Type **Efirstname** into the New Tag dialog. You can use the sequential color selected by InDesign or choose from the Color pull-down menu (**Figure 4.18**). Click OK.

   The Efirstname tag appears in the Tags panel.

4. Create a tag for Elastname.

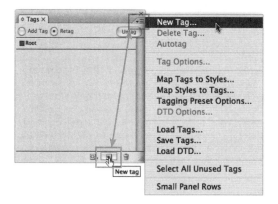

Figure 4.17 InDesign allows you to create, edit, and delete tag names through the Tags panel.

Figure 4.18 InDesign assigns colors sequentially from the Color drop-down list. Feel free to change these color assignments. The colors have no effect on the XML or the structure.

Designer's XML Rule #3

Tag names created in InDesign must match exactly those from the XML file. No exceptions.

Lesson 4-7B: Editing Existing Tag Names

To edit existing tag names, do the following:

1. Double-click the **root** tag in the Tags palette.

   The Tag Options dialog appears.

2. Change the tag name to **dataroot**.

   Note the case and spelling as you type.

3. Click OK.

Lesson 4-7C: Importing Tag Names

To import tag names from an existing InDesign or XML file, do the following:

1. Select Load Tags from the Tags panel menu (**Figure 4.19**).

Figure 4.19 By loading tag names from existing InDesign documents or the actual XML itself, you will avoid all the pitfalls of misspellings and case sensitivities. If the XML file is available, it's always the first choice.

2. Select **employees.xml**.

You could also select **1card.indt** or **6cards.indt**. Because these InDesign templates already have the identical XML structure you're looking for, you can obtain the needed tags from them as well.

3. Click Open.

The Tags panel is populated by all the tag names used in the XML file (**Figure 4.20**).

Figure 4.20 Tag names are listed in alphabetical order, *not* in the order in which they appear in the XML structure.

InDesign assigns colors for the tag names sequentially from the default color list.

Lesson 4-8: Creating a Structured Layout

In most cases, structured layouts start on your master pages:

1. Display the A-Master.

2. Create a text frame within the visible margins (**Figure 4.21**).

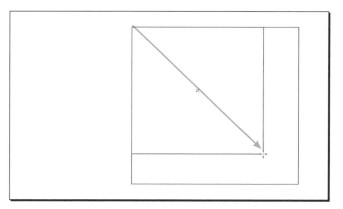

Figure 4.21 By drawing a text frame on the master page, you are creating a target you'll need for autoflowing the XML content later.

WARNING *In most cases tags should not be applied to items on the master page. Doing so will cause the XML, when it's imported, to populate the placeholders on the master page. The resulting content will then appear on every page of your document.*

3. Display page 1.

4. Command-Shift-click to override the master text frame on page 1.

The text frame should display a bounding box and in and out ports, indicating that it has been overridden.

5. Insert the Text cursor in the frame and create text placeholders for your XML content (**Figure 4.22**).

First Last
Title
Phone
Email

Figure 4.22 What you type for the XML placeholders doesn't matter as much as how you tag them. You could just as easily use A, B, C, D... or 1, 2, 3, 4.

What you type is unimportant. You can use any text you want for the placeholders; here is what we used: **First Last**, **Title**, **Phone**, **Email**. Use single hard returns or spaces to break lines or separate placeholders.

Placeholder Order is Elemental

Note the order in which we typed the placeholders for this exercise. You may have thought that this sequence was arbitrary or accidental or based on the needs of the client or simply a design aesthetic. None of these answers comes close to the truth. Instead, the sequence of the placeholders was dictated, in turn, by the order of the same elements contained in the XML file itself. Without outside help, InDesign must adhere to this sequence. Any element out of order will be ignored and *not* imported into your layout. In some cases the entire import may fail.

If you want to shuffle elements around—say, placing the last name first, the simplest method is to create a new XML file using the elements in desired sequence. Another method, available in InDesign CS3, is to apply an XSLT *(eXtensible Stylesheet Language Transformation)* to resequence the XML upon import. The use of XSLTs with InDesign is covered in **Chapter 11**.

You can also apply the XSLT outside of InDesign by using a third-party XML parser. There are several XML parsers available as shareware and freeware on the Internet, but their use and applicability are outside the scope of this book.

---

6. In the last line of the text frame after the Email placeholder, press Return/Enter to insert a hard return.

Although you may not be in the habit of normally doing so, you must add a single hard return after the last item: **Email**. The extra hard return at the end of the business card ensures that each record occupies its own distinct card.

Designer's XML Rule #4

Always insert a hard return after the last element of any dynamic, structured layout.

The placement and spacing you saw in the sample business cards were specified by styles using exact font and paragraph formatting. To duplicate that look, you will need similar styles of your own. Luckily, you can save some time by importing them from one of the templates we've already explored.

7. Display the Paragraph Styles panel.

8. Select Load All Text Styles… from the Paragraph Styles panel menu (**Figure 4.23**).

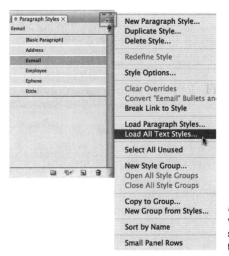

Figure 4.23 There's no point in wasting time setting up Paragraph styles when you can load them from an existing template.

9. Select **1card.indt** in the Open a File dialog. Click Open.

The Load Styles dialog appears.

10. Make sure all the style names are checked. Click OK.

The styles from **1card.indt** appear in the Paragraph Styles panel.

11. Apply paragraph styles to your placeholders that match their names. Because there are no "First" or "Last" styles, apply the Employee style to the first line.

The placeholder formatting should now match **1card.indt** (**Figure 4.24**).

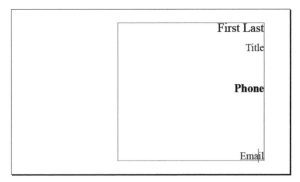

Figure 4.24 The basic layout is complete but lacks its XML structure.

Styles Essential to XML Magic

You may think that XML is responsible for all the magic you have seen so far, but that's not entirely the case. InDesign's Paragraph styles are a major contributor, too. Although the XML structure differentiates one employee's data from another, by itself it hasn't a clue about how to place this information on our layout. That's where the placeholders come in by holding the space for each piece of data and by formatting the text. If you poke around the styles we imported, you will discover the typeface, size, leading, and other formatting characteristics that we chose to create the cards as they appear. But if you're not careful you might miss one minor but essential setting.

Click in the first line and select Keep Options from the Paragraph panel menu. You'll notice that the Start Paragraph command is set for **In Next Column** (**Figure 4.25**). This setting is irrelevant in a single-card layout, but without it, when we tag the structure with the dataroot element, all the overset text would simply flow into the first text frame. Instead, when the next employee name appears and assumes the formatting, In Next Column forces the first line to jump to the next text frame in our layout, which happens to be on the next page (business card).

The In Next Column and In Next Frame settings work with either the single- or multiple-card layouts, but the On Next Page setting only works with the single-card design.

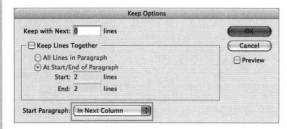

Figure 4.25 Without the Keep Option: In Next Column, part of the XML magic wouldn't happen at all.

Lesson 4-9: Tagging Placeholders

Okay, now all the elements are in place to finish our structure. The final step in the process is to apply XML tags to the various placeholders. Tags identify which elements get imported from the XML file and where they land into your layout. This is the way you should tag the placeholders:

1. Select the Text tool.

2. Select the word *First*. Be careful *not* to select the space between the words *First* and *Last*.

WARNING InDesign provides several shortcut methods for selecting text—for example, double-, triple-, and quadruple-clicking. Abstain from triple- and quadruple-clicking during the tagging process. The reason is simple: Quadruple-clicking to select a line or paragraph automatically selects the hard return, too. Because the imported XML replaces anything that resides within the tag brackets, you may suddenly see the spaces between your elements disappear, along with tabs and hard returns.

3. Click `Efirstname` in the Tags panel (**Figure 4.26**).

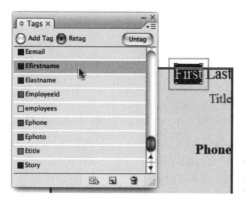

Figure 4.26 Careful, careful! Mind how you tag that element. Tagging seems simple enough, but plenty of errors can be caused during this process.

- Brackets appear at the beginning and end of the word [**First**].

- The bracket color matches the color of the `Efirstname` element in the Tags panel.

- The color of the text frame has also changed.

Designer's XML Rule #5

Do *not* tag spaces, tabs, and hard returns unless you want the XML to replace them.

---

4. Switch to the Selection tool and click the text frame.

The text frame is tagged with the `Story` tag (**Figure 4.27**).

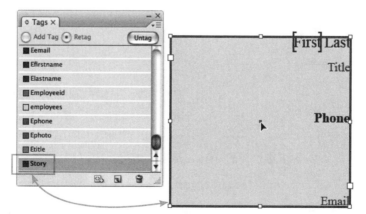

Figure 4.27 See, we told you! InDesign demonstrates it has a mind of its own sometimes— it tagged text frame with the `Story` element. If you had missed this error, you wouldn't realize something was wrong until later. When you try to import the XML, InDesign would ignore your placeholders altogether because `Story` is not part of the structure.

Whoa! **Story** is *not* one of the elements from the XML file, so where did it come from? The answer: InDesign created it. If you remember from **Lesson 4-4**, the text frame was tagged with the **employees** element. Because you did not tag the text frame yourself, InDesign did it for you. And instead of using one of the existing tags, it created one of its own.

Unfortunately, this presumptuous bit of creativity is totally unacceptable, and for good reason. By using **Story**, which is not an element in your XML file, InDesign has broken the structure. If you tried to import XML at this moment it would fail.

But don't worry, there's an easy fix.

5. Select the **Story** element in the Structure pane (**Figure 4.28**).

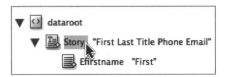

Figure 4.28 To fix the text frame, first click on the **Story** element in the Structure pane.

6. Click **employees** in the Tags panel (**Figure 4.29**).

Figure 4.29 Click the **employees** element in the Tags panel to rename the **Story** tag in the Structure pane.

- **Story** is replaced by **employees** in the Structure pane.

- The color of the text frame matches the **employees** element in the Tags panel.

7. Apply the appropriate tags to the remaining placeholders.

All placeholders are tagged properly (**Figure 4.30**).

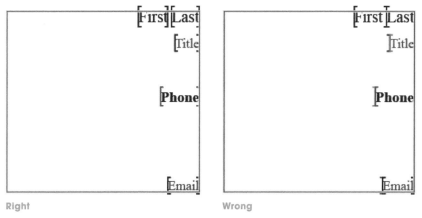

Right   Wrong

Figure 4.30 On the left you can see what correctly tagged placeholders look like. To the right you can see tags enclosing spaces and hard returns alike. The simplest fix is to select the whole mess, untag it, and start over from scratch.

Lesson 4-10: Preserving Paragraph Formatting

The project is nearly ready, but not quite. Should you try to import the XML file at this point and flow the content to additional pages, you would receive a disturbing surprise: The first card created by the XML would be okay, but all additional cards generated would ignore your carefully applied text formatting (**Figure 4.31**). Egads!

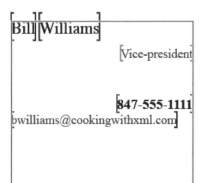

Figure 4.31 Don't import the XML yet! This is what will happen if you try. For some reason, InDesign refuses to clone the formatting on every element. Map tags to Paragraph and Character styles to preserve the formatting.

To preserve all your hard work, you need to lock down the original design, which is based largely on Paragraph styles. You do this by creating a formal relationship (mapping) between the XML tags and your Paragraph styles. InDesign gives you two ways to access this feature:

1. Select Map Tags to Styles from the Tags panel menu, or the Structure pane menu (**Figure 4.32**).

Figure 4.32 You can access the mapping feature from the Structure pane or the Tags panel.

The Map Tags to Styles dialog appears.

2. Click Map by Name.

This option automatically pairs tags to styles when their names match (**Figure 4.33**).

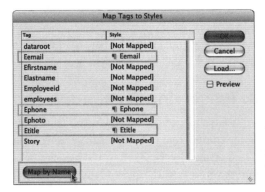

Figure 4.33 With a little foresight you can automate the mapping procedure by naming your styles after the XML tags or vice versa. As always, spelling and case matter.

All the placeholder tags are matched except for `Efirstname` and `Elastname`. There are no styles named for these tags. Instead, map the Employee Paragraph style to each. (You could get away with mapping the Employee style to one or the other, but we'd rather be safe.)

3. Match the Employee style to the `Efirstname` tag in the Map Tags to Styles dialog (**Figure 4.34**).

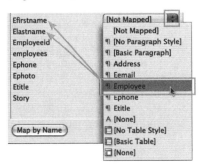

Figure 4.34 Tags that don't have a style match can be assigned to any Paragraph or Character style in the list. There are no limitations or rules here. Go ahead and create a style for each tag or assign many tags to one style. It's up to you.

4. Click OK.

Congratulations! Your document is completely structured and ready for XML.

Designer's XML Rule #6

For some reason InDesign won't clone the formatting on some tagged elements. For example, the first line of card two may pick up the formatting from the last line of card one. To keep this from happening and to preserve the desired formatting, always map the tags to the styles.

Lesson 4-11: Testing Your Structure

Let's test the structure and see if everything works.

1. Select **dataroot** in the Structure pane.

2. Import **employees.xml**.

3. In the XML Import Options dialog, select only the following checkboxes:

- Clone repeating text elements

- Only import elements that match existing structure

- Do not import contents of whitespace-only elements

4. Click OK.

The XML content should replace your placeholders as in **Lesson 4-1**.

5. Drag **dataroot** to the text frame.

- The text frame changes color, indicating it is now tagged for the element **dataroot**.

- The overset icon should be visible in the out port.

6. Load the overset text.

7. Create a new page from the A-Master.

8. Autoflow the text into the master text frame on page 2.

- Six pages should appear in the Pages panel.

- Each page contains one of the six employees.

- Each page is formatted identically.

XML Troubleshooting Tips

Here are some of the potential glitches that can trip up your XML workflow:

■ Items are not tagged.

■ Items are tagged out of sequence.

■ Spaces, tabs, or hard returns were unintentionally included within tagged placeholders.

■ Dataroot was not selected before importing XML.

■ The wrong XML file or tag names were used.

■ Incorrect XML Import Options were selected.

Lesson 4-12: Press-Ready Docs

By this point you should be ready to tackle the 6-up layout. The steps and techniques for a sheet of cards are nearly identical to the single-card lesson; only the logistics vary a bit. Follow these steps:

1. Create a New Document with the specifications shown in **Figure 4.35**.

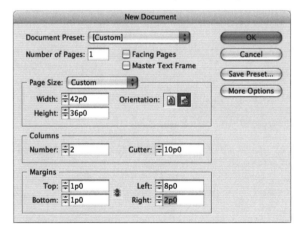

Figure 4.35 These specs create the 6-up layout.

2. Display A-Master.

3. Select Layout > Create Guides.

The Create Guides dialog appears.

4. Create row guides from the specifications shown in **Figure 4.36**.

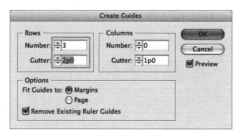

Figure 4.36 Create Guides is a great timesaver for setting up multiple ruler guides. Notice the options for fitting the guides to *Margins*, or to *Page*, and to *Remove Existing Ruler Guides*.

5. Select the Text tool.

6. Draw a text frame in the area defined by the guides for the first card structure.

7. Switch to the Selection tool.

8. Click the out port of the text frame.

9. Option-drag (Alt-drag) (semi-autoflow) a new text frame in the second column, first row (**Figure 4.37**).

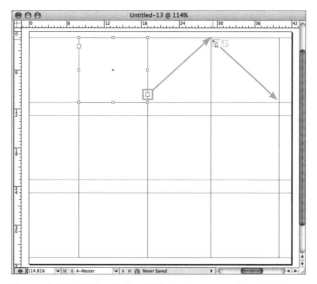

Figure 4.37 Hold the Option (Alt) key to access the dotted serpentine arrow of semi-autoflow. This technique saves some time by reloading the text frame icon automatically after drawing a new frame.

10. **Option-drag** (Alt-drag) text frames in the remaining rows and columns.

You now have six linked master text frames.

11. Display page 1.

12. Override the first master text frame.

13. Repeat **Lessons 4-8**, **4-9**, and **4-10** to create a structured layout in this text frame. The layout is ready for XML (**Figure 4.38**).

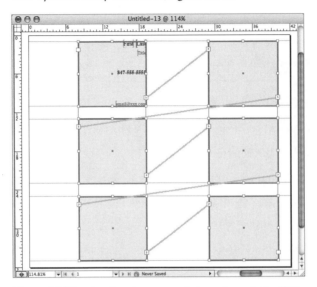

Figure 4.38 The structured press-ready layout awaits the XML.

14. Select **dataroot** in the Structure pane.

15. Import **employees.xml**.

16. In the XML Import Options dialog, select only the following checkboxes:

- Clone repeating text elements
- Only import elements that match existing structure
- Do not import contents of whitespace-only elements

17. Click OK.

- The XML content should replace your placeholders as in the original example.
- Only the first record is displayed in your layout.
- The threaded frames are tagged for the **employees** element.

18. Drag **dataroot** to the text frame.

- All six employees appear in the layout
- All frames should be identically formatted.

That's it, you've passed the first test. You have learned the foundational concepts that will allow you to create successful XML workflows. In the coming chapters you will expand this knowledge and understanding and fill your toolbox with all sorts of useful XML tips and tricks.

Review

Remember what you learned in this hands-on tutorial; these important lessons will be invaluable in the next chapter:

- How to create, import and edit tags

- Proper placeholder tagging techniques

- XML element sequence and nesting

- Mapping tags to styles

Story Editor Makes a Great XML Editor

We can't say enough about good tagging techniques. Applying tags properly and in the correct sequence is essential to successful XML workflows. One tool that will become invaluable to you in this process is InDesign's Story Editor. This becomes plainly evident the moment you open your first XML workflow within it.

Although the colorful brackets are handy in your layout to identify the tagged elements, they often get lost or obscured in the hubbub of text and graphics. But in Story Editor the XML structure literally SHOUTS for attention (**Figure 4.39**). The colorful brackets from the layout are replaced by pentagons displaying not only the tag color but the entire tag name. The good-sized polygons are easy on the eyes and cut down on a lot of squinting. We use the Story Editor frequently during the tagging process to screen for problems in sequencing or tagging structure (**Figure 4.40**).

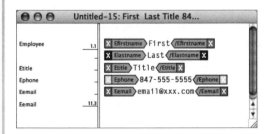

Figure 4.39 Correctly tagged placeholders as they should appear in the Story Editor.

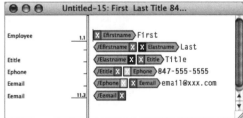

Figure 4.40 Incorrectly tagged XML placeholders. Compare this image with Figure 4.39.

The Wrong Way

You might think "The Wrong Way" is an odd title for a section. Why would you want to teach someone the "wrong" way to do something? The reason is simple: We are firm believers that you learn as much from your mistakes as from your successes. We are also confident that as you learn more about XML and structured layouts, you may think of various alternative techniques for creating dynamic workflows. In addition to learning the "right" way to build a dynamic document with XML, you should have some experience in knowing when a particular method *won't* work. We know this because extensive experimentation and trial-and-error (lots of error!) is how we learned so much about how XML works with InDesign.

Like all early explorers and pioneers setting off in any field to discover new worlds and establish new ways of life, we wandered into the XML/InDesign wilderness alone and mostly unaided. Some tried to help and gave us tantalizing glimpses of what was possible in this brave new world, but there were few concrete examples. Most of the things we thought XML could do were simply conjecture. Over several months of investigation, often filled with frustration and frequent failure, we developed the methods we're now teaching you.

In this chapter, you learned how to create a structured layout using tagged text that automatically generates single or multiple business cards. There's no doubt that our approach works, but is our preferred method the only one? The simple answer is no.

In the following lessons we briefly explore the "floating frame" technique: an alternate XML method we toyed with for weeks without success. By learning why it fails, it may lay for you (as it did for us) a better foundation for understanding how XML does (and does not) function with InDesign.

Lesson 4-13: Floating Frames Method

For designers experienced with corporate identity projects, our preferred method, using a single frame containing tagged and styled text, may not have been your first choice. Instead, your design may have favored several, independent frames like the one in **Figure 4.41**.

Let's take a few minutes to explore an alternative method for creating a structured, dynamic layout:

1. Create a new document as in **Lesson 4-6**.

2. Select the Text tool.

3. Draw individual text frames for each element on your business card. You will need one for the employee's **name**, **title**, **phone**, and **email address**. Remember to make the frames large enough to hold the longest name, title, and so on.

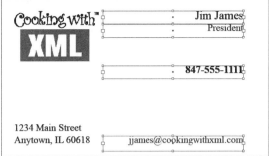

Figure 4.41 Here you see two possible methods for laying a typical business card. Normally, the choice would be a personal preference and nothing more. You will see how alternative B is the "wrong way" in most XML workflows.

4. Type placeholder text into each of your text frames.

5. Load all text styles from **1card.indt** as in **Lesson 4-8**.

6. Apply the styles to each placeholder as appropriate.

7. Load the XML tags names from the **employees.xml** file, as in **Lesson 4-7C**.

8. Switch to the Selection tool.

9. Select the frame containing the title placeholder.

10. Click `Etitle` in the Tags panel.

    The frame containing the title changes color, indicating it is tagged for the `Etitle` element.

11. Tag the frames containing the phone and email placeholders as appropriate.

Lesson 4-14: Creating Nested Elements

Now we confront one of several problems we're going to face during this lesson. The only frame left untagged contains the placeholders for both the first *and* last names. So the question is which tag do you use? `Efirstname`? `Elastname`?

The answer is simply that neither will actually solve the problem. If the frame is tagged for the first name only, the first name lands in the frame; if the frame is tagged for the last name, you guessed it, only the last name appears.

The solution is to nest the elements in one frame. Here's how you do it:

1. Select the Text tool.

2. Select the placeholder for the first name.

3. Click `Efirstname` in the Tags panel.

    The placeholder displays tag brackets for the `Efirstname` element.

4. Tag the last name placeholder with **Elastname**.

   The layout is completely tagged (**Figure 4.42**), but we're not quite done yet.

5. Save file as **mycardtest1.indd**.

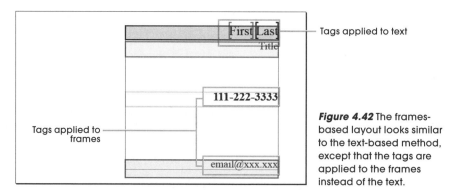

Figure 4.42 The frames-based layout looks similar to the text-based method, except that the tags are applied to the frames instead of the text.

Lesson 4-15: Modifying Element Order

Observe the hierarchy of the elements (**Figure 4.43**). Hopefully, you recognize at least four problems in the *structure*. First, the root element is named incorrectly. Second, the elements are not in the same order as they appear in the XML file itself. Third, the dreaded "**Story**" element seems to have reared its ugly head again. And fourth, there is no **employees** element at all.

Figure 4.43 Study the Structure pane carefully. Note the order of the elements and how they are nested. Usually, the first sign of trouble can be seen here.

The first two problems are solved easily:

1. Select the **Root** element in the Structure pane.

2. Click **dataroot** in the Tags panel (**Figure 4.44**).

   The **Root** element is renamed **dataroot**. One problem solved.

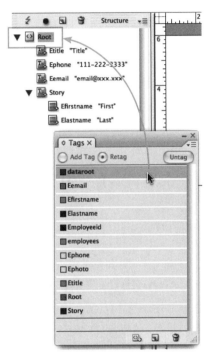

Figure 4.44 Changing the name of an element can be done quickly and painlessly within the Structure pane.

3. Select the **Story** element in the Structure pane.

4. Drag the **Story** element to the top of the list, just below **dataroot** (**Figure 4.45**).

   The **Story** tag and the placeholders for **Efirstname** and **Elastname** have moved to the top of the list.

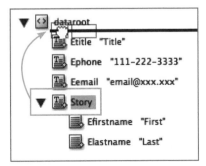

Figure 4.45 It takes a calm hand, keen eye, and practice to be able to move critical elements within the structure correctly. Always check the results before you proceed to the next task. As you have already seen, the success of your XML workflow depends upon it.

Lesson 4-16: Renaming Structural Elements

Two problems have been solved, but the presence of the Story element and lack of an employees element have effectively broken our structure.

Here's a partial solution to the dilemma that doesn't require reconstructing the XML file itself:

1. Select the Story element in the Structure pane.

2. Click employees in the Tags panel.

The Story element has been renamed employees.

Simply renaming the Story element hasn't entirely fixed our problem. Follow along and watch carefully:

3. Select dataroot in the Structure pane.

4. Import **employees.xml**. Select only the following import options:

- Clone repeating text elements

- Only import elements that match existing structure

- Do not import contents of whitespace-only elements

Lesson 4-17: Troubleshooting XML Structure

Observe the results of the import (**Figure 4.46**). Only the first and last names imported correctly. Look at the Structure pane. See how the imported content inserted itself between the first employees element and the placeholders for Etitle, Ephone, and Eemail? Because the placeholders were not part of the employees element, they were **ignored** when the XML was imported.

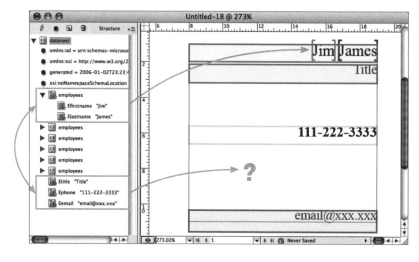

Figure 4.46 The first and last name imported correctly, but where's the rest of the data? See how the faulty structure caused the XML to ignore the placeholders for the title, phone number, and email address.

As we explained in **Chapter 1**, proper XML structure is ignored at your peril. Here's a simple fix to this problem:

1. Select Undo from the Edit menu.

The layout returns to the previous state: The XML content is purged from the Structure pane and the generic First and Last name placeholders are restored.

2. Drag the `Etitle` element into the `employees` element in the Structure pane (**Figure 4.47**).

The `Etitle` element appears as a child element of `employees`.

Very important: Note that the actual placement of the placeholder on the layout has *not* changed.

 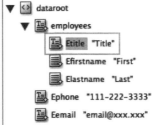 

Figure 4.47 Creating the proper structure may take several steps. Here we dragged the Etitle element into the employees element (left). It appears in the wrong position of the structure (middle). So, we move it to its proper location (right).

3. Drag the `Etitle` element below `Elastname` in the Structure pane.

`Etitle` now appears in its proper location within the XML structure.

4. Repeat steps 2 and 3 with the `Ephone` and `Eemail` elements.

The placeholder structure now mimics the desired XML structure.

5. Select File > Save.

Let's try importing the XML file again:

6. Select **dataroot** and import **employees.xml**.

- The XML content imports successfully this time.

- All placeholders are properly replaced and display the expected data from the XML file.

Lesson 4-18: Creating Multiples

You may be thinking right now that all looks well with our current document and you're finished—but this isn't called the "wrong way" for nothing. Although the content imported correctly into the placeholders on page 1, you're going to have problems generating cards for the remaining five employees. Although you will have to backtrack a little when it fails, let's take a look at what happens:

1. Drag A-Master to the Page panel to create a new page.

2. Display page 2.

3. Drag the `employees` element for the second employee to page 2.

All the information for the second employee appears in a single text frame (**Figure 4.48**).

Figure 4.48 When you try to flow one of the other records into the layout InDesign doesn't clone the individual structured frames from page 1. And there's no way to make it do so short of scripting or third-party plug-ins.

Now you know why it's called the wrong way. Without scripting or third-party plug-ins, there's no way (that we know of) to get InDesign to create multiple pages automatically from the structured layout as it appears after step 4 in **Lesson 4-17**. It is possible to create all six cards, just not automatically as you did in our other method.

This is what you have to do to automate the process to build multiples:

4. Select File > Revert.

The XML content disappears from the Structure pane and the tagged placeholders revert to their appearance after Lesson 4-17, step 5.

5. Select page 1 in the Pages panel.

6. Select Duplicate Spread from the Pages panel menu (**Figure 4.49**).

A duplicate page appears in the panel, which includes all the placeholders as in page 1.

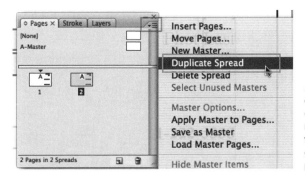

Figure 4.49 By using the existing structured layout on page 1 to create a new page, instead of the A-Master, you can get around the cloning problem.

7. Observe the Structure pane (**Figure 4.50**).

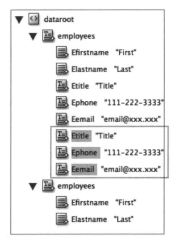

Figure 4.50 After duplicating page 1, as you can see here, an unwelcome surprise is waiting for you in the Structure pane. For some unknown reason, the Etitle, Ephone and Eemail elements from page 2 are nested within the employees element on page 1.

STOP! Do you see what just happened? When you duplicated page 1, InDesign did as you asked and then promptly screwed up the perfectly good structure. This is the real kicker: If you look at page 2, you see the exact same placeholders as on page 1, which is great. But a glance at the Structure pane tells you that the page 2 title, phone, and email placeholders were incorporated into the page 1 employees element! Egads!

You know enough about XML by now to know that this won't fly. If you don't fix this problem, the imported XML will ignore the title, phone, and email placeholders on page 2 as it did after **Lesson 4-16,** step **4.**

Here's how you can once again rescue this errant structure:

8. Select one Etitle, Ephone, and Eemail element from the Structure pane. Hold Shift to select consecutive elements, or Cmd (Ctrl) to select non-consecutive elements.

9. Drag the selected elements below `Elastname` in the second `employees` element in the Structure pane (**Figure 4.51**).

The three elements now appear as child elements in the correct position in the structure (**Figure 4.52**).

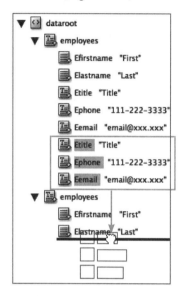

Figure 4.51 Although it's an added step, it's easy to Shift-select all three elements and drag them down to where they belong. You will have to do the same manual troubleshooting for any new page you want to create.

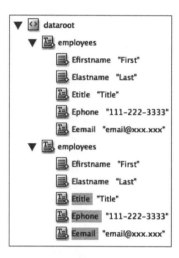

Figure 4.52 Finally, both pages display properly structured layouts that are ready for XML.

Lesson 4-19: Payoff = Unlimited Possibilities

To create sufficient pages for the six new employees, you have to repeat steps 5–9 in **Lesson 4-18** four more times. It's a lot of extra work for what seems to be no reward at all. But, there's a potential advantage to using the floating frames method that you may not see yet. Before you import the XML try this:

1. Reposition the placeholders in your layout; see **Figure 4.53** for one suggestion.

You can put the placeholders literally anywhere on the card as long as the elements stay in the proper order within the Structure pane.

Now you can import the XML file:

Figure 4.53 Once you've created a valid structure, have fun with your floating frames. This screenshot gives you one suggestion.

2. Select `dataroot` and import **employees.xml**.

The XML imports properly into all the cards no matter where you positioned the placeholders. In fact, each of the six cards can feature individualized designs.

You'll have to decide whether this little bit of design flexibility is worth all the effort. It certainly isn't to us. But there are some valuable lessons in the following review section to take away from this vain procedure nonetheless.

Review

- InDesign can import XML content into any properly structured layout.

- InDesign cannot clone the position and formatting of independent text frames without a lot of manual assistance.

- The actual position of a placeholder frame on the page is irrelevant to its position within the Structure pane.

- Elements can be manually rearranged in the Structure pane to conform to the desired XML structure.

In most cases, structured layouts will put a crimp in your "creative" expression no matter what you do. So the one aspect we like about this frame-based method is that it allows more freedom to "design" a layout. Understanding the structure and knowing how to control the flow of data onto the page can vastly expand your XML capabilities.

5

Anchored Objects

In this chapter you will learn how to:

- Use anchored objects in a structured document

- Tag anchored objects

- Clone non-tagged elements

- Work with multisection XML

This chapter continues your education in InDesign's XML capabilities by adding some very useful tools and techniques. **Chapter 4** shows you how InDesign uses XML to create multiple, data-driven layouts quickly and easily. We're going to ramp it up now by introducing the capability of cloning *untagged* text and anchored objects.

InDesign has always supported inline objects. Like PageMaker before it, you could slip a graphic or a text frame anywhere into a paragraph or an empty line. Added in InDesign CS2, the *anchored* object is an amazing feature that breaks the invisible barrier of the text frame's edge.

NOTE   Download all applicable files for Chapter 5 from www.peachpit.com/indesignxmlguide and copy them to a folder on your hard drive (approximately 2 MB).

Sample Project: Cookbook

Lesson 5-1: Anchored Objects

Scenario: You work for a large specialty publisher, which prints cookbooks among other things. The production department sent over the layout for the latest project and the XML file to supply the content. Your task is to merge the layout with the data and get the book ready for press.

1. Open **cookbook.indt** from the Chapter 5 folder.

2. Show the Structure pane, tag markers, and tagged frames (*See* **Chapter 2**).

3. Select View > Show Frame Edges (Cmd-Shift-H/Ctrl-Shift-H), if they are hidden.

By their very nature, recipes and cookbooks are ideal candidates for an XML work-flow. Like the business cards in **Chapter 4**, recipes are simply *records* within a *data-base* (cookbook), and conform easily to our description of a structured document.

Take a second to observe the layout of the cookbook in **Figure 5.1**. The first thing you should notice, prominently sitting at the top of the page, is the tagged, anchored text frame holding the placeholder text: "Section Title." Below it sits another tagged text frame that contains placeholder text for a recipe. Predictably, the recipe (like most) consists of three basic parts: a title, a list of ingredients, and a set of directions.

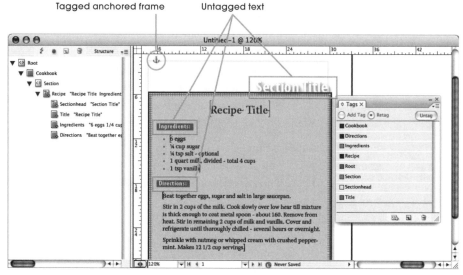

Figure 5.1 The basic structure is similar to **Chapter 4**'s business card with a couple of exceptions: the anchored text frame at the top of the page and the two *untagged* subheads that introduce the ingredients and directions.

The observant among you will not only see the tag markers sprinkled throughout the layout but also notice that several text elements on the page in fact don't display any obvious tags at all, specifically the placeholder text "Section Title" and the words "Ingredients" and "Directions."

What's up? Did some production artist slip up? Nope. There's good reason these items look the way they do. Let's import the XML and watch the magic.

4. Select View > Show Text Threads (Cmd-Shift-Y/Ctrl-Shift-Y), if they are hidden. Using the Selection tool, drag the anchored frame an inch or two away from its current position.

   Note how the text frame is not inline or attached to any other object.

5. Press Cmd-Z/Ctrl-Z to undo the move.

   The frame should return to its original position.

6. Select Import XML from the File or Structure pane menu.

7. Select **recipes.xml** from the Chapter 5 folder. Make sure the Show XML Import Options checkbox and the Merge Content radio button are selected. Click Open.

   - Selecting the XML Import Options checkbox is a no-brainer in most XML workflows. It is an essential choice for specifying how the XML will be applied to your document and structure. We leave it checked by default.

   - Selecting the Merge Content or Append Content radio buttons depends on whether you need to replace the existing content or simply want to insert additional records into the document. In this case, we want to completely replace the existing placeholder text. Therefore, Merge Content is selected.

Designer's XML Rule #7

Select Merge Content to replace all existing placeholder text. Select Append Content to insert additional records.

---

8. Select only the following checkboxes in the XML Import Options dialog:

   - Clone repeating text elements

   - Only import elements that match existing structure

   - Do not import contents of whitespace-only elements

9. Deselect all other checkboxes. Click OK.

   In a few seconds the XML content replaces the placeholder text and a complete recipe for Clam Dip appears on the screen.

Pretty cool. But you ain't seen nothin' yet.

Lesson 5-2: Multisection XML

Remember how in **Chapter 4** we dragged one of the employee icons from the Structure pane to the layout, and it replaced all of the existing employee's contact information? Let's see what happens if we do the same thing in this document.

1. In the Structure pane, click the Root element to reveal the Cookbook child element (see "Expanding the Structure" in **Chapter 2**).

2. Click the Cookbook element to reveal the four Section elements.

3. Click the first Section element to reveal nine Recipe elements (**Figure 5.2**).

   If text snippets are still turned on, you should see Clam Dip beside the first **Recipe** element. If you don't see text snippets next to each **Recipe** element, select Show Text Snippets from the Structure pane menu.

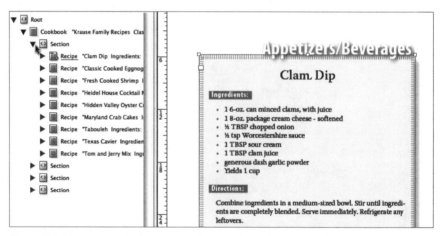

Figure 5.2 Open up the first Section element to reveal Clam Dip, the first of nine recipes in the section. The four sections of the cookbook hold 61 total recipes.

4. Drag the second Recipe icon from the Structure pane anywhere over the main text frame on page 1.

   The recipe for Classic Cooked Eggnog instantly replaces the recipe for Clam Dip, and the text for the title, ingredients, and directions automatically assumes the identical formatting and positions.

   We can't tell—are you barefoot yet? Well, the next trick should settle it once and for all.

5. Click on the second Section element to reveal 13 Recipe elements.

6. Drag the first Recipe element icon from the second section to the main text frame on page 1.

The recipe for Artichoke Bread instantly replaces the recipe for Classic Cooked Eggnog. Note that, in addition to the text for the title, ingredients, and directions changing and formatting automatically, the section title in the anchored frame changes too!

Now, we know book publishers are sitting there thinking, "I can't print a book one page at a time!" We totally sympathize. So let's ramp it up a bit.

In **Chapter 4**, you saw how you can create business cards one at a time by dragging the individual employee icons or all at once, by dragging the root element to the layout. The cookbook layout is no different.

7. Drag the first Section element icon to the main text frame.

The recipe for Clam Dip replaces Artichoke Bread. The section title reverts back to Appetizers/Beverages. But, more importantly, the main text frame displays a red plus sign indicating that it now contains overset text.

8. Using the Selection Tool, click the red plus sign to load the overset text.

9. Select Layout > Pages > Add Page or press Cmd-Shift-P/Ctrl-Shift-P to add a new page to the layout.

A new blank page appears on the screen displaying a single master text frame. Note that no anchored frame is evident on page 2.

10. Hold the Shift key to activate autoflow and click anywhere in the main text frame on page 2.

Seven additional pages are added to the document automatically. The nine recipes are identically formatted and, most important of all, each displays the section title in an anchored frame at the top of the page.

In case you were wondering, it doesn't matter whether there are 9 recipes or 900, they would all appear on their own page, fully and identically formatted.

Wow! You'll probably never wear socks again.

There's one last bit of magic left in this lesson. Let's try to flow all the recipes from all the sections all at once. Can you figure out how to do it? Right, drag the **Cookbook** element to the layout. **Cookbook** is the parent element that contains all the **Section** elements.

11. Drag the Cookbook element icon from the Structure pane to any main text frame on any page.

The color of the main text frame changes to indicate that it is now tagged for the Cookbook element. Page 9, the last page of the Appetizer/Beverage section, now displays a red plus sign indicating overset text.

Designer's XML Rule #8

You can drop an XML parent icon on any linked text frame in a multipage structured document. Note: An anchored frame is *not* linked to the structured flow. Therefore you can't use it to flow additional records.

---

12. Using the Selection tool, click the red plus sign to load the overset text.

13. Press Cmd-Shift-P/Ctrl-Shift-P to add a new blank page.

14. Hold the Shift key to activate autoflow and click anywhere on the main text frame on the new page.

This time the autoflow process will take a while, maybe even a minute or so, depending on the speed of your computer. When it's finished you will be greeted by a 61-page cookbook, completely formatted and ready for press (well, maybe not *totally* ready, but you understand what we mean).

You may want to consider moving to Florida or someplace warm. We hear they walk around barefoot all the time.

Bugs in the Cupboard

If you are performing this magic in InDesign CS2 you may notice a small bug in your cookbook. The section title has a tendency of ignoring the formatting you apply to the anchored text frame and popping to the top of the frame on the newly created pages (**Figure 5.3**). Eeeks, a bug! In fact, this bug can appear in any XML structure that employs anchored frames in CS2.

Figure 5.3 A bug in InDesign CS2 causes anchored frames to shift or ignore formatting, as in this example where the text aligns to the top of the frame. Reimporting the XML seems to fix the problem.

Don't worry, although there's no way to kill the bug (except by upgrading to CS3), you can fix the problem by reimporting the XML. That's right. Simply click the root element in the Structure pane and select File > Import XML. Choose the same XML file and leave all the checkboxes selected as in Lesson 5-1, step 8. When the XML imports and replaces the existing content, all the section titles realign to the bottom of the frames as intended.

> **Designer's XML Rule #9**
>
> Reimport the same XML file with the identical settings to correct frame creep (CS2 only).

Are you excited? Are you ecstatic and breathless waiting to learn how to do this trick yourself? Then let's get to it.

Lesson 5-3: Starting the Cookbook

As in most design projects there are usually several ways to approach things. You can start with the data structure (as we have done so far) and create the design to match it. Or create the design first and conform the data to it afterwards. Either way, you need to make the decision at some time during the process. This is one of the reasons we like using databases and spreadsheets in our XML workflow. The ability to export the data in multiple ways gives you unlimited freedom to create any type of project and use the data in almost any way. In later chapters we examine methods to manipulate the data; for now let's look at how to construct the structured layout based on an existing XML file.

1. Create a new document with the specifications shown in **Figure** 5.4.

Master Text Frame

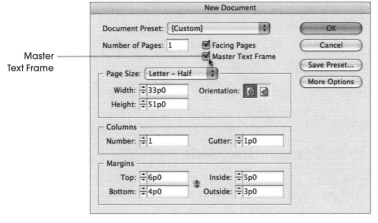

Figure 5.4 Don't forget to select the Master Text Frame checkbox. You could create a master text frame manually, but this option speeds up the process and reduces the chances of any mistakes.

2. Import the XML file **recipes.xml**. Deselect all checkboxes in the XML Import Options dialog.

The Structure pane opens, and the Tags panel fills with tag names automatically.

NOTE As we describe earlier, when all the checkboxes are deselected, the entire contents of the XML file are loaded into the Structure pane.

3. Open the Root, Cookbook, and Section parent elements in the Structure pane to reveal the first Recipe element.

4. Drag the first Recipe element to the master text frame on page 1.

The master text frame is overridden by the **Recipe** element. It changes color to reflect the color of the **Recipe** element in the Tags panel. The contents of the first recipe appear in the frame. You may also notice tag brackets surrounding each part of the recipe too.

Using the actual XML file for our starting point is a great method for getting the structured document off on the right foot. Because the Recipe element was placed directly from the Structure pane onto the page, you can be certain that the elements are in the exact order they appear in the XML itself. Some elements may not be needed, nor wanted, in the final design, but it's an easy task to delete them. With all the elements already on the page and in the correct order, the hard part is over.

Before we proceed to the next lesson, it's important to understand how the XML data is structured. By using the Text tool and the Tags panel, as we describe in "Identifying Tagged Elements" in **Chapter 2,** you can derive the names and order of the elements appearing in the text frame. Or you may find it easier to simply switch to InDesign's Story Editor, where the XML tags are plain to see.

The elements should be in the following basic order:

- Sectionhead

- Title

- Ingredients

- Directions

But there's something missing.

Lesson 5-4: Send in the Clones

By now you may also have noticed that the words *Ingredients* and *Directions* appear nowhere in the XML data, except in the tag names themselves (and tag names don't print). So, are you wondering how they got into each of the 61 recipes of the cookbook?

The answer: *cloning.* Not the cloning you see in headlines or *Star Wars*, but text and object cloning made possible through the magic of InDesign's XML features.

In **Chapter 4**, it is cloning that creates the six business cards with exactly the same formatting and structure. Cloning not only makes it possible to insert the words *Ingredients* and *Directions* into each and every recipe, it also creates and formats the anchored frame holding the section title as well.

Let's start with the easy ones first.

1. Select Edit > Edit in Story Editor or press Cmd-Y/Ctrl-Y.

   ■ Story Editor appears, displaying the Clam Dip recipe and the tag markers. It will be easier to get the cloned text into the proper location using Story Editor, where the tags are easier to see.

   ■ Note the blank line at the top of the text window.

   Before we begin setting up the structure, it's important to clean up the layout by removing any extraneous spacing or hard returns.

2. Insert the cursor in the first line and press Delete to remove the extra hard return.

*NOTE Be careful not to delete any tag markers. Luckily, InDesign warns you if you accidentally try to delete a tag that is being used (see "Untagging Graphics and Text" in **Chapter 2**).*

3. Insert the text cursor in front of the opening Ingredients tag.

4. Type the word **Ingredients:** (including the colon—**Figure 5.5**).

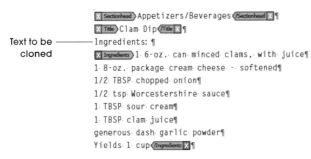

Text to be cloned

Figure 5.5 Using Story Editor, it's easy to see where to insert the cloned text. By putting the word **Ingredients:** in between tags and on a line of its own, you make InDesign clone the text and the paragraph return for each of the recipes.

5. Press the Return/Enter key to insert a paragraph return.

*NOTE It may seem oddly trivial to observe here that the key that inserts a new paragraph is named **Return** on Macs and **Enter** on Windows-based PCs, but it's actually an important distinction. That's because there's another Enter key located on your numeric keypad that must never be used for this purpose. The reason is simple: In InDesign the Enter key on the numeric keypad inserts a column break, not a paragraph return.*

Designer's XML Rule #10

Text to be cloned must be outside of any tagged placeholder element. Remember, items within the tags—such as the placeholder text—are completely replaced by the imported XML content.

---

6. Insert the text cursor on the same line, in front of the opening Directions tag.

7. Type the word **Directions:** and press the Return/Enter key to insert a paragraph return.

   Each sectionhead is now on its own line.

8. To start the process of creating the anchored frame, select the text *Appetizers/Beverages.*

9. Click the Untag button in the Tags panel (see "Untagging Text" in **Chapter 2**).

   The Sectionhead tags are removed from the text.

10. Press Cmd-X/Ctrl-X to cut the text.

    The section title is cut into memory, but the cursor remains in the position originally occupied by the tags.

11. Press Cmd-Y/Ctrl-Y or select Edit > Edit in Layout to return to Layout view.

    You must return to Layout view because InDesign does not allow you to insert an anchored object in Story Editor.

12. Select Object > Anchored Object > Insert.

    The Insert Anchored Object dialog appears.

13. Create an anchored object with the specifications shown in **Figure 5.6**.

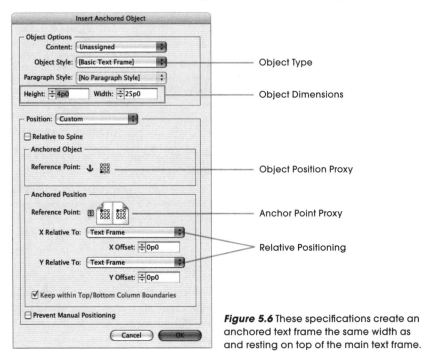

Figure 5.6 These specifications create an anchored text frame the same width as and resting on top of the main text frame.

14. Click `Sectionhead` in the Tags panel to apply the tag to the anchored text frame.

The frame adopts the color of the **Sectionhead** tag.

15. Using the Text tool, insert the cursor into the anchored frame. Press Cmd-V/Ctrl-V to paste the text cut in step 7.

The Target of the Tag is the Object

It may not make sense that you are tagging the anchored frame and not the text within the frame, until you realize that the contents of anchored objects are not considered part of the flow of the frame in which they are inserted (**Figure 5.7**). Tagging the text would cause InDesign to ignore or skip over the placeholders (because they are not part of the frame and not within the structured document), and the text in the anchored frame would not be replaced at all. Additionally, this means that anchored objects can hold only one tagged element because their entire contents are replaced based solely on the tag applied to the object. Confused yet?

Think of it this way: The anchored object itself is the placeholder for the XML element. When the XML is imported, the content of the element replaces whatever's inside the object at the time.

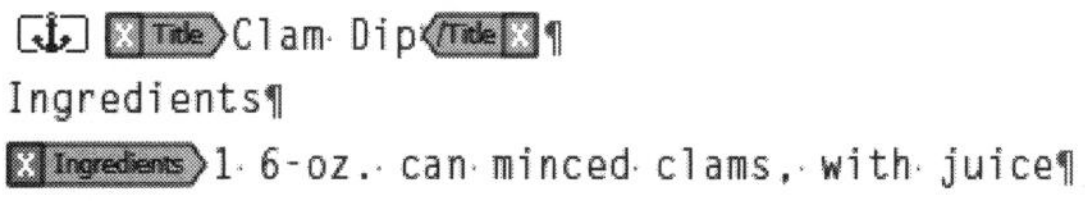

⌖ ⬛Title⟩Clam·Dip⟨Title⬛¶
Ingredients¶
⬛Ingredients⟩1·6-oz.·can·minced·clams,·with·juice¶

Figure 5.7 An anchored object tagged for the `Sectionhead` element shows no obvious tagging signs within Story Editor. To match the XML structure, insert the anchored object before the opening `<Title>` tag as shown here.

This completes the final XML placeholder for the structure. You could skip to Lesson 5-7 and import the data right now to create your own version of the cookbook. But you'd discover that the paragraph styles we add in Lesson 5-5, besides making the book easier to look at, are essential for getting the recipes to paginate properly (see "Styles Essential to XML Magic" in **Chapter 4**).

Lesson 5-5: Formatting the Structure

There's no magic to creating paragraph and character styles for a structured document. Styles simply make the task of standardizing the formatting of text easier. Often we employ specific styling to help position the content on the page or even to start new pages with page or column breaks as we demonstrate in **Chapter 4**. We don't want to waste space (or time) here creating the desired formatting, so let's just import the styles from the cookbook template used in Lesson 5-1.

1. Select Load All Text Styles from the Paragraph Styles panel menu.

2. Load all the Paragraph and Character styles from **cookbook.indt** in the manner described in **Chapter 4**, Lesson 4-8.

   The styles from the cookbook template appear in the Paragraph Styles panel.

3. Select Load Object Styles from the Object Styles panel menu. Select and open **cookbook.indt**.

   The Load Styles dialog opens. All object styles from the template are selected automatically.

4. Click OK to load all object styles from the template.

   The styles from the cookbook template appear in the Object Styles panel.

You can apply these styles to various text and frame elements manually, but we like to work a little faster and more efficiently. (Why do things yourself when someone else can do it?)

To apply styles automatically, do this:

5. Select Map Tags to Styles from the Tags panel or the Structure panel menu.

   The Map Tags to Styles dialog opens.

6. Click the Map by Name button.

   If the Preview checkbox is selected you will see the layout format automatically. However, a couple elements did not change. The text *Ingredients* and *Directions* did not change because they are not tagged and were not mapped to any style. These words and any other untagged element have to be styled manually. But the good news is: 90 percent of the work is already done.

7. Click OK.

8. Using the Text tool, insert the cursor in the text *Ingredients*. Click Subhead in the Paragraph Styles panel.

   The text formats appropriately.

9. Repeat step 8 on the text *Directions*.

   The entire layout is now formatted and ready for importing XML.

Structure – Importing XML ≠ Magic

As the structure and layout begin to resemble the sample cookbook template used in Lesson 5-1, and your eye wanders over to the long list of imported recipes in the Structure pane, you may be tempted to think that your project is finished—that perhaps you can just start dragging recipes to the layout to finish the cookbook. Resist the urge! The magic doesn't work that way.

By now you should realize that structure, by itself, isn't enough. The magic you have seen up to this point—which includes cloning, formatting, and everything else—is a result of the process of importing XML into a structured layout *and* the choices made in the XML Import Options dialog. In fact, the data currently displayed in the Structure pane is functionally useless in an XML workflow. Don't believe it? Try it yourself. Drag any of the recipe elements to the layout and see what happens. But be ready to press Cmd-Z/Ctrl-Z to undo the damage.

You'll discover that the text that appears in the frame looks little like the XML placeholders it replaces. If you drag the recipe over before applying styles, all the text appears in the frame, but the anchored frame disappears as will the text *Ingredients* and *Directions*. Drag the recipe into the frame after applying the styles, and you will see only the text from the `<sectionhead>` element, because the style Recipe Title is formatted with a page break to force each recipe to start a new page.

In fact, the only way to make the cookbook work properly is to delete all the unused recipes *before* re-importing the XML.

Lesson 5-6: The Wrong Way

We'll take a brief detour on the way to creating the cookbook to illustrate an important point about importing the XML properly. As it now appears, the layout is nearly identical to the cookbook template, with one exception: the long list of unused recipes.

If you tried the little experiment suggestion in the nearby sidebar "Structure – Importing XML ≠ Magic," you know that the recipe elements in the Structure pane are currently useless. But perhaps you think they might become more usable after importing the XML. Let's take a second to disabuse you of that notion.

1. Select the Root element in the Structure pane.

2. Select Import XML from the File or Structure pane menu.

3. Select and open **recipes.xml**.

4. Select only the following checkboxes in the XML Import Options dialog:

    ■ Clone repeating text elements

    ■ Only import elements that match existing structure

    ■ Do not import contents of whitespace-only elements

5. Deselect all other checkboxes. Click OK.

The XML content imports, replacing the placeholders. (Actually, since we used the first recipe as XML placeholders, you'll just have to take our word for it.)

6. Drag the second Recipe icon to the layout.

- All the text from the first recipe disappears, replaced only by the section title. You can see by the red plus sign indicating that the rest of the recipe text is in overset land. (Again, take our word for it or press Cmd-Y/Ctrl-Y to check it out yourself in Story Editor.)

- Since all the recipe elements already exist in the Structure pane incorrectly, even re-importing the XML again didn't correct the problem.

> **Designer's XML Rule #11**
>
> If the structure is faulty in any way, the cloning and formatting process will fail, partially or entirely.

7. Press Cmd-Z/Ctrl-Z to undo step 6.

The placeholders return, along with all the proper formatting.

Lesson 5-7: The Right Way

Ok, you knew this was coming...to get this design to work properly, first you must delete all the additional recipes in the Structure and then re-import the XML. Otherwise, the rest of the structure can be left exactly the way you see it.

1. Select the second Recipe icon in the Structure pane.

2. Hold the Shift key and select the last icon in the Structure pane.

All elements are selected except for those above the first **Recipe** icon. These must remain unchanged.

3. Click the trash can icon at the top of the Structure pane or press the Delete key.

The selected icons disappear.

4. Select the Root element.

5. Import **recipes.xml** as in Lesson 5-6 using all the same settings.

- You may notice that the XML Import Options dialog remembers the last settings used.

- The Structure pane repopulates with all the cookbook elements.

6. Drag the second Recipe icon to the main text frame.

It replaces the content and assumes all the proper formatting.

7. Drag the Section icon to the text frame.

The text frame changes to match the color of the **Section** tag color and the red plus sign appears indicating overset text.

8. Create a new page and flow the overset text as described in steps 8–10 in Lesson 5-2.

InDesign creates eight more pages to accept the additional recipes, as before.

9. Drag the Cookbook icon to the main text frame.

The text frame changes to match the color of the **Cookbook** tag color, and the red plus sign appears on the last page indicating overset text.

10. Create a new page and flow the overset text as described in steps 12–14 in Lesson 5-2.

InDesign creates 61 total pages for the entire cookbook, as before.

As you can see, the newly imported XML works just as the XML did in Lesson 5-2. We hope you're starting to understand that it's not the XML alone, nor the formatted structure that's responsible for the magic. It's the relationship between the placeholders, the formatting, and the XML import options and how they work together that makes it all possible.

Review

In this chapter we broke the boundaries of the text frame by adding anchored objects to the XML workflow. Here's what we learned:

- How to use anchored objects in a structured document

- How to tag anchored objects

- How to create and clone non-tagged elements

- How to work with multisection XML

6

Inline and Anchored Graphics

In this chapter you will learn how to:

- Work with inline graphics in an XML workflow

- Clone untagged anchored objects

- Work with anchored graphics

- Use nested styles to format untagged elements

So far we've explored the various ways text can be utilized in an XML workflow. We even threw a curve into the mix by introducing anchored objects in **Chapter 5**. But the only graphics used in our files were static. By now you're wondering if using XML means boring, text-only documents. Fortunately, the answer is a resounding no!

In this chapter we show you how to incorporate graphics into your XML workflow. The concept for this chapter came to us one day when we were browsing through a bookstore and stumbled across an ideal candidate for this type of project. There on the display rack was a pocket atlas, one you might find at your local library or in your high school book bag. Chock-full of facts and images and using a repeating page layout, it was the epitome of a structured document.

NOTE *Download all applicable files for Chapter 6 from www.peachpit.com/indesignxmlguide and copy them to a folder on your hard drive (approximately 3 MB).*

Sample Project: Atlas

Lesson 6-1: Anchored Objects, the Sequel

Scenario: You work for a publisher that specializes in printing maps and atlases. The production department sent over the layout for the latest project along with the XML file and support files to supply the content.

1. Open **atlas.indt** from the Chapter 6 folder.

NOTE *In CS3, make sure the Open Normal radio button is selected in the Open a File dialog so you create a new document whenever opening a template file (.indt).*

2. Show the Structure pane, tag markers, and tagged frames.

3. Select View > Show Frame Edges (Cmd-Shift-H/Ctrl-Shift-H), if they are hidden.

With the frame edges turned on, you should notice three anchored frames in the layout. One frame holds the flag, another the map, and the third is just for show. We discuss the strategy of using the third anchored frame in the sidebar "Anchored Object Strategy" later in the chapter. For now, let's concentrate on learning how to combine text and graphics in your XML workflow.

Whenever you approach a project built by someone else, get into the habit of dissecting the structure to understand the order and placement of the tagged placeholders, and identify any elements to be cloned before proceeding to the next step (**Figure 6.1**).

4. Select the dataroot element in the Structure pane. Import **world_atlas.xml** from the Chapter 6 folder.

5. Select only the following checkboxes in the XML Import Options dialog:

    ■ Clone repeating text elements

    ■ Only import elements that match existing structure

    ■ Do not import contents of whitespace-only elements

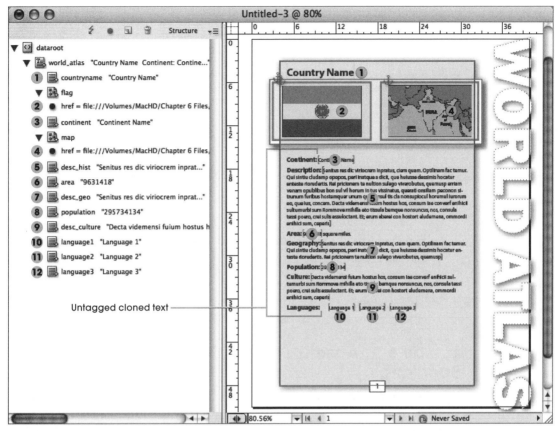

Figure 6.1 Use the Structure pane and the Selection and Text tools to match the XML elements with their placeholders in Layout view.

6. Deselect all other checkboxes. Click OK.

- After a few seconds an atlas entry for the United States appears, replacing the placeholder items.

- Nine other countries are listed in the Structure pane.

Ready for some more magic?

7. Drag the second element icon from the Structure pane to the main text frame. Be careful to avoid the anchored frames!

The entry changes, displaying information now for China, replacing the text and pictures for the United States completely. Wow!

8. Drag the dataroot icon to the main text frame.

- The frame changes color, matching the tag color for **dataroot** in the Tags panel.

- The entry for the United States replaces China.

- A red plus appears in the out port of the main text frame, indicating overset text.

9. Using the Selection tool, click the out port on the main text frame to load the overset.

10. Press Cmd-Shift-P/Ctrl-Shift-P to add a new blank page based on the atlas master page.

11. Autoflow the overset text starting on the new page 2.

- Eight more pages appear, identical to the first, displaying entries for nine additional countries.

- Note how the flags and maps alternate positions on the left and right sides. This is caused by the Relative to Spine setting specified in the Object style applied to the anchored frame.

Lesson 6-2: Absolutely Graphical, Relatively Speaking

If you've been paying attention to how often we've mentioned that XML is a plain-text language, getting pictures to appear automatically in a structured layout may seem downright miraculous. But it's really not that spectacular if you know anything about Web design (**Figure 6.2**).

Recall that, like XML, HTML is also a plain-text language, and it certainly doesn't seem to have any problems dealing with graphics. Why? Because HTML doesn't *create* the graphics; it simply references them in the code. In other words, it tells the browser where the graphics are stored on the Internet. For example, to insert a graphic called **logo.jpg** on a Web page, you insert the following code in the HTML:

```
<img src="logo.jpg">
```

Written this way, the reference indicates that the image file **logo.jpg** is saved in the same server and folder as the HTML file that is referencing it. If the graphic is stored elsewhere, you also have to include some path information indicating on what server and in which folder it can be found.

Figure 6.2 Although HTML is a plain-text language, it has no problems supporting graphics. The HTML code simply tells the browser which graphic to load and where to find it.

Paths come in two varieties: *absolute* or *relative.* Absolute paths leave nothing to chance, including the exact location of the graphic down to the server name, as in the following:

```
<img src="http://www.cookingwithxml.com/images/logo.jpg">
```

Relative paths are more open and flexible. They simply indicate where an image can be located in *relation* to the current Web page or document, such as:

```
<img src="images/logo.jpg">
```

The preceding reference tells the browser that **logo.jpg** is located in the subfolder **images**.

Absolute and relative references both have advantages and disadvantages. For example, using an absolute path tells the browser exactly where to find the graphic. That's great if the graphic file is located in static location and you have to move the Web page files around, because the browser will always find the graphic—it's in a fixed location. But if the *graphic* is moved, the path reference is suddenly wrong.

Relative references are great if the graphic is stored in the same location as the Web page or within a subfolder. Because the reference is relative, the entire folder (containing the Web page *and* the image) can be copied to a new location, or server, without breaking the path.

But how does this all relate to graphics in an XML workflow? XML uses a similar method to reference graphics, which can also be written as either absolute or relative. To re-create the same graphic reference cited earlier in XML, you would type the following:

Absolute: `<image href="file:http://www.cookingwithxml.com/images/logo.jpg" />`

Relative: `<image href="file://images/logo.jpg" />`

Let's see how the graphics are referenced within the atlas XML file.

1. Launch TextEdit or Notepad, or your favorite XML editor.

2. Open **world_atlas.xml** from the Chapter 6 folder.

3. Scroll down to the sixth line: `<flag href="file://images/us-flag.pdf" />`.

It should be pretty obvious that this piece of code references the name and location of the U.S. flag graphic used in the atlas. Because the reference doesn't spell out the hard drive or Web server name, we can also deduce that this is a relative reference. Therefore, the file **us-flag.pdf** should be located in a subfolder called **images**. Let's check it out.

4. Switch to the Mac Finder or Windows Explorer.

5. Navigate to the Chapter 6 folder.

6. Locate and open the **images** subfolder (**Figure 6.3**).

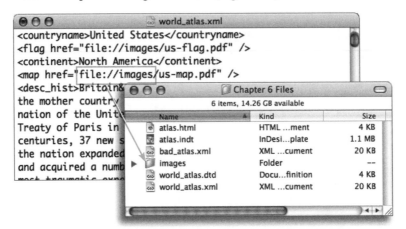

Figure 6.3 Using a relative path, the graphic can be in the same location as the XML file or within a subfolder.

Within the **images** subfolder you should find all the graphics used in the atlas, including **us-flag.pdf**. InDesign is able to find and import these graphics because they are stored in a subfolder relative to the location where the XML file is found. As with all relative references, you can move the XML file to any computer or hard drive you please, just as long as you also move the **images** subfolder to the same location.

So, the important thing to understand is that the XML file doesn't *create* the graphic; it simply *identifies* which graphic to import and where it can be found.

Lesson 6-3: Building the Atlas Template

With the experience of putting together the cookbook in **Chapter 5** under your belt, building the structured layout for the atlas should be a simple matter. As always we start with the basic document setup:

1. Create a new document with the specifications shown in **Figure 6.4**.

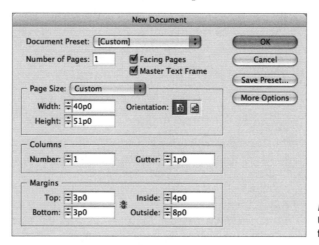

Figure 6.4
Use these specs for
the atlas template.

2. Import **world_atlas.xml**.

    The XML Import Options dialog appears.

3. Deselect all checkboxes in the XML Import Options dialog. Click OK.

    The XML content loads into the Structure pane.

4. Option-click/Alt-click on the triangle in front of the dataroot element in the Structure pane

    All elements are revealed.

5. Observe the first Flag element in the Structure pane.

You should notice that the icon clearly indicates that the Flag element is a graphic (see Table 2.1 in **Chapter 2**). In place of the *data* text snippet you'll see the icon for an XML attribute and, beside it, the *attribute* text snippet.

6. Double-click on the attribute icon for the Flag element in the Structure pane.

The Edit Attribute dialog opens (**Figure 6.5**).

Figure 6.5 Since XML doesn't create or support graphics itself, it simply stores the location of the graphic file instead. This is an example of an absolute graphic reference.

Observe the attribute's Name and Value. The name, HREF, stands for *hypertext reference* and is used in HTML to display a graphic on a Web page. The Value attribute stores the path describing the exact location of the graphic file. Whenever a graphic is placed in InDesign and tagged with an XML element, the program constructs this attribute automatically using an *absolute* reference (see Lesson 6-2).

7. Click OK to close the dialog.

8. Drag the first world_atlas icon from the Structure pane to the main text frame on page 1.

The text data, map, and flag of the United States appear in the text frame as a continuous, unformatted flow. The flag and the map appear at 100 percent scale as inline graphics.

Stop a moment to enjoy the miracle you just witnessed. The magic might not seem that impressive unless you remember that the Structure pane itself contains no graphics, just path statements like the one we observed in step 6 and earlier in Lesson 6-2. Yet that's all InDesign needs to track down the proper graphic and place it in your layout. Fantastic!

NOTE *Although there's no limitation on the size of the image or graphic that can be imported, for the purpose of this project we created each flag and map at exactly the same scale so they would fit precisely in the frames provided in the layout.*

In the Structure pane you should see ten total entries for the atlas, but to build the structure you only need the one element already placed in the layout. In fact, as we describe in **Chapter 5**, the remaining elements must be deleted or they will wreck the structure. As long as you delete the superfluous elements before importing the XML, it doesn't matter when you do it. So, now is as good as any other time.

9. Select the second world_atlas icon in the Structure pane.

10. Hold the Shift key and select the last icon in the Structure pane.

All elements are selected except for those above the first word_atlas icon.

11. Click the trash can icon at the top of the Structure pane or press the Delete key.

The selected icons disappear. This removes the XML elements from the Structure pane as well as from the document pages.

Now you're ready to start building the formatted structure.

Lesson 6-4: Anchoring Graphics

The graphics placed automatically by flowing XML into a document appear in the text as *inline anchored objects*. This default behavior comes in handy in many XML workflows. In this particular layout we want the graphics to appear in specific locations on the page. In this lesson we set up the proper relationship for the anchored graphics.

Before we begin, it's important to observe some key aspects of our current structure.

1. Reveal the contents of the `world_atlas` element in the Structure pane and observe the `Flag` and `Map` child elements.

Note how each is on a line of its own and separated by the **continent** element. No matter what you do in the final structure, it's vital that these elements (as well as all the others) remain in the order currently displayed so they match the structure of the imported XML.

2. Using the Selection tool, click on the flag graphic.

Selection handles appear around the inline graphic.

3. Select Object > Anchored Object > Options.

The Anchored Object Options dialog appears.

4. Enter the specifications in the dialog shown in **Figure 6.6**.

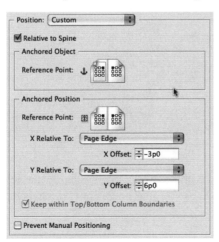

Figure 6.6 These specifications reposition the flag graphic to the desired location.

Anchors Aweigh

The use of Inline objects has been around a long time, but the anchored object is a relatively new feature to InDesign, having made its debut in CS2. Unlike inline objects, which must sit dutifully within a line of text or in their own paragraph, anchored objects can be positioned virtually anywhere on the page, even outside the text frame itself! To learn more about the use and limitations of anchored objects, refer to the InDesign Help file, or check out *Real World Adobe InDesign CS3* and *InDesign CS3 for Macintosh and Windows Visual Quickstart Guide,* both from Peachpit Press.

5. Click OK.

6. Using the Selection tool, click on the map graphic.

Selection handles appear around the inline graphic.

7. Select Object > Anchored Object > Options.

The Anchored Object Options dialog appears.

8. Enter the specifications in the dialog shown in **Figure 6.7.**

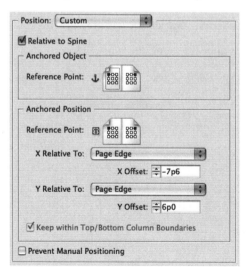

Figure 6.7 These specifications reposition the map graphic to the desired location.

9. Click OK.

Moving the two anchored graphics to the top of the page has left some unwanted gaps in the text. Getting rid of the extra space won't hurt the structure—if you're careful (**Figure 6.8**).

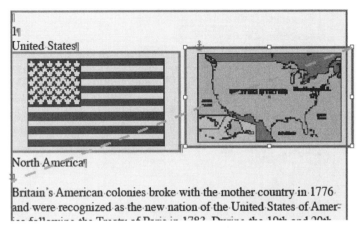

Figure 6.8 Here the map graphic has been floated from its original position in its own paragraph, leaving an undesirable hole in the text. The dashed line indicates the location of the frame's anchor marker.

10. Press Cmd-Y/Ctrl-Y to switch to Story Editor or select Edit > Edit in Story Editor.

11. Insert the cursor after the first anchor icon. Press the Delete key.

The **continent** placeholder moves up behind the icon.

NOTE *When deleting the paragraph return and other spacing between the tagged place-holders, be careful not to delete any tags or placeholders.*

12. Delete the paragraph return after the second icon.

Now it's time to insert the background frame as an anchored object.

13. Select the blank first line of text and the content and tags of the subsequent countryID element. Press the Delete key.

- The **countryname** element shifts to the first line.

- The cursor should still be inserted before the **countryname** tag.

14. Press Cmd-Y/Ctrl-Y to return to Layout view. (Anchored objects can only be inserted in Layout view.)

15. Select Object > Anchored Object > Insert.

The Anchored Object Options dialog appears.

16. Enter the specifications in the dialog shown in **Figure 6.9**.

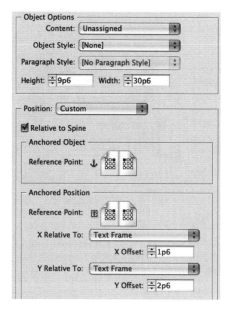

Figure 6.9 These settings create an anchored object used as the background for the flag and map graphics.

17. Click OK.

A new anchored object appears near the top of the page.

> ### Anchored Object Strategy
>
> The new frame in step 15 will be used as the background for the flag and map graphics, the same way it was used in the earlier template example in Lesson 6-1. It won't be tagged and has no significance to the structure—it's purely for show. Therefore, you might think that it could be simply inserted in the document the same way you added the master frame. But you'd be wrong.
>
> Because the map and flag are anchored graphics and integrally part of the text flow, the background frame can't be separately free floating. A free-floating object must be either behind the text frame (and any anchored objects) entirely or in front of it. No free-floating object can be inserted between an anchored object and the text frame from which it originates. Inserting it as the first item in the text flow places the background frame at the bottom of the object layer hierarchy and automatically behind all the text in the frame, as well as any anchored objects inserted therein.

18. Set the background frame color to Paper. Set the stroke color to Black. Set the stroke width to 2 points.

All anchored objects are in their desired locations.

Lesson 6-5: Creating Object Styles

One potential problem that can disrupt XML workflows is that anchored objects can shift from their desired locations during cloning when their positions are manually formatted. To prevent object shifting altogether, formalize the design using Object styles.

To create Object styles do this:

1. Using the Selection tool, click on the anchored background frame.

Selection handles should appear around the active anchored graphic.

2. Select New Object Style from the Object Styles panel menu.

- The New Object Style dialog appears.

- All formatting options are selected by default, except for Paragraph styles.

- The dialog should automatically pick up the formatting applied to background frame.

If you have never used it (or changed the settings) before, all checkboxes in the New Object Style dialog are checked by default, except for the Paragraph styles settings. By having the formatted frame selected, all the specifications you just applied will be automatically captured when the new Object style is created. The settings we are most interested in are Fill, Stroke, and Anchored Object Options, but make sure all the boxes remain checked to maintain consistent formatting. For anchored graphic objects, the Paragraph styles settings are irrelevant, but come in handy for anchored text frames like the one used in the cookbook in **Chapter 5**.

3. Name the style Backframe. In CS3, select the Apply Style to Selection checkbox. Click OK. In CS2, apply the style to the background frame.

4. Select the flag graphic.

5. Select New Object Style from the Object Style panel menu.

6. Name the style Flag. In CS3, select the Apply Style to Selection checkbox. Click OK. In CS2, apply the style to the flag graphic.

7. Select the map graphic.

8. Select New Object Style from the Object Style panel menu.

9. Name the style Map. In CS3, select the Apply Style to Selection checkbox. Click OK. In CS2, apply the style to the map graphic.

All objects are now styled properly.

> **Designer's XML Rule #12**
>
> Format all anchored objects with Object styles to prevent shifting and to ensure consistent positioning during cloning.

Lesson 6-6: Send in the Clones, the Sequel

In **Chapter 5**, we added the words *Ingredients* and *Directions* to the structured layout so they could introduce the appropriate parts of each recipe. These words were then cloned automatically when the XML file was re-imported later. In the atlas template from Lesson 6-1, you may remember seeing bolded words introducing each of the descriptive paragraphs of data. As you can see in your current layout, the XML data itself features no such words, which means you must add them manually to the layout before the template can be complete.

We learned in the cookbook example that cloned text must be inserted outside the tagged placeholders. But unlike in the cookbook, the words you add to the atlas structure will not be on a line/paragraph of their own—they will be in the same paragraph as the XML placeholders.

But before we proceed, we have to take care of a bit of housekeeping. You may have noticed that some of the text has slipped under the anchored frames and become inaccessible. Addressing the problem now will save you some trips to Story Editor or other equally undesirable contortions.

1. Use the Text tool to select the text **United States** in the first line.

2. Format the text as Myriad Pro, Bold, 18-pt. on 20-pt. leading, 11 picas space after the paragraph.

   The hidden text moves out from under the anchored frames.

3. Select the main text frame in your layout. Press Cmd-Y/Ctrl-Y to switch to Story Editor (it's easier to see the tags in Story Editor).

4. Type **Continent:** including a single space directly in front of the opening continent tag.

5. Type **Description:** including a single space directly in front of the opening desc_hist tag.

6. Type **Area:** including a single space directly in front of the opening area tag.

7. Type **Geography:** including a single space directly in front of the opening desc_geo tag.

8. Type **Population:** including a single space directly in front of the opening population tag.

9. Type **Culture:** including a single space directly in front of the opening desc_culture tag.

10. Type **Language:** including a single space directly in front of the opening Language1 tag.

11. Delete the paragraph return after the closing Language1 tag.

12. Insert the cursor between the closing Language1 tag and opening Language2 tag. Select Type > Insert White Space > Em Space.

13. Delete the paragraph return after the closing Language2 tag.

14. Insert an em-space between the closing Language2 tag and opening Language3 tag.

15. Insert a single paragraph return after the Language3 tag but delete any other extraneous paragraph returns or spacing that creeps into your structure.

NOTE *Inserting one extra paragraph return at the end of a structured layout is necessary to get it to clone properly.*

16. Apply the Basic Paragraph style to the empty line.

The structure now includes all the text and objects that will be cloned, as shown in **Figure 6.10**. You're nearly finished.

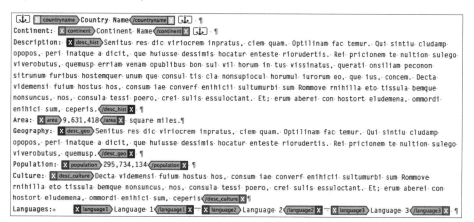

Figure 6.10 Note the location of the anchor icons and the untagged text introducing the paragraphs.

Lesson 6-7: Formatting the Structure

By this time, formatting the structure should be second nature to you. If you've been paying attention, you understand that formats applied to the XML placeholders transfer to the imported data and then are cloned on each page of the layout. All sorts of glitches can happen to a structured layout as it's being cloned, and we've determined that you preclude most of the problems by creating and applying Paragraph, Character, and Object styles to the structured layout before importing the XML whenever possible.

Paragraph styles have sufficed in our workflow up until now. But to make the atlas and other documents look good, you'll discover that Character styles are equally important. And the most powerful application of Character styles also happens to be one of our favorite InDesign wündertools: nested styles.

Nested styles, like Lerner and Lowe, or chocolate and peanut butter, are happy confluences of two great things. The tool combines Paragraph and Character styles in an ingenious way that is also ideal for a structured XML workflow. It allows you to apply Character styles automatically to parts of paragraphs based on their intrinsic structure. How much better can it get?

For example, each paragraph of atlas data is introduced by one of the words you typed in Lesson 6-6 (Continent, Description, Population, and so on). In the original template, each of these words is formatted differently than the text in the rest of the paragraph. You could format these words manually and hope they retain the format as the placeholders are being replaced and cloned, but that's like hoping the tooth fairy will leave a winning lottery ticket under your pillow.

The problem with the atlas is that the introductory words are *un*tagged. Using the tools you have learned so far, there's no way to guarantee that these words will maintain their formatting during cloning—except by using nested styles.

Let's see how nested styles work in a structured layout:

1. Select the word **Continent:** (including the colon).

2. Format the text as Myrid Pro, Regular, 9-pt., with 10-pt. leading. Add 6-pt. spacing after the paragraph.

3. Select New Paragraph Style from the Paragraph Styles panel menu.

4. Name the style continent. Match the spelling and case of the XML tag exactly as it appears in the Tags panel. In CS3, click the Apply to Selection checkbox. Click OK.

   - The continent style appears in the Paragraph Styles panel.

   - In CS3 the Paragraph style is automatically applied.

5. In CS2, apply the continent style to the paragraph.

6. Select Bold from the Font pull-down menu and increase the font size to 11 pt.

7. Select New Character Style from the Character Styles panel menu.

8. Name the style **Bold title**. Click OK.

The Bold title style appears in the Character Styles panel.

9. Click the Clear Overrides button at the bottom of the Paragraph Styles panel.

The format of the selected text returns to the Paragraph style's default format.

10. Double-click continent in the Paragraph Style panel.

The Paragraph Style Options dialog appears.

11. Select the Drop Caps and Nested Styles tab in the Paragraph Styles Options dialog.

12. Click the New Nested Style button. Assign the specifications shown in **Figure 6.11**.

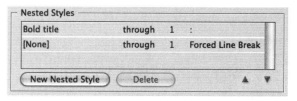

Figure 6.11
These specifications automatically format the first word (and colon) as the Bold title Character style.

13. Click OK.

The paragraph style updates to apply the Bold title style to the Continent: text at the beginning of the paragraph.

Lesson 6-8: Creating Styles for Each XML Element

Because each of the subsequent paragraphs needs to be formatted identically to this one, we could use the continent style for all of them and map it manually to each of the XML elements. But we prefer to have Paragraph styles named for each of the XML elements.

1. Select Duplicate Style from the Paragraph Styles panel menu.

■ The Duplicate Paragraph Style dialog appears.

■ The Style Name field displays the text *continent copy*.

2. Change the name to **desc_hist**. Match the spelling and case of the XML tag exactly as it appears in the Tags panel.

Note that the new style is based on the continent style.

3. Click OK. Apply the desc_hist style to the paragraph.

4.   Repeat steps 1 through 3 until you have created and applied a style for each of the XML elements applied to placeholder paragraphs, except for Language2 and Language3. Because the Language2 and Language3 elements share a paragraph with the element Language1, only one style is needed.

5.   Select the text *United States* in the first line of the layout and create a new Paragraph style named **countryname**.

Note how the New Paragraph Style dialog picks up the formatting of the existing text. But one setting has not been applied yet. As is, the imported XML content will form a continuous text flow filling every text frame top to bottom. That means if one atlas entry doesn't use the entire page, the next entry will automatically start in the remaining space. Egads! Don't worry; we describe the solution in "Styles Essential to XML Magic" in **Chapter 4**.

6.   Select the Keep Options tab in the New Paragraph Style dialog.

7.   Select On Next Page from the Start Page pull-down menu. Click OK.

8.   Apply the countryname style to the paragraph.

The structured layout is nearly complete.

Lesson 6-9: Mapping Tags to Styles

For the cloning to work properly when the XML is re-imported, the relationship between the XML tags and the newly created paragraph styles has to be formalized. This is done by mapping the tag names to the Paragraph styles.

1.   Select Map Tags to Styles from the Tags panel or the Structure pane menu.

     The Map Tags to Styles dialog appears.

2.   Click the Map by Name button.

     The XML elements will be matched to their style counterparts automatically.

NOTE   All the elements will have a style match except for dataroot, world_atlas, countryID, flag, map, Language2, *and* Language3.

3.   Click the Preview checkbox to review the formatting.

     The text in the layout should format according to the mapping specifications.

4.   If everything seems formatted appropriately, click OK. Otherwise confirm that the tags are mapped to the correct Styles and then click OK.

Before testing the atlas, let's save the file.

5. Select File > Save As.

6. Name the document **my_atlas** and save it as an InDesign template in the Chapter 6 folder.

7. Close the file.

Lesson 6-10: Testing the Template

Nervous? Let's see if your structured atlas design works.

1. Open **my_atlas.indt to create a new document**.

2. Select the dataroot element in the Structure pane.

3. Import **world_atlas.xml**.

4. Select only the following checkboxes in the XML Import Options dialog:

- Clone repeating text elements

- Only import elements that match existing structure

- Do not import contents of whitespace-only elements

5. Deselect all other checkboxes.

6. Cross your fingers and click OK.

- After a few seconds the United States entry appears, replacing the placeholder items.

- All the entries are formatted as specified.

- All ten countries are listed in the Structure pane.

7. Drag the dataroot element to the main text frame.

- The frame color changes to match the dataroot element.

- The text frame displays a red plus (+) indicating it contains overset text.

8. Create a new page and autoflow the remaining content into the main text frame on page 2.

InDesign flows the content onto page 2 and creates 8 additional pages for the remaining data.

Quick, it's not too late to list your socks on eBay!

Lesson 6-11: Troubleshooting the Structure

If you followed the instructions carefully, everything should have worked as in the sample template in Lesson 6-1. If something messed up, first try to identify the error. Next, press Cmd-Z/Ctrl-Z to reverse the process and then check the following items in the structured document for errors before trying it again:

- Placeholders tagged properly

- Placeholders in the proper order

- Tags mapped to the proper styles

- One untagged and unformatted paragraph return at the end of the placeholder text

- Extraneous elements deleted from Structure pane

- Root element selected before importing

- Correct options selected in XML Import Options dialog

Fix any problems and then try it again.

Lesson 6-12: Broken World

Although there's only one way to create a functioning XML workflow, there are unlimited ways of creating a broken one. Lesson 6-11 can help you track down a problem originating in your structured document, but what do you do if the error is coming from the XML itself?

There's not enough space in this book to discuss every possible error you can encounter in an XML file, but we'd like to show you at least one common problem you may experience and its simple solution.

1. Open **atlas.indt**.

2. Select the dataroot element in the Structure pane.

3. Import **bad_atlas.xml**.

4. Select only the following checkboxes in the XML Import Options dialog:

   - Clone repeating text elements

   - Only import elements that match existing structure

   - Do not import contents of whitespace-only elements

5. Deselect all other checkboxes. Click OK.

The Find: us-flag.tif dialog appears (**Figure 6.12**).

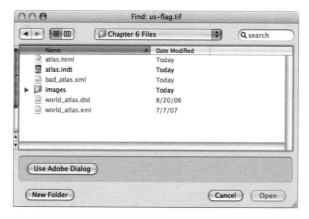

Figure 6.12 If InDesign can't find the referenced graphical element, it asks you to do so using this dialog.

If you look in the title bar of the dialog you can see that InDesign is looking for a file called **us-flag.tif**. Unfortunately all the graphics used in this workflow are saved as PDFs, not TIFFs. In other words, a simple typo has ground this workflow to a halt. But, instead of crashing or doing some other undesirable reaction, InDesign politely asks us to locate the missing file. Using this dialog you can track down the actual location of **us-flag.tif** or simply redirect InDesign to a proper replacement.

6. Navigate to the **images** subfolder and select **us-flag.pdf**. Click Open.

The Find: us-map.tif dialog appears.

7. Select **us-map.pdf** in the **images** subfolder and click Open.

- The remainder of the XML import should proceed without further error.

- The atlas entry for the United States replaces the placeholder text and graphics.

If this happens to you during a real project, open the XML file in your favorite editor (see **Chapter 3**) and examine the file and path names. Make any corrections necessary and save the file.

Review

We've come a long way in the last three chapters. If Chapter 6 feels like a blur, here's a recap to put it back in focus. You learned:

- How XML works with inline graphics
- How to clone untagged anchored objects
- How to work with anchored graphics
- How to use nested styles in a structured document

7

Targeted XML Import

Chapter Objectives

In this chapter you will learn how to:

- Import XML into specific elements

- Import XML to update data in place

- Import XML to delete empty elements

- Edit XML to create proper element structure

- Combine XML files for complex workflows

It occurred to us that the number of readers producing world atlases (Chapter 6) any time soon is small, so we looked around for other more common projects to demonstrate. The candidate that came to mind immediately, ideal for an XML workflow, is the traditional product catalog or pricelist.

In this Chapter you will learn everything you need to know to set up and complete a typical product catalog using an XML workflow.

NOTE   Download all applicable files for Chapter 7 from www.peachpit.com/indesignxmlguide and copy them to a folder on your hard drive (approximately 8 MB).

Sample Project: Product Catalog

Thousands of catalogs are printed each year for every conceivable market and category, including consumer electronics, industrial equipment, parts, and accessories, professional services, and many, many more. Although most of these items are available online today, one office supply distributor revealed to us that sales still increase dramatically when their printed catalog arrives in customer mailboxes and, in turn, subsequently dip when the interval between catalogs becomes too long.

Common sense would seem to dictate that publishing catalogs more frequently would drive sales and increase profits. Unfortunately, traditional production methods are way too expensive. In most markets the cost of producing catalogs more frequently far outstrips any gains in sales.

You probably already know that, next to the printing itself, the biggest cost in creating a catalog is the time and labor involved in design and production. Literally hours and days are devoted simply to transcribing and formatting product descriptions, prices, and SKU numbers. To address the need for increasing the frequency of catalog releases, some companies have resorted to expensive third-party solutions to help automate the process. These plug-ins and programs can cost thousands of dollars and often require lengthy periods of instructor-led training before a design department can get up and running. We've got a better way: the XML way!

Lesson 7-1: Targeted XML Import

Scenario: Your company specializes in selling classic books, as well as adaptations on audio tape, VHS, and DVD. You are developing a print catalog to augment your company's online store. The goal is to create a multi-section catalog design that lists the products both by format and by author. You have access to a catalog template started by a coworker, the XML files used by the Web-based store, and the product images, which are saved in JPEG format.

1. Open **BookCatalog.indt** from the Chapter 7 folder.

2. Show the Structure pane, tag markers, and tagged frames.

3. Select View > Show Frame Edges, if they are hidden.

Examine the structured layout in front of you. (It may help to switch to Story Editor (**Figure 7.1**) to get the full flavor of the design's complexity.) You should be able to identify one tagged anchored frame and nine tagged text placeholders. The layout also takes full advantage of Paragraph, Character, and Object styles throughout. Let's check out what kind of magic we have in store for you.

> ⚓ X producttype › Format ‹ /producttype X › : ¶
> X productname › Title ‹ /productname X › ¶
> Author: · X artistfirstname › Firstname ‹ /artistfirstname X › · X artistlastname › Lastname ‹ /artistlastname X › ¶
> X description › Type· a· descrption· of· the· product· here.· Limit· the· description· to· no· more· than· 250· words. ‹ /description X › ¶
> X company › Publisher· or· Studio ‹ /company X › ,· X year › Date· released ‹ /year X › ¶
> Order· #· X productid › 000-000000 ‹ /productid X › » $ X price › 0.00 ‹ /price X › ¶
> #

Figure 7.1 It's easy to see the structure in Story Editor.

4. Select the Inventory element in the Structure pane.

5. Import **Books.xml**.

- The Import XML dialog appears.

- The Show XML Import Options checkbox is selected.

- The Import into Selected Element checkbox is selected.

Targeted Import Hits the Mark

InDesign inserts, updates, or replaces the tagged content depending on whether the structure of the imported XML matches that of the existing data, element for element. By default, this process starts at the root element in the Structure pane. When checked, the Import into Selected Element option can be used to target the imported XML to an element other than the root. By selecting an element in the Structure pane before importing—as you did in step 4—you cause InDesign to turn on this option by default (**Figure 7.2**).

Note: When the imported XML doesn't match the existing structure, it is always inserted into the structure.

Figure 7.2 It's not hard to miss this option in the XML Import dialog, but it makes a world of difference to your workflow.

6. Click Open.

The XML Import Options dialog appears.

7. Select only the following checkboxes in the XML Import Options dialog:

- Clone repeating text elements
- Only import elements that match existing structure
- Do not import contents of whitespace-only elements

8. Deselect all other checkboxes. Click OK.

A second BK element appears in the Structure pane, but otherwise nothing else happens.

What's up? No magic? No miracles? No nothin'? What went wrong? Let's see if you can figure out the "problem" in the project.

9. Press Cmd-Z/Ctrl-Z.

The layout should return to its original configuration.

10. Launch TextEdit or Notepad, whichever is appropriate for your operating system.

11. Open **Books.xml** from the Chapter 7 folder.

A quick scan of the XML shows that the structure matches the names and order of the elements in the file perfectly. But a more careful examination reveals one small, seemingly insignificant, difference: In InDesign, the root element in the Structure pane is named Inventory but there is no such element in the XML file! Although the structure of the placeholders matches in all other aspects, trying to import the XML into an element that didn't match its own structure caused the import process to fail just as surely as it would have had the elements been misspelled or out of order.

We purposely threw this curve ball at you for two reasons. First, just to see if you were paying attention. And second, to demonstrate a cool trick we call *Targeted XML Import.*

12. Select the BK element in the Structure pane.

BK is a child element of Inventory.

13. Import **Books.xml**.

- The Import XML dialog appears.
- The Show XML Import Options checkbox is selected.
- The Import into Selected Element checkbox is selected.

14. Select only the following checkboxes in the XML Import Options dialog:

- Clone repeating text elements

- Only import elements that match existing structure

- Do not import contents of whitespace-only elements

15. Deselect all other checkboxes. Click OK.

- In a few seconds the placeholder text in the layout is replaced by the data entry for the book *A Connecticut Yankee in King Arthur's Court.*

- A total of 35 book entries appear in the Structure pane.

16. Drag the BK element from the Structure pane to the main text frame on page 1.

- The color of the frame changes to match the **BK** element.

- Page 1 fills with the content stored in the Structure pane.

- Each entry displays an anchored frame.

- Most of the anchored frames contain images depicting the book covers.

- The text frame displays a red plus (+) sign indicating overset text.

By selecting, or *targeting*, the **BK** child element in the Structure pane, you correctly matched up the structure in the layout to the structure of the XML file. In the next lesson you'll see why this is so important.

Lesson 7-2: Targeting Multisection Structures

Up until now we have used single XML files for each project. These files run the gamut from simple to complex. In this lesson, we explore how one structure can be used to import content from multiple XML files.

1. Open **BookCatalogSection.indt**.

2. Show the Structure pane, tag markers, and tagged frames.

3. Select View > Show Frame Edges, if they are hidden.

The document features the identical structure based on the **BK** child element as in the previous lesson with a special bonus: two additional structured layouts based on child elements named **AB** and **MV** (**Figure 7.3**).

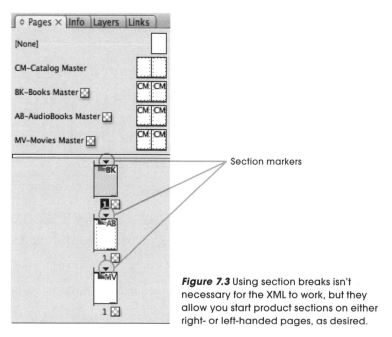

Section markers

Figure 7.3 Using section breaks isn't necessary for the XML to work, but they allow you start product sections on either right- or left-handed pages, as desired.

4. Select the BK element in the Structure pane.

5. Import **Books.xml**. Click Open.

   ■ The Import XML dialog appears.

   ■ The Show XML Import Options checkbox is selected.

   ■ The Import into Selected Element checkbox is selected.

6. Select only the following checkboxes in the XML Import Options dialog:

   ■ Clone repeating text elements

   ■ Only import elements that match existing structure

   ■ Do not import contents of whitespace-only elements

7. Deselect all other checkboxes. Click OK.

   ■ The data entry for the book *A Connecticut Yankee in King Arthur's Court* appears in the layout.

   ■ The BK element in the Structure pane fills with 35 book entries.

8. Drag the BK element from the Structure pane to the main text frame on page 1.

The page fills with products, as in Lesson 7-1.

9. Select the AB element in the Structure pane.

10. Import **Audiobooks.xml**. Click Open.

- The Import XML dialog appears.

- The Show XML Import Options checkbox is selected.

- The Import into Selected Element checkbox is selected.

11. Repeat steps 6 and 7.

- The data entry for the audio book *Anna Karenina* appears in the layout.

- The **AB** element in the Structure pane fills with 11 audiobook entries.

12. Drag the AB element from the Structure pane to the main text frame on the page that begins the audiobook section.

The page fills with audiobook entries and cover images.

13. Select the MV element in the Structure pane.

14. Import **Movies.xml**. Click Open.

- The Import XML dialog appears.

- The Show XML Import Options checkbox is selected.

- The Import into Selected Element checkbox is selected.

15. Repeat steps 6 and 7.

- The data entry for the DVD *A Farewell to Arms* appears in the layout.

- The **MV** element in the Structure pane fills with 24 DVD and VHS entries.

16. Drag the MV element from the Structure pane to the main text frame on the page that begins the movies section.

The page fills with movie entries and cover images.

All three child elements—**BK**, **AB**, and **MV**—are filled with content.

Lesson 7-3: Inserting Pages in a Multisection Structure

In previous sample projects you used autoflow to automatically create pages from the overset text. Unfortunately, this feature doesn't work properly with multisection documents. Let's explore two alternative procedures for inserting additional pages to accommodate the overset text:

1. Show the Pages panel, if it's not visible.

NOTE *The three page icons displaying section markers. Each page icon is formatted by its own master page, customized for its specific product category.*

2. Using the Selection tool, click on the red plus (+) at the bottom of page 1 to load the overset text.

The arrow cursor changes to indicate that the overset text is loaded.

3. Select and drag one of the BK-Books Master icons from the masters section of the Pages panel and drop it to the right of the icon for page 1 (**Figure 7.4**).

A new blank BK-formatted page appears in the panel between the first and second pages.

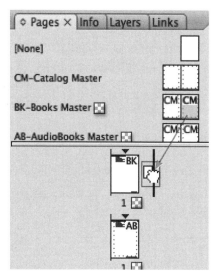

Figure 7.4 When you drag the master page to the correct spot, a black bar appears beside page 1 to indicate that the new page will be inserted between the first and second pages.

4. Click the loaded text icon over the main text frame on the new page 2.

- The page fills with book entries.

- The lower right corner of the text frame displays a red plus (+) indicating additional overset text.

Dragging master pages to the panel is okay for onesies and twosies, but if you need to add two or more pages at a time, here's a better way:

5. Select Insert Pages from the Pages Panel or select Layout > Pages > Insert Pages.

The Insert Pages dialog appears.

6. Enter the specifications shown in **Figure 7.5**. Click OK.

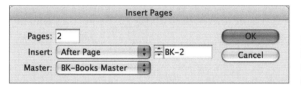

Figure 7.5 Use the Insert Pages dialog any time you need to add two or more pages at a time.

7. Load the overset text from page 2 and flow it manually onto the new pages.

8. Insert additional pages as necessary to flow the remaining entries in each of the three sections.

All the catalog data should now be displayed within the document.

Lesson 7-4: Multipurpose XML Import

That was fun. Targeted XML Import offers important advantages to complex work-flows. It allows you to import XML of widely differing structures into one document, or the same XML file for a variety of purposes. Let's explore one example where you can—with small modifications—use the same XML file in multiple ways:

1. Open **BookCatalogPricelist.indt**.

2. Show the Structure pane, tag markers, and tagged frames.

3. Select View > Show Frame Edges, if they are hidden.

Observe the Structure pane. Note the MV and MV2 elements contained in the root element **Inventory**. The MV element is structured to populate the Movie data entries on pages 1–3.

4. Navigate to page 3.

The MV2 element has been delegated to create a six-column pricelist on page 3.

5. Select the MV element in the Structure pane.

6. Import **Movies.xml**.

7. Select only the following checkboxes in the XML Import Options dialog:

   - Clone repeating text elements

   - Only import elements that match existing structure

   - Do not import contents of whitespace-only elements

8. Deselect all other checkboxes. Click OK.

   Pages 1–3 fill automatically with the text and images for the movie product entries.

A Rose Is Still a Rose

Before you import the XML for the pricelist, take a closer look at the structure of the placeholders on page 3. Show the Tags panel and insert the Text cursor in any of the tagged elements. Notice that the names have been slightly altered. Although we're still using the same XML content, the tag names had to be changed to facilitate the formatting of the pricelist. Why? If you thought about it for second you could probably figure it out for yourself. The reason is simple: The XML elements in BK, AB and MV are already mapped to paragraph styles that format the main catalog entries on pages 1–3. If you import the exact same XML file into the pricelist, it would adopt the exact same formats, too. So we cheated a bit by duplicating the XML file in advance and appending the number 2 to the end of each element name and saving as Movieprice.xml. This minor change allows us to map the same data to a whole new set of Paragraph and Character styles. Later in Lesson 7-11 we show you how to do this for yourself.

---

9. Select the MV2 element in the Structure panel.

10. Import **Moviesprice.xml** as in steps 6 and 7. Click OK.

    The placeholder text is replaced by the first data entry from the imported XML.

    NOTE The elements used in the structure filter the XML upon import, allowing only data for the format, title, director, year, order number, and price to enter the layout.

11. Drag the MV2 element to the text frame containing the pricelist.

    The text frame fills with the movie data formatted line-by-line into the pricelist.

    NOTE You may notice a blank line at the top of the pricelist. The extra line is not in the place-holder, it's not in the XML, it simply appears when you drag the MV2 element to the text frame. These phantom spaces will plague your workflow from time to time, and although they're annoying, they're also perfectly harmless. Just go ahead and delete any lines that are not supposed to be there. Once deleted, they will not appear again, even if you re-import or update the XML.

Lesson 7-5: Advanced Targeted XML Import

If you were thinking that Targeted XML Import was going to involve a bunch of tedious drudge work in the Structure panel, pay attention to this lesson. Here we combine all the XML data we've used up until now in the catalog (and a bit more) to give you a glimpse at what's possible. The only limitation to this technique is your imagination and skill in assembling the XML file.

1. Open **BookCatalogInventory.indt**.

2. Show the Structure pane, tag markers, and tagged frames.

3. Select View > Show Frame Edges, if they are hidden.

Examine the entire document carefully. You'll notice six distinct structured layouts, two for each of the sections: Books, Audiobooks, and Movies.

4. Select the Inventory element in the Structure pane.

5. Import **Inventory.xml**.

6. Select only the following checkboxes in the XML Import Options dialog:

   - Clone repeating text elements

   - Only import elements that match existing structure

   - Do not import contents of whitespace-only elements

7. Deselect all other checkboxes. Click OK.

Depending on the speed of your computer, the process can take up to a minute or more. Upon completion, each of the structured layouts has been populated by the content in the XML file. One file, six distinct sections—can it get any better?

8. Insert pages as necessary in each of the sections and flow the remaining data entries, as shown in Lesson 7-3.

9. Click the Preview button at the bottom of the Toolbox to see the completed catalog as it would print.

   - The frames and XML structure are hidden. You should see only text and pictures.

   - The entire catalog is complete with entries and pricelists in place for the Books, Audiobooks and Movies sections.

10. Click the Normal button at the bottom of the Toolbox. Do not close the file, but proceed to the next lesson.

    All the frames and the XML structure should be visible again.

Lesson 7-6 Updating XML Content

You can probably see how an XML workflow can help you create data-driven documents more quickly and easily with fewer errors overall, but perhaps you're not convinced yet on the need to switch. Maybe it's time to bring out the big guns. One of the banes of the catalog designer's existence has to do with the constant need to update prices and product photos, sometimes right up to press time. We've heard numerous horror stories of how prices and photos had to be changed even as plates were being hung. XML can't change the industry but, fortunately, it can help save your sanity.

1. Launch TextEdit, Notepad, or your favorite XML editor.

2. Open **Inventory.xml**.

3. Scroll down to the first product in the file: A Connecticut Yankee in King Arthur's Court.

4. Locate the <price> element and change the price from 4.95 to 6.50. Be sure not to delete any of the tags or other code elements.

5. Scroll down to the next product: A Farewell To Arms.

6. Change the price from 18.15 to 20.50.

7. Continue down through the products and alter several more prices. Note the changes that you make.

8. Save the file as **updatedInventory.xml** and close it.

9. Switch to InDesign; select the Inventory element in the Structure pane.

10. Import **updatedInventory.xml**.

11. Select only the following checkboxes in the XML Import Options dialog:

    - Clone repeating text elements

    - Only import elements that match existing structure

    - Do not import contents of whitespace-only elements

12. Deselect all other checkboxes. Click OK.

    - The modified XML data replaces the existing content, completely updating all the prices automatically.

    - Most importantly: Nothing else has changed! The positions and formatting of all the unaffected text and graphics are in position and ready for press.

Updating data on the fly is probably one of the most impressive aspects of an XML workflow. It allows designers to work on a design, without regard to the status of the product data, and update information right up to the last minute. In the past, we waited as long as possible before importing data, because we knew it would change. We wanted to minimize the number of manual corrections we'd have to make. Now there's no reason to delay. Set up the catalog, import the data, get everything formatted and positioned perfectly. As long as you're using an XML workflow you can simply smile when the inevitable calls comes: "The prices have changed!"

"No sweat," you say. "I have XML on my side."

However, there's one big caveat: The changes you made to the XML file just now were minor—modifications that probably wouldn't affect layout or text flow. If you make larger, or more aggressive, changes to the XML, the effects on the layout can be unpredictable. Just because updates can be fast in XML doesn't mean they'll be without hassle altogether. Don't make it your standard procedure to wait to the last minute to perform updates.

Remember what your mother told you: "Just because you can doesn't mean you should."

Lesson 7-7: Deleting Empty Elements

You probably noticed in the previous lessons the numerous empty anchored frames in each of the catalog sections. This is not an unusual situation for catalog designers as new items are added frequently, often even before product photos can be taken. In fact, any time you assemble hundreds or thousands of products into a single catalog, you're guaranteed to end up with some empty data elements. In our sample catalog we anticipated the situation and designed it in such a way that empty elements (and therefore empty picture frames) didn't affect the look or flow of the data. Not every design can be so accommodating, and empty frames can leave unacceptable holes in your layout. Fortunately, InDesign provides a feature to automatically delete these potential troublemakers before they can cause you any grief.

1. Select the Inventory element in the Structure pane.

2. Import **Inventory.xml**.

   The XML Import Options dialog appears.

3. Select only the following checkboxes in the XML Import Options dialog:

   - Clone repeating text elements

   - Only import elements that match existing structure

   - Do not import contents of whitespace-only elements

   - Delete elements, frames, and content that does not match imported XML

4. Deselect all other checkboxes. Click OK.

After a few moments, depending on the speed of your computer, the text and graphics reflow through the entire catalog, and all the empty graphic frames are deleted automatically.

That last checkbox selected is the key. By selecting "Delete elements, frames, and content that does not match imported XML" in the XML Import Options dialog, you ordered InDesign to strip out any anchored frame that did not contain a picture. This option will remove empty text elements, too.

Understanding the Full Importance of Empty Elements

Deleting empty elements sounds like a no-brainer. Who wants a bunch of empty lines of text and image frames lying around cluttering up the place? Well, there are two potential issues that arise when deleting empty elements. First, it's important to understand that when InDesign removes the placeholder and the XML tag markers for each empty element from the layout, it does *not* remove paragraph returns, tabs, spaces, or any untagged text that are part of placeholder. These unwanted elements have to be removed manually.

Second, removing tagged elements can prevent you updating the content when you re-import XML, as you did in Lesson 7-6. Remember, there is a one-for-one relationship between the tagged placeholders and the imported content. If you select "Only import elements that match existing structure" in the XML Import Options, updated data from the file can't land in the layout if there isn't a placeholder in the layout waiting for it.

The safe bet is to maintain a version of the file that preserves all the elements in place and then hold off deleting empty elements until you're ready for press.

Delete Option a Must for Data Updates

The option "Delete elements, frames, and content that does not match imported XML" has an important secondary purpose that is vital for updating data in any XML workflow. When updating prices, photos, and other data, it's a certainty that, just as products will be added to the catalog, from time to time products will have to be completely removed, too. When checked, the "Delete elements..." option also deletes complete products that are no longer contained in the XML (**Figure 7.6**).

Unchecked, InDesign imports new items and even swaps out old products that are still represented in the XML, but if the product has been removed from the XML the program ignores it and leaves it in the layout. Scary!

☐ Do not import contents or whitespace-only elements

☑ Delete elements, frames, and content that do not match imported XML

☐ Import CALS tables as InDesign tables

Figure 7.6 Whenever you update XML data in an existing layout, this option should be your first choice.

Lesson 7-8: Beginning the Catalog Structure

The structure of the catalog is only slightly different from that of the atlas you created in **Chapter 6**. You could probably create this type of layout with your eyes closed by now. As usual, the XML workflow takes advantage of InDesign's full set of features.

1. Create a new document using the specifications shown in **Figure 7.7**.

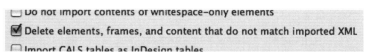

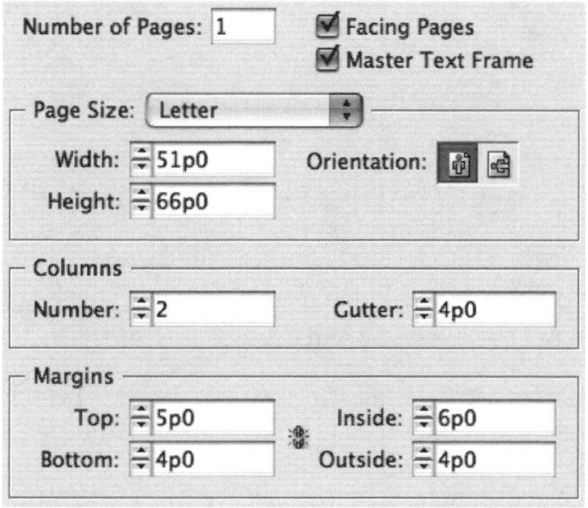

Figure 7.7 These settings will create the basic catalog layout.

2. Show the XML structure, tag markers, and tagged frames.

3. Import **rawBooks.xml**.

4. Deselect all checkboxes in the XML Import Options dialog. Click OK.

5. Option-click/Alt-click on the triangle in front of the `dataroot` element.

The entire XML content is revealed.

6. Drag the first `Book` icon from the Structure pane to the main text frame on page 1.

The text entry for *A Connecticut Yankee in King Arthur's Court* appears in the frame.

Note that this entry does not contain an image element. A master placeholder must contain all the elements desired in the final product. A quick scan of the Structure pane shows that the first **Book** element doesn't contain a cover image, but the second one does.

7. Drag the second `Book` icon from the Structure pane to the main text frame on page 1.

The entry for *A Farewell to Arms* completely replaces the first entry.

Right about now you're probably wondering what you did wrong. The first line of the layout displays the text **978-0684837888.jpg** but where's the picture? The simple answer: It's still somewhere on your hard drive, and **978-0684837888.jpg** is the name of the file.

The file you imported in step 3 is the raw (unmodified) XML generated by the database for this project. Because XML supports only text, we can store only the *name* of the graphic in the database. But there's a small problem: The database program exports the XML reference for a graphic like this:

```
<image>978-0684837888.jpg</image>
```

We could include the entire path—relative or absolute—but it wouldn't improve the reference at all:

```
<image>/Mac HD/chapter 6 files/images/978-0684837888.jpg</image>
```

Neither statement enables InDesign to import the graphic, as you see in previous lessons both in this chapter and in Chapter 6. Instead, for the reference to work (see **Chapter 6**, Lesson 6-2), it would have to look like this:

```
<image href="file://images/978-0684837888.jpg" />
```

In the first and second examples, the filename is being stored as *data* within the element, but the correct structure, shown above this paragraph, is constructed as an empty element (see "Data Content Types Key" in **Chapter 1**) where the image filename is referenced merely as an *attribute*.

Getting the database to export the image name and path as an empty element to an XML file is beyond our meager programming and scripting capabilities. Instead, we resort to a simple but tried-and-true method available to every designer using a Mac or PC: Find and Replace.

Before you work on the XML files, save the InDesign document to be safe.

8. Save the file as an InDesign template. Name the file **myBookCatalogInventory.indt**.

Lesson 7-9: Editing Raw XML for Import

By now your XML skills and savvy should be sufficient to pull back the curtain a bit and let you have a little peek at the wizard and machinery at work behind the scenes. In our previous sample projects we provided perfectly formatted XML files and structured documents, and everything worked right out of the box. Unfortunately, the real world is rarely that neat and orderly. You'll find that, more often than not, you have to dig into the XML file itself to edit the code, or even completely reformat it.

In this lesson we show you one of the most common fixes we make in an XML workflow.

1. Launch TextEdit or Notepad or your favorite XML editor.

2. Open **rawBooks.xml**.

3. Note the first `<image>` element.

As we describe in Lesson 7-8, the element is not structured correctly to import the graphic in InDesign. For it to work, the entry `<image>978-0684837888.jpg</image>` must be reconstructed to look like this: `<image href="file://images/978-0684837888.jpg" />` as well as all the other 28 `image` elements. Before you totally freak out, we assure you that the change is a lot easier than it sounds. It's a simple two-step process using the Find/Replace command.

NOTE *CS3 and other programs can create complex search and replace routines using wild-cards and Boolean expressions that can complete this operation in one step. Look up GREP expression in the CS3 help file for more information.*

4. Select the opening tag `<image>` and press Cmd-C/Ctrl-C to copy it.

5. Activate the Find command.

The Find/Replace dialog appears. (In some programs the copied element may appear automatically in the Find field.)

6. Insert the cursor in the Find field. Press Cmd-V/Ctrl-V to paste the element in the Find field if the element doesn't appear automatically.

7. Type `<image href="file://images/` in the "Replace with" field (**Figure 7.8**). Click the Next/Find Next button.

    The next `<image>` element in the code is highlighted.

TextEdit (Mac)

Notepad (Windows)

XML Spy (Windows)

,oXygen/> (Mac/Windows)

Dreamweaver CS3 (Mac/Windows)

Figure 7.8 We use the Find/Replace feature often to fix image and other faulty references. Here are a sample of the Find commands from our favorite Mac and Windows programs.

8. Click the Replace button.

    ■ The opening `<image>` tag is replaced by the code `<image href="file://images/`.

    ■ The next `<image>` tag is selected.

    Before you proceed to replace the rest of the `<image>` tags, carefully check the change; some programs will not allow you to Undo this process if find you make a mistake. The text should now look like this: `<image href="file://images/978-0684837888.jpg</image>`.

9. If the text has changed properly, click the Replace All button. The program will replace all the text that matches the search field to the end of the file. You may need to repeat the command once to catch any elements you may have missed at the beginning of the file.

All opening ‹image› tags are replaced.

Now you need to perform the second half of the element reconstruction.

10. Select a closing ‹/image› tag. Press Cmd-C/Ctrl-C to copy it.

11. Activate the Find command if the Find dialog is not visible.

12. Select any text displayed in the Find field. Press Cmd-V/Ctrl-V to paste the closing ‹/image› tag.

Any previous text displayed in the Find field is replaced by the closing ‹/image› tag.

13. Select any text displayed in the "Replace with" field and type " /> (double-quote, space, slash, right-angle bracket).

14. Click the Next button.

The next closing ‹/image› element in the code is highlighted.

15. Click the Replace button.

- The closing ‹image› tag is replaced by the code " />.
- The next ‹/image› tag is selected.

Before you proceed to replace the rest of the ‹/image› tags, carefully check the change. The entry should now look like this: ‹image href="file://images/978-0684837888.jpg" />. By reconstructing the element thusly you have created an element that will import the cover image properly.

16. If the text has changed correctly, click the Replace All button.

All closing ‹/image› tags are replaced.

17. Select File > Save As.

18. Save the file as **myBooks.xml**.

19. Repeat steps 2–17 with the file **rawAudiobooks.xml**. Save the file as **myAudiobooks.xml**.

20. Repeat steps 2–17 with the file **rawMovies.xml**. Save the file as **myMovies.xml**.

All the ‹image› elements are now reconstructed in the proper way, and the file is ready to use.

Lesson 7-10: Creating the Master Product Placeholder

The **myBooks.xml** file, created in lesson 7-9, can now be used to create the books section of the product catalog template. First, let's start with a clean layout in **myBookCatalogInventory.indt**:

1. In InDesign, select the text frame on page 1 and delete it.

2. Select the BK element in the Structure pane. Press the Delete key.

   The content of the Structure pane is deleted.

3. Drag the A-Master icon and drop it on page 1.

   The master is reapplied to the page.

4. Import **myBooks.xml**. Click Open.

   ■ The Import XML dialog appears.

   ■ The Show XML Import Options checkbox is selected.

   ■ The Import into Selected Element checkbox is grayed out.

5. Deselect all checkboxes in the XML Import Options dialog. Click OK.

   The XML content fills the Structure pane.

6. Option-click/Alt-click on the triangle in front of the BK element.

   The entire XML content is revealed.

7. Drag the first Book icon from the Structure pane to the main text frame on page 1.

   The text entry for *A Connecticut Yankee in King Arthur's Court* appears in the frame.

As we note in Lesson 7-8 the first entry doesn't contain an **image** element. For the master placeholder to work properly it must contain all the elements desired in the final layout. As before, you'll see that the second **Book** element contains everything you need.

8. Drag the second Book icon from the Structure pane to the main text frame on page 1.

   The entry for *A Farewell to Arms* completely replaces the first entry, displaying a cover image at the top of the text.

9. Before proceeding, select and delete all the unused Book elements from the Structure pane.

The **BK** and the **Book** entry for *A Farewell to Arms* are the only elements remaining in the Structure pane.

10. Select the text frame containing the book entry. Press Cmd-Y/Ctrl Y to switch to Story Editor.

- Story Editor appears.

- Note the blank line above the anchor icon.

NOTE For the purposes of the following lessons, whenever the Delete key is mentioned the instructions refer to the small Delete key on the right side of most keyboards (Mac and Windows). The large Delete key on Mac keyboards will be referred to as the Backspace key, as it's called on Windows-based keyboards. On Mac laptops that have only one Delete key, you can achieve the described action by holding the Fn (Function) key before pressing the Delete key.

To achieve the desired layout you will delete the unneeded paragraph returns and arrange the placeholders so the data appears thusly:

```
Book:
A Farewell To Arms
Author: Ernest Hemingway
The tragic tale of love and loss during WWI.
Charles Scribner's Sons, 1929
Order # 978-0684837888          $18.15
```

11. Delete the paragraph return in the empty line so the anchor icon moves up to the first line.

The blank line is deleted, and the anchor icon moves up to the first line.

12. Delete the paragraph return after the anchor icon so that producttype moves up to the same line.

The **producttype** element moves up behind the anchor icon.

13. Insert the cursor after the closing producttype tag. Type : (colon).

14. Insert the cursor in front of the artistfirstname. Type **Author:** (including the colon).

15. Insert a space after the closing artistfirstname. Delete the paragraph return so artistlastname moves up to the same line.

The **artistlastname** element moves up to the same line and directly after **artistfirstname**.

16. Insert a comma and one space after the company closing tag. Delete the paragraph return so year moves up to the same line.

The **year** element moves up to the same line separated from the **company** element by a comma and one space.

17. Type **Order #** (don't forget the number sign) in front of the opening productid tag.

18. Insert a tab after the closing productid tag. Type **$** (dollar sign). Delete the paragraph return so price moves up to the same line.

■ The **price** element moves up to the same line as **productid**.

■ There should be one extra paragraph return at the end of the entry.

Before the physical structure of your template is finished, you have to adjust the position of the anchored image. In its current inline position, if the graphic frame ends up empty (as several have in the previous lessons) it would leave an unacceptable hole in the layout. But by floating the placeholder outside the text flow, empty frames won't even be noticeable (**Figure 7.9**).

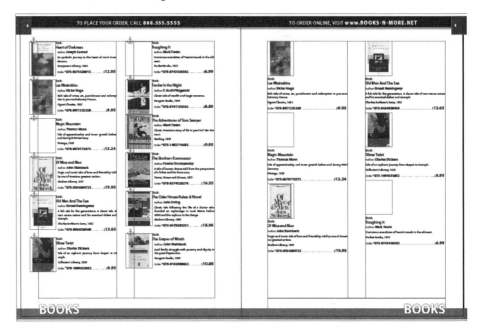

Figure 7.9 If you compare a layout of anchored frames (left) to one featuring inline graphics (right), you can see clearly see the advantages to using anchored frames.

19. Press Cmd-Y/Ctrl-Y to switch to Layout view.

20. Select the anchored graphic. Select Object > Anchored Object > Options.

The Anchored Object Options dialog appears.

21. Enter the specifications as shown in **Figure 7.10**. Click OK.

The anchored object repositions to the left and is aligned to the top of the data entry.

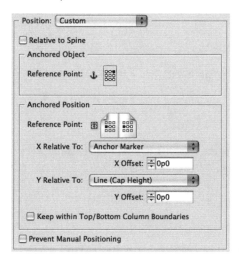

Figure 7.10 These settings float the image to the left side of each product entry.

22. Select New Object style from the Object Styles panel menu. Name the style **Cover-image**. In CS3, click the Apply to Selection checkbox. Click OK. In CS2, apply the Cover-image Object style to the anchored frame.

- The new style named Cover-image appears in the panel.

- The master placeholder is structured and should appear as in **Figure 7.11**.

Figure 7.11 Each product section features a similar placeholder.

23. Press Cmd-S/Ctrl-S to save the changes to the file **myBookCatalogInventory.indt**.

Before you import the catalog data, let's create the XML and structure needed for a pricelist to create a true multisection catalog, similar to the one in Lesson 7-4.

Lesson 7-11: Creating Multipurpose XML

You could use the existing **myBooks.xml** file as is for both the book listings and the pricelist. But as we explain in the sidebar "A Rose Is Still a Rose," the elements in the file are already mapped to Paragraph and Character styles used for the catalog. To use the same content for a different purpose *and* in a different format requires that we first make a small modification to the XML structure and save it as a separate file.

1. Open **myBooks.xml** in TextEdit, Notepad, or your favorite XML editor.

2. Activate the Find/Replace command.

3. Type > in the Find What field.

   This entry will find the closing bracket for all XML elements.

4. Type **2>** in the Replace With field.

   This text will insert the number 2 before the closing bracket in all XML elements.

5. Press the Find Next button.

   The next closing bracket in the file is selected.

6. Press the Replace button.

   - The number 2 is inserted before the selected bracket.

   - The next closing bracket in the file is selected automatically.

7. If the replacement was made correctly, press Replace All.

   The number 2 is inserted before every closing bracket in the file.

8. Save the file as **myBooksprice.xml**.

If you are working in an XML editor, when you try to save the file the program will warn you that the structure is not well-formed (see "Well-formed XML" in **Chapter 1**). Unfortunately, TextEdit and Notepad won't make a peep, so it's important to understand proper XML construction before you play around with the structure in a non-XML-aware application. In the process of inserting the number 2 into all the elements, two of the elements in the file have essentially been broken. Luckily, it's just as easy to fix the problem as it was to create it in the first place.

One of the errors in the very first line of the code. The processing instruction in line 1 now looks like `<?xml version="1.0" encoding="UTF-8"?2>`. Note the 2 between the ? and the >. No text or numbers may appear in this position.

9. Delete the 2 in the processing instruction so it looks like this:

   ```
   <?xml version="1.0" encoding="UTF-8"?>.
   ```

In line 15 of the XML file, the image element looks like this: `<image href="file://images/978-0684837888.jpg" /2>`. Note the 2 was added between the / (slash) and the >. As with the processing instruction earlier, this is an invalid construct in XML. If you scroll down through the file you will notice that all the `<image>` elements are structured incorrectly as well. Let's go back and fix the elements that are broken

10. Select the text `/2>` in the image element on line 15. Press Cmd-C/Ctrl-C to copy the text.

11. Activate the Find/Replace command. Insert the cursor in the Find What field. Press Cmd-V/Ctrl-V to paste.

12. Select any existing text in the Replace With field and type `/>`. Click the Next button.

The text `/2>` is selected.

13. Click the Replace button.

- The text `/2>` is replaced by the text `/>`.

- The next `/2>` is selected automatically.

14. If the change was made correctly, click the Replace All button. Otherwise correct any errors and then click the Replace All button.

The elements are all correctly structured.

15. Save the file.

16. Open **myAudiobooks.xml.** Repeat steps 2–15. Save as **myAudiobooksprice.xml.**

17. Open **myMovies.xml.** Repeat steps 2–15. Save the file as my **myMoviesprice.xml.**

You have created XML for each section of the catalog.

Lesson 7-12: Creating the Pricelist Structure

You have all the components needed for a multisection catalog at hand. In this lesson you will insert three sections and add pricelists based on the XML saved in Lesson 7-11.

1. In InDesign, access the Structure pane in **myBookCatalogInventory.indt** and reveal the entire XML contents. Observe the structure.

The solitary **Book** (child) entry is contained within the **BK** (parent) element.

Before we can create a multisection catalog, we have to create a multisection XML structure in the current document. As is, the existing structure can only support one section.

2. Select New Tag from the Tags panel menu.

The New Tag dialog appears.

3. Name the tag **Inventory**. Click OK.

Inventory appears in the Tag panel.

4. Select the BK element in the Structure pane.

5. Click Inventory in the Tags panel to rename the BK element.

The **BK** element is renamed **Inventory** in the Structure pane.

This structure is no better than the previous one, but you're not finished, yet.

6. Select New Element from the Structure pane menu. Select BK from the drop-down menu. Click OK.

A **BK** element appears in the Structure pane as a child element of **Inventory**.

7. Drag the Book element into the BK icon (see **Chapter 4**, Lesson 4-15).

■ The **Book** element becomes a child element of the new **BK**.

■ The structure is now ready for a multisection workflow.

8. Select Inventory in the Structure pane. Import **myBooksprice.xml**. Click Open.

Note that the Import into Selected Element checkbox is selected by default.

9. Deselect all checkboxes in the XML Import Options dialog. Click OK.

A **BK2** element appears below **BK** in the Structure pane.

10. Drag the A-Master icon to the Pages panel beside the page 1 icon.

A new page appears in the panel.

11. Navigate to page 2.

12. Using the Text tool, create a new text frame from the left to the right margins, approximately 3 picas tall, at the top of the page.

In this frame you will create a descriptive header for the pricelist to identify the columns of data. The header must be inserted in a separate non-structured frame or it would be cloned along with the rest of the placeholders.

13. Type **2008 Book Pricelist**. Press Enter/Return to create a new paragraph.

14. Type **Format**. Press the Tab key. Type **Title**. Inserting a tab character between each, type the words **Author**, **Year**, **Order #**, and **Price**.

15. Create a second text frame directly below the first that extends to the bottom of the page.

16. Drag the first Book2 element from the Structure pane to the new text frame.

- The entry for the book *A Connecticut Yankee in King Arthur's Court* appears.

- Note that this entry does not contain an **image** element.

17. Before proceeding, delete all unplaced Book2 elements in the Structure pane.

Only the entry for the book *A Connecticut Yankee in King Arthur's Court* remains in the Structure pane in the **dataroot2** element.

18. Insert the cursor in the data entry and press Cmd-Y/Ctrl-Y to switch to Story Editor.

- The data entry appears in Story Editor displaying its tag structure.

- Note the blank first line.

- Note the absence of an **image** element.

As in previous examples, each XML data element occupies its own line in the text frame, separated by paragraph returns. For the purpose of creating the pricelist, you will delete certain elements altogether and all paragraph returns except the last one. Then you will insert tabs between all the placeholders, except the gap between **artistfirstname2** and **artistlastname2**, which gets a single space.

19. Delete the blank first line. Select and delete the entire description2 placeholder, including the opening and closing tags.

The **producttype2** placeholder moves up to the first line.

20. Insert a tab after the closing producttype2 tag. Delete the paragraph return.

A tab character is inserted between the **producttype2** and **title2** elements on the same line.

21. Insert a tab after the closing title2 tag. Delete the paragraph return.

A tab character is inserted between the **title2** and **artistfirstname2** elements on the same line.

22. Insert a space after the closing artistfirstname2. Delete the paragraph return.

The **artistfirstname2** and **artistlastname2** elements appear the same line separated by a single space.

23. Repeat step 21 with each of the remaining elements until they all are on the same line with a single tab character or space inserted between them, as shown in **Figure 7.12**.

- All element placeholders are on a single line separated by tabs.

- There is a single paragraph return at the end of the line.

The first section of the catalog is complete. It contains structured placeholders for the product entries and pricelist.

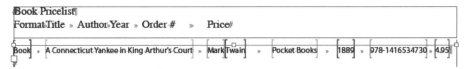

Figure 7.12 The pricelist displays information for the format, title, author, year, order number, and price. The photo and description tags and placeholders are deleted.

Lesson 7-13: Creating New Catalog Sections

Depending on your preferences, a catalog can be created in one file or in multiple files using InDesign's book feature. For this example, we keep it simple by using InDesign's section feature.

1. Show the Pages panel.

The current document contains two pages in one section.

2. Select the A-Master in the Pages panel. Select Master Options for "A-Master" from the Page panel menu.

3. Rename the page prefix **BK** and the page Name as **Books**. Click OK.

- The BK-Books master appears in the Pages panel.

- Icons for pages 1 and 2 display the BK prefix.

4. With the BK-Books master selected, choose Duplicate Master Spread "BK-Books" from the Pages panel menu.

A new master spread called BK-Books copy appears in the Pages panel.

5. Select Master Options for "BK-Books copy" from the Pages panel menu. Change the master page prefix and name to **AB-Audiobooks**. Click OK.

The new master page is renamed AB-Audiobooks.

6. Repeat steps 4–5 to create a third set of master pages. Name them **MV-Movies**.

7. Drag the AB-Audiobooks master down beside page 2 to create two new pages.

Two AB pages appear in the Pages panel as pages 3 and 4.

NOTE *You can create two pages simultaneously by dragging the AB-Audiobooks name itself or by selecting and dragging both AB-Audiobooks master page icons at once.*

8. Click on the first AB page. Select Numbering & Section Options from the Pages panel menu.

9. Enter the specifications shown in **Figure 7.13**. Click OK.

The page is number 1 in the new AB section.

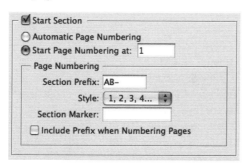

Figure 7.13 These specifications set up the Audiobooks section pagination.

10. Repeat steps 7–9 to create a new section with two pages using the MV-Movies master.

The document contains six total pages in three sections.

Lesson 7-14: Inserting Additional XML Structures

Before the catalog template can be complete, you first have to create product and pricelist structures for the Audiobook and Movie sections.

1. Select the `Inventory` element and import the XML content, as in Lesson 7-8, steps 2–4, for each section in the following order:

- myAudiobooks.xml

- myAudiobooksprice.xml

- myMovies.xml

- myMoviesprice.xml

2. In the XML Import Options dialog deselect all checkboxes before clicking OK.

- Each new element is added consecutively.

- The Structure pane displays six child elements—BK, BK2, AB, AB2, MV, MV2— within the **Inventory** root.

3. Navigate to page 1 of the AB section.

4. Option-click/Alt-click on the triangle in front of the AB element in the Structure pane.

   The data from myAudiobooks.xml is revealed.

5. Drag the first Audiobook element to the main text frame on AB-1.

   The master text frame is filled by the audiobook data entry.

6. Structure the entry as in Lesson 7-10, steps 8-18. Apply the Object style named Cover-image to the anchored graphic frame. The completed structure is shown in **Figure 7.14**.

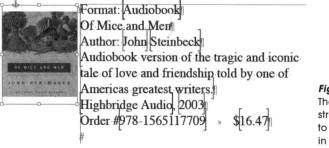

Figure 7.14
The audiobook structure is identical to the books structure in section 1.

7. Navigate to page 2 of the AB section.

8. Using a child from the AB2 element in the Structure pane, create the pricelist structure for the audiobooks section as shown in Lesson 7-12, steps 12–22. The completed audiobooks pricelist structure should appear as shown in **Figure 7.15**.

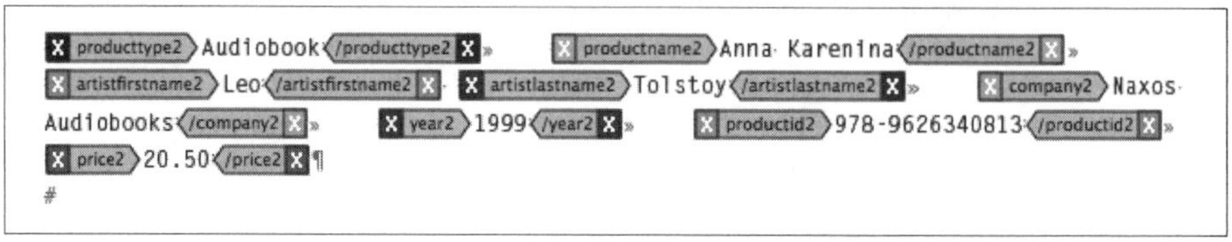

| X | producttype2 | Audiobook | /producttype2 | X | » | X | productname2 | Anna Karenina | /productname2 | X | » |
| X | artistfirstname2 | Leo | /artistfirstname2 | X | » | X | artistlastname2 | Tolstoy | /artistlastname2 | X | » | X | company2 | Naxos Audiobooks | /company2 | X | » | X | year2 | 1999 | /year2 | X | » | X | productid2 | 978-9626340813 | /productid2 | X | » | X | price2 | 20.50 | /price2 | X | ¶

Figure 7.15 The audiobook pricelist structure (as it appears in Story Editor) is identical to the books pricelist structure in section 1.

9. Create product (**Figure 7.16**) and pricelist (**Figure 7.17**) structured placeholders for the MV-Movies section using the appropriate elements from the Structure pane.

The placeholders in all three sections are complete and ready for formatting.

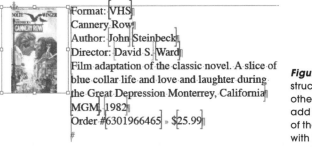

Figure 7.16 The product data structure is identical to the other sections except that you add the first and last name of the movie's director along with the author's name.

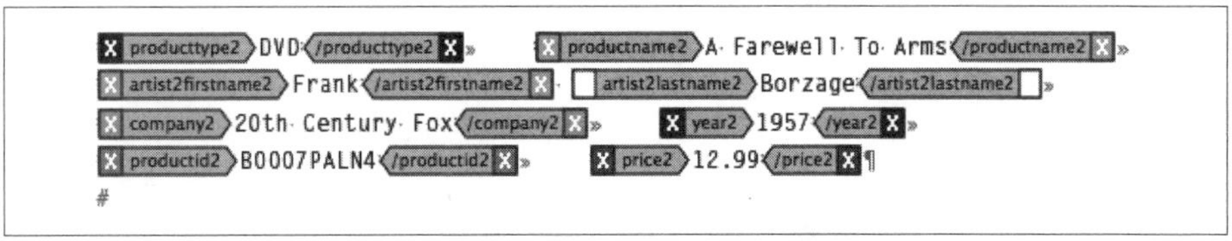

Figure 7.17 The movies pricelist structure is identical to the other sections except for the replacement of the author's placeholder with those of the director's first and last name.

Lesson 7-15: Formatting the Structure

To complete the template the final task is to assign Paragraph styles to the data entries.

1. Load all styles from **BookCatalogPricelist.indt**.

2. Select Map Tags to Styles from the Tags panel menu.

3. Click the Map By Name button.

   All tags are mapped automatically to correspondingly named Paragraph and Character styles, the tags that do not have matching styles are left unmapped.

4. Map the producttype2 tag to the Pricelist Paragraph style. Click OK.

   The placeholders throughout the layout adopt the formats specified by the Paragraph styles.

5. Apply Pricelist Main Head to the first line of the pricelist header.

6. Apply Pricelist Header to the second line of the pricelist header.

Because the design combines elements together in several places, we make liberal use of nested styles to format the text. Take a few minutes to check out the specifications before proceeding.

7. Save and close the file.

The master placeholders for the catalog section are in place and formatted, and you're ready to import data.

Lesson 7-16: Combining Multiple XML Data Files

The placeholder structures in the template you just saved should be similar if not exactly like the template **BookCatalogInventory.indt** used in Lesson 7-5. If you study the Structure pane of the new template shown in **Figure 7.18**, in the `Inventory` root element you'll see the six child elements, `BK`, `BK2`, `AB`, `AB2`, `MV`, and `MV2`, which correspond to the XML files you created in Lessons 7-9 and 7-11. You could import these files one at a time, targeting the specific element as in Lesson 7-2, but we have a better idea. By combining all six into one XML file you can import all the data in one operation, savings tons of time and effort.

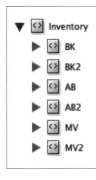

Figure 7.18 You could manually select each child element and import the XML files one by one, but why? By combining the files in the correct order, you can automate the process.

1. Open **myBooks.xml** in TextEdit, Notepad, or your favorite XML editor.

2. Select File > Save As. Name the file **myInventory.xml**. Click Save.

Note that the root element is named `<dataroot>`.

3. Select the `<dataroot>` tag. Type `<Inventory>`. Remember to match the spelling and case of the element used in your template structure.

4. Scroll to the bottom of the XML code, locate and select the closing `</dataroot>` tag.

5. Type `</Inventory>`. Remember to match the spelling and case of the element used in your template structure.

6. Save the file.

By adding the `<Inventory></Inventory>` tags at the beginning and end, you have matched the root structure of your template. Now all you have to do is insert the code from other XML files to complete the structure

7. Open **myBooksprice.xml**.

8. Select and delete the processing instruction: `<?xml version="1.0" encoding="UTF-8"?>`.

9. Press Cmd-A/Ctrl-A to select all the code in the file. Press Cmd-C/Ctrl-C to copy the code. Close the file. Don't save the changes.

10. In **myInventory.xml**, insert the cursor in front of the closing </Inventory> tag. Press Cmd-V/Ctrl-V to paste the code from **myBooksprice.xml**.

The code for the books section pricelist is inserted between the closing </BK> and closing </Inventory> tags.

11. If the file is properly structured, press Cmd-S/Ctrl-S to save it.

12. Repeat steps 7–11 to insert the code from the files: **myAudiobooks.xml**, **myAudiobooksprice.xml**, **myMovies.xml**, and **myMoviesprice.xml** in the same sequence.

NOTE *It is vital that the code is inserted to match the sequence of the XML structure in the template.*

13. If the file is properly structured, press Cmd-S/Ctrl-S to save it. Close the file.

Lesson 7-17: Importing Combined XML

Well, this is the moment of truth. Everything you did up until now has led to this point. Let's see whether all your hard work has paid off. Cross your fingers.

1. Open **myBookCatalogInventory.indt**.

2. Select the Inventory element in the Structure pane.

3. Import **myInventory.xml**.

4. Select only the following checkboxes in the XML Import Options dialog:

- Clone repeating text elements

- Only import elements that match existing structure

- Do not import contents of whitespace-only elements

5. Deselect all other checkboxes. Click OK.

After a moment the XML content populates the Structure pane and replaces the placeholder in each individual section.

6. Show page 1 in the BK-Books section. Drag the first BK element to the main text frame.

- The frame color changes to match the **BK** element tag color.

- The frame fills with identically formatted book entries.

- A graphic frame is anchored to the left of each data entry.

- The overset (+) symbol appears at the bottom of the frame.

7. Click the overset symbol to load the remaining text. Insert two pages after BK-1, based on the BK-Books master. Flow the content manually into each of the pages. Insert additional pages as necessary until all the overset content is exhausted.

8. Navigate to the pricelist in the BK-Books section. Drag the first BK2 element from the Structure pane to the pricelist frame.

   ■ The frame color changes to match the BK2 element tag color.

   ■ The pricelist fills with identically formatted product data.

9. Repeat steps 6-8 for the Audiobook and Movie sections until all the product and pricelist data has been inserted.

   All the product data and images are now displayed.

There's one last chore. You're ready to send the catalog to the press and you want to remove all the empty frames before sending out the file. Can you remember how to do it?

10. Select the Inventory element in the Structure pane. Re-import **myInventory.xml**.

11. Select the following checkboxes in the XML Import Options dialog:

    ■ Clone repeating text elements

    ■ Only import elements that match existing structure

    ■ Do not import contents of whitespace-only elements

    ■ Delete elements, frames, and content that does not match imported XML

12. Deselect all other checkboxes. Click OK.

    The XML content is imported once more, but this time the anchored frames for products that don't have cover photos are removed.

It's a thing of beauty. With a little advance prep work you have created a complete product catalog with a few clicks of the mouse. We don't know how we're ever going to get that silly grin off your face.

Review

In this chapter you learned how to:

■ Import XML into specific elements

■ Import XML to update data in place

■ Import XML to delete empty elements

■ Edit XML to create proper element structure

■ Combine XML files for complex workflows

8

Variable Data

Chapter Objectives

In this chapter you will learn how to:

- Build nested XML sub-structures

- Create variable-text driven layouts

- Flow complex XML data into anchored objects

Okay, we've got to confess we have mixed feelings about this project, probably similar to the way Oppenheimer felt about creating the A-bomb. On one side, the tricks you learn in this chapter are definitely among the coolest in the XML/InDesign world. On the other hand, we've all seen clunky examples of personalized direct mail where the customized areas are plopped into a shell of a layout. We would like this chapter to show you that variable data elements can be well integrated into a good design, with control and finesse just like any other project.

Sample Project: Direct Mail Postcard

Variable data printing is the technological first cousin to the lowly mail merge. Both start with a basic design, boilerplate text and graphics, and a list of names and addresses. The most basic examples simply drop the name and address onto the envelope or mailing panel, whereas advanced designs interweave the data throughout the design, making each piece a custom-printed brochure or sales piece. The effect is both dramatic and cost-effective. Most direct-mail campaigns can expect a one- to two-percent response rate. Variable data projects can achieve responses as high as 20 to 40 percent! Why the huge difference?

The reason is simple: A normal direct mail piece is a generic advertisement or flyer that speaks only to a general audience. It's like someone yelling, "Hey, you!" in a crowd. It's easy to ignore. On the other hand, a variable data project customizes the message using specific data—name, address, personal interests and so on—captured in a computer program. It's like yelling, "Hey, George!" If your name is George, it's hard to resist the urge to turn around to see who's calling you. It's at this moment that the sales pitch has a chance to work.

To demonstrate what kinds of results can be achieved with variable data, we have designed a sample direct-mail postcard for this chapter that uses every XML trick we know to increase the customer response rate.

NOTE *Download all applicable files for Chapter 8 from the www.peachpit.com/indesignxmlguide and copy them to a folder on your hard drive (approximately 10 MB).*

Lesson 8-1: Direct Mail Postcard

Scenario: You work for a direct marketing firm that has been hired by a national pet store chain to design a promotional postcard for dog biscuits. The postcard will be mailed to customers who filled out either a paper-based or online questionnaire that asked them for their name and address, as well as the name and breed of their dog. This information was entered into a computer database that has been made available to you for this project.

1. Open **Postcard.indt**.

A postcard layout appears.

NOTE *CS3 users: Feel free to use the file **Postcard_CS3.indt**, which was specifically prepared to take advantage of the special features available only in InDesign CS3's Effects dialog. Otherwise, both files are identical.*

2. Show Tag Markers, Tagged Frames, Structure, and Frame Edges.

3. Observe the layout and tagged elements (**Figure 8.1**).

- You should see a main text frame, containing the placeholder for the mailing address, and five other text and picture frames that are tagged and anchored within it.

- Note the tagged placeholders within the anchored frames.

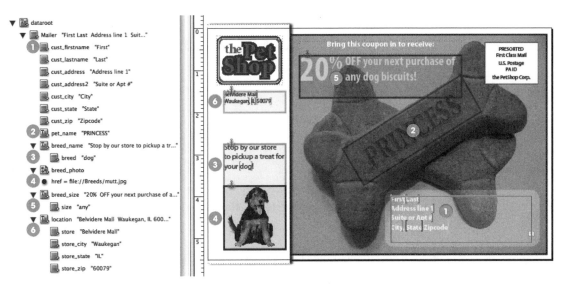

Figure 8.1 The postcard uses every XML trick you have learned so far and a few you haven't to create a coupon personalized to each customer.

The postcard is a coupon designed to bring customers into the store by offering them a discount specifically targeted to their pet and their locality. The first thing to notice is that almost every text and graphic element on the postcard is customized with XML data. Besides the obvious—the customer's name and address—note how the name of the customer's dog is displayed and formatted as if it's a part of the actual biscuit. To heighten the personalization we've added the name and picture of their dog's breed in one frame and targeted the discount to the biscuit size that's best suited to the size of their dog. Finally, the coupon displays the return address of the store closest to the customer's ZIP code. In effect, the customer receives a coupon that has been created and printed just for them and their pet. Is this even possible?

In the past, it was just not an option to print one-off, customized pieces like this cost effectively. When dealing with the time-consuming and tedious process of setting up traditional presses, printing one copy of a flyer or brochure costs almost the same as printing 1,000. At best, customization has been limited to niche markets: regional promotions or topical twists, such as *university alumni* or *big and tall*. The introduction of digital printing presses, such as the Ryobi 3404 and the HP Indigo 5000, among others, has changed all that. More like giant laser or inkjet printers than traditional plate-based presses, these devices have revolutionized the print industry. Some of the presses make it possible to print press-quality, short-run, four-color jobs more quickly and cheaply than you could using traditional means, whereas others allow you to print brochures, postcards, or other marketing pieces totally customized for each recipient.

4. Navigate to page 1. Select dataroot in the Structure pane.

5. Import **Petshop.xml**. Select the following checkboxes in the XML Import Options dialog:

   ■ Clone repeating text elements

   ■ Only import elements that match existing structure

   ■ Do not import contents of whitespace-only elements

6. Click OK.

   ■ After a minute or more, depending on the speed of your computer, the place-holder text on page 1 is replaced by the first entry in the XML file.

   ■ The Structure pane displays 200 customer entries.

   ■ Note how the mailing label is tagged for the **dataroot** element already.

   ■ Note the overset (+) symbol displayed on the text frame.

This mailing label was built for and tagged with the **dataroot** element. Therefore the structure has automatically received all the fully formatted XML content.

7. Click the overset (+) symbol to load the text. Press Cmd-Shift-P/Ctrl-Shift-P to insert a new page.

   A new blank postcard layout appears.

8. Autoflow the text into the main text frame on the new page.

   ■ InDesign flows the XML data into the text frame and creates 198 additional pages (**Figure 8.2**).

   ■ Each page contains the name and address of a new recipient and displays the name and breed of their pet, as well as the location of their nearest PetShop store.

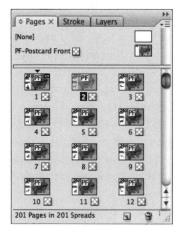

Figure 8.2 The only thing more amazing than creating 200 customized postcards is knowing that you can actually print them at press quality at a reasonable price.

Come on, admit it. This is one of the coolest things you've ever seen! The only thing that would have made it better would have been if your own name and your dog's name had appeared on the postcard, too. And that's the point of variable data printing.

9. Navigate to the PF-Postcard Front master page. Observe the objects positioned on the master page.

There are only two text frames on the page: One contains coupon boilerplate, and the other is set up for the mailing label.

10. Navigate to page 1. Observe the elements on page 1.

On the master page there are two text frames, yet on each of the finished postcards there are seven! Where did the extra five frames come from? Answer: They are all cloned from anchored frames in the structured master placeholder. This project is our most complex XML workflow so far. It combines both text and graphic anchored frames and also introduces a new concept that we call *nested XML sub-structures.*

11. Close the document. Do not save the changes.

NOTE   *In CS2, we have experienced a creeping sensation in this layout, where some or all of the anchored frames ignore their assigned Object styles and start to inch away from their intended positions on subsequent pages. To smash this bug, simply re-import the XML file into the finished layout. This process will reapply the Object styles and force the anchored frames back to their assigned positions. Although we have not seen the problem occur in CS3, this solution should work in either version.*

Lesson 8-2: Nested XML Sub-structures

In **Chapter 5** you learn how to insert text in anchored frames. In **Chapter 6** you learn how to insert graphics into anchored frames. In **Chapter 7** you learn how to target specific elements within a structure. In this chapter you bring all these skills together to build a marketing piece that's amazingly sophisticated and yet incredibly simple to produce. But, before you can fully understand what's needed to get this magic to work, it'll help if you perform some preliminary detective work first.

1. Open **Postcard.indt** to create a new untitled document.

2. Insert the Text cursor into the frame containing the placeholder for the mailing label. Press Cmd-Y/Ctrl-Y to switch to Story Editor.

- Story Editor appears.

- The address information occupies four lines of the window.

- Each placeholder is tagged for the appropriate address element.

- Five anchor icons appear at the end of the fourth line.

3. Using the Text cursor, select the first anchor icon. Show the Tags panel.

   The pet_name tag highlights.

4. Select each of the anchor icons in turn, and note which tag name highlights.

5. Press Cmd-Y/Ctrl-Y to switch to Layout view. Show the Structure pane, if it isn't open.

6. Reveal and observe the XML structure. Note the names and order of the elements (**Figure 8.3**).

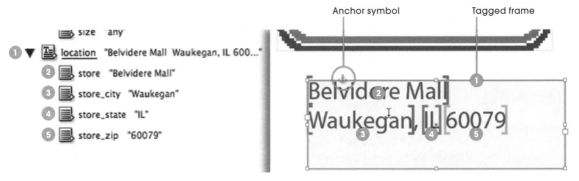

Figure 8.3 The elements in the Structure pane match the structure of the placeholders. Note the nested text elements within **breed_name**, **breed_photo**, **breed_size**, and **location**.

7. Insert the Text cursor in the text frame containing the store address. Press Cmd-Y/Ctrl-Y to switch to Story Editor.

   The contents of the text frame appear in Story Editor (**Figure 8.4**).

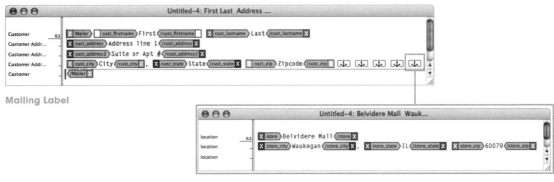

Figure 8.4 The mailing label (top) and the return address (bottom) in Story Editor are two separate and independent structures.

You can see from poking around in the layout how the anchored text frames—like the one holding the store address—contain miniature structures of their own. Such sub-structures can hold 1 or 100 or more XML elements. This capability of nesting structures one within another opens up almost unlimited design possibilities using an XML workflow. As in most aspects of how XML works with InDesign, your main limitations are your own imagination and your ability to create the XML content. We can't help with the imagination part, but we can show you how to create the XML used for this project.

8. Close the file. Don't save any changes.

Lesson 8-3: Creating XML Sub-structures

The Structure pane gives you a clue to how the XML must be put together. But getting the data into this form doesn't happen automatically—at least not for designers who don't know much programming or scripting. Your company may already have programmers on staff who can create the perfect push-button solution; that's great. For the rest of us, here's our method.

First, we create a database to capture the desired information (**Figure 8.5**). It's deployed on the company's Web site and can be accessed by customers via Internet from home or at a kiosk whenever they visit their local store. Customers are asked to enter their name, address, and details about their pet and are promised discounts and coupons for products and services as an incentive to provide the information. The system can capture data about any type of pet, but for the purposes of this chapter we restrict the discussion to dogs.

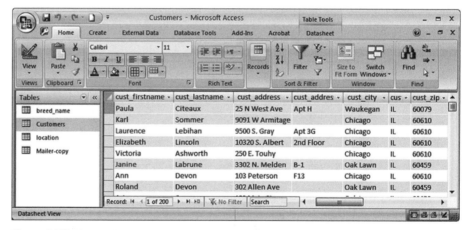

Figure 8.5 Storing customer information in separate fields facilitates sorting, filtering, and otherwise targeting specific customers or regions for promotional purposes.

Next, the marketing manager develops a promotional campaign to increase traffic in the stores: discounted dog biscuits. We review and select the necessary fields from the database and create a query to collect the pertinent information (**Figure 8.6**). The results are exported to XML. But the data isn't usable yet.

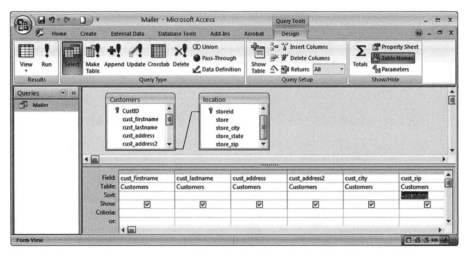

Figure 8.6 By using the query to pre-sort the data by ZIP code, the XML data reflects the same order, saving the store money when mailing the finished piece.

1. Open **Petshop.xml** and **raw_Petshop.xml** in TextEdit, Notepad, or your favorite XML editor. Tile the windows for each file side by side.

   The XML files are displayed in two separate windows sharing the screen.

2. Scroll down to the first `<store>` element in both windows and compare the code in each (**Figure 8.7**).

Figure 8.7 Without help from programming or scripting, the raw data doesn't assume the proper structure. You can rewrite the code manually or, even easier, use the Find/Replace command.

It should be pretty obvious that the code in the **raw_Petshop.xml** file is missing some elements. In **Petshop.xml** the address of the store is nested within the `<location>` element. In a workflow that doesn't use anchored frames this type nesting is unnecessary. In a workflow that uses anchored frames it's essential.

In **Chapter 5**, you learn that the contents of anchored frames are not part of the normal text flow and that the frame itself, not the contents, must be tagged, or else no XML data will enter the frame. This anchored frame technique is used to insert the section title at the top of each recipe page. By nesting one or more elements inside the element assigned to the anchored frame, it's possible to insert multiple elements within the frame. Unfortunately, this nesting isn't created automatically by the database without a bunch of scripting and programming, well beyond the scope of this book. Of course, there's nothing stopping you from adding the necessary elements manually, one at a time; but we prefer the Find/Replace command.

Nesting structures need to be created for three of the five anchored frames in the postcard. Let's modify them in the raw XML to sequence them as they are needed for use in InDesign:

3. Locate and select one of the opening ‹breed› tags. Press Cmd-C/Ctrl-C to copy it.

4. Activate the Find/Replace command. Insert the cursor into the "Find what" field and press Cmd-V/Ctrl-V to paste the tag name.

The tag name appears in the field.

5. Insert your cursor into the "Replace with" field, type ‹breed_name›, and then press Cmd-V/Ctrl-V to paste.

The two elements **‹breed_name›‹breed›** are displayed in the "Replace with" field.

6. Click the Find button. Click the Replace button.

The program should find and replace the first **‹breed›** tag with **‹breed_name›‹breed›**.

7. If the replacement occurred properly, click the Replace All button. Otherwise, Undo, fix the problem, and import the XML again.

The **‹breed_name›** tag has been inserted before all **‹breed›** tags.

WARNING *Don't press the Replace All button more than once. This action would double up the* **‹breed_name›** *element in the structure and thereby break the XML.*

So far, so good. But before the structure can be complete you have to close the ‹breed_name› element and then nest all the other elements destined for anchored frames. While you're at it, you might as well reconstruct the **‹breed_photo›** element—as you did in **Chapter 7**—so the photo will import automatically along with the XML data.

8. Repeat steps 3-7 to find and replace the elements as shown in **Table 8.1**.

Table 8.1 *Elements to Find and Replace*

FIND WHAT	REPLACE WITH
</breed>	</breed></breed_name>
<size>	<breed_size><size>
</size>	</size></breed_size>
<store>	<location><store>
</store_zip>	</store_zip></location>
<breed_photo>	<breed_photo href="file://Breeds/
</breed_photo>	" />

9. Save the file as **my_Petshop.xml** in the Chapter 8 folder, the same directory that contains the image folder. Close the file and exit the program.

The file is now properly structured for the postcard workflow.

NOTE An XML editor is an invaluable asset whenever you edit or create XML, because it can ensure your code is well-formed and/or valid.

Lesson 8-4: Creating the Postcard Structure

To make the job a little easier, we provide a file that's partially started.

1. Open **blank_Postcard.indt**.

2. Show Tag Markers, Tagged Frames, Structure, and Frame Edges.

3. Observe the layout (**Figure 8.8**).

4. Import **my_Petshop.xml**. Deselect all checkboxes in the Import XML Options dialog. Click OK.

   The XML content fills the Structure pane.

5. Drag the first Mailer element from the Structure pane to the mailing label master text frame. Delete all other Mailer elements from the Structure pane.

   - The text frame fills with the content from the first XML entry.

   - There is only one Mailer element in the Structure pane.

*NOTE You do not always have to use the first parent element for the master placeholder. In this case, the first entry in this XML file happens to contain the **cust_address2** element, but you may notice that this is not the case with every entry. A master placeholder must contain every element permitted in the final layout. For purposes of setting up the master placeholder, if an entry does not contain all the necessary elements simply select another that does.*

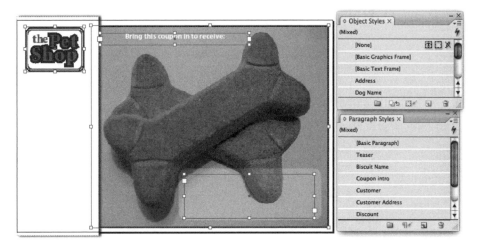

Figure 8.8 The master page layout features the company logo, dog biscuit photo, master text frame for the mailing label, and a translucent rectangle background for the mailing label, plus essential Object, Paragraph, and Character styles.

> **Designer's XML Rule #13**
>
> A master placeholder must contain all elements desired in the final document structure.

Throughout the process of creating the master placeholder, you have to keep one eye glued to the Structure pane to ensure your final structure contains all the desired elements in the correct order.

6. Insert the cursor in the text on page 1. Press Cmd-Y/Ctrl-Y to switch to Story Editor.

NOTE For the purposes of the following lessons, whenever the Delete key is mentioned, the instructions refer to the small Delete key on the right side of most keyboards (Mac and Windows). The large Delete key on Mac keyboards will be referred to as the Backspace key.

7. Insert the cursor in the blank first line. Press the Delete key to remove the extra paragraph return.

NOTE The goal here is to eliminate the extra paragraph returns without deleting the placeholders or their tags. Depending on where the cursor is inserted you may need to alternate between the Delete and Backspace keys. At the end of the lesson, you want to see the five anchor icons on one line, outside and immediately following the **cust_zip** *placeholder.*

8. Insert the cursor after the closing cust_firstname tag. Insert one space; press the Delete key to remove the paragraph return.

   - The placeholder for **cust_lastname** moves up to the same line as **cust_firstname**.

   - The first and last name placeholders are separated by a single space.

Let's move the city, state, and ZIP placeholders into the same line.

9. Insert the cursor after the closing cust_city tag. Type **,** (comma); insert one space; and press the Delete key to remove the paragraph return.

   - The placeholder for **cust_state** moves up to the same line as **cust_city**.

   - The city and state placeholders are separated by a comma and a single space.

10. Insert the cursor after the closing cust_state tag. Insert one space; press the Delete key to remove the paragraph return.

    The placeholders for the customer's city, state, and ZIP are all on the same line.

The mailing label placeholder is complete. All remaining elements will be inserted into anchored frames.

Lesson 8-5: Creating Placeholders in Anchored Frames

The first anchored element is pet_name. The dog name placeholder is designed to look like it's part of the biscuit itself. But before you create the dog name placeholder, you need to determine what size and angle text frame works best with the photo of the dog biscuit. You could print the postcard to paper and measure the available space using an ordinary ruler; or you could use a powerful feature built into InDesign.

1. Switch to Layout view. Using the Measure tool, draw a line in the usable space the length of the dog biscuit at its center (**Figure 8.9**). Note the length in the D1 field and angle as displayed in the Info panel. Measure the height of the biscuit at the center.

2. Switch to Story editor. Select the text placeholder for the pet_name element. Click the Untag button in the Tags panel.

   The tags surrounding the placeholder disappear.

3. Press Cmd-X/Ctrl-X to cut the dog's name. Press the Backspace key to delete the preceding paragraph return and move the text cursor to the previous line, immediately following the cust_zip closing tag.

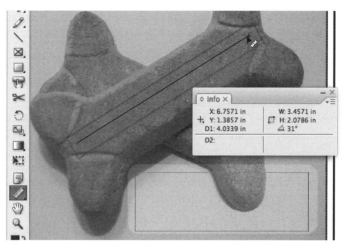

Figure 8.9 The Measure tool can be used to obtain lengths (top), widths (bottom), and angles from any object in your layout. It is stashed in the Tools panel with the Eyedropper.

4. Switch to Layout view.

NOTE Throughout the chapter, when switching back and forth between Layout view and Story Editor, the instructions assume that you leave the cursor at the last position described.

5. Select Object > Anchored Object > Insert. Enter the specifications shown in **Figure 8.10**. Click OK.

- The anchored frame appears above the mailing label.

- The text cursor is automatically inserted in the anchored frame.

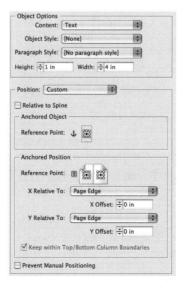

Figure 8.10 These specifications will create a text frame for the dog's name based on the measurements obtained in step 1.

6. Press Cmd-V/Ctrl-V to paste the dog's name into the frame. Apply the Biscuit Name Paragraph style to the text in the frame.

7. Using the Selection tool, select the frame. Click pet_name in the Tags panel to apply the tag to the frame.

NOTE *The tag* **<pet_name>** *must be assigned to the frame itself, not the text within it. As a matter of fact, as long as it's tagged, the placeholder frame could be empty and still perform properly.*

Designer's XML Rule #14

A tag must be applied to an anchored frame before content can flow into it.

---

8. Click Dog Name in the Object Styles panel to assign the style to the frame.

   The text is formatted with a drop shadow and other effects that make it appear three-dimensional.

NOTE *These effects look good to us. Feel free to experiment with the settings to make the name appear any way you like. In CS2, your choices are restricted but respectable. In CS3, using the new Effects dialog, the sky's the limit. Remember to capture all your settings in the Object style assigned to the frame.*

The frame is not yet at the proper position or angle.

9. Using the Selection tool, drag the anchored frame to the center of the dog biscuit. Rotate the frame 31 degrees. Reposition it to the center of the biscuit as necessary.

   - The dog name appears as if it is part of the biscuit itself.
   - The override symbol (+) appears in the Dog Name Object style.

10. Right-click on the Dog Name Object style. Select Redefine Style from the context menu.

    - The frame's new position and angle are saved into the Object style definition.
    - The pet_name placeholder is complete.

NOTE *In this project, more than any other, Object styles are essential.*

Lesson 8-6: Creating Placeholders with Sub-structures

The pet_name placeholder is typical of the anchored frames you create in **Chapter 5**, it doesn't contain a sub-structure. The breed_name, breed_size, and location elements, on the other hand, all exhibit parent/child relationships that require sub-structure placeholders to work properly.

1. Select the mailing label text frame and switch to Story Editor.

2. Select the opening breed_name tag marker, but do not select any text or other markers. Click the Untag button in the Tags panel.

   ■ The **breed_name** tag disappears.

   ■ The **breed** tag and text remain.

3. Delete paragraph returns as necessary (see the Note in Lesson 8-4, step 7) to move the breed placeholder up and just after the pet_name anchor icon.

NOTE   *As you're creating this (or any) structure it helps to have a good memory to remember which icons belong to specific anchored frames. But don't fret if you lose track. Simply select the icon in question and check the Tags panel for the assigned tag.*

4. Select the breed placeholder text including the opening and closing tags. Press Cmd-X/Ctrl-X to cut the placeholder. Switch to Layout view.

NOTE   *Whenever we talk about placeholders we automatically mean the text or photo and its XML tags.*

5. Select Object > Anchored Object > Insert. Enter the specifications shown in **Figure 8.11**. Click OK.

   ■ The anchored frame appears above the mailing label

   ■ The cursor is automatically inserted in the frame.

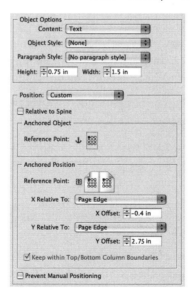

Figure 8.11 These specifications will create an anchored text frame for the **breed_name** placeholder.

6. Using the Selection tool, select the new anchored frame and apply the breed_name tag to it.

7. Using the Text tool, insert the cursor into the anchored frame and type **Stop by our store to pick up a treat for your**. Add a space, then press Cmd-V/Ctrl-V to paste the breed placeholder. Option/Alt click the Teaser Paragraph style to apply it to the text in the frame.

NOTE *The **breed_name** placeholder is the first of the nested sub-structures in the layout. For the content to import properly, the anchored frame must be tagged for the parent element before any child elements are inserted into the frame. Performing these steps out of sequence will break the structure and require retagging work later. Always check the Structure pane to confirm that the elements are properly named and ordered.*

8. Apply the Teaser Object style to the frame.

   ■ The frame repositions to the left edge of the postcard.

   ■ The **breed_name** placeholder is complete.

NOTE *Watch out for the override symbol (+) whenever you apply Object or Paragraph styles. Overrides can be the cause of text and objects failing to format properly. To remove overrides, select the item and press the "Clear overrides" button in the appropriate panel.*

Lesson 8-7: Converting Objects from Inline to Anchored

The next element in the structure that needs your attention is the photo for the dog breed. During XML import the photo is placed automatically into an anchored frame, but the frame is positioned *inline* and currently hidden in the overset text of the mailing label. To complete this placeholder, you need to float the frame out of the text and over to the left edge of the postcard in Layout view and then move the anchor icon up to the last line of the mailing label in Story Editor. Because you're presently in Layout view, let's take care of the frame's position before you deal with the anchor icon.

1. Using the Selection tool, drag the bottom right corner of the mailing label down to the right far enough to expose the inline photo.

2. Using the Selection tool, select the photo. Right-click on the photo and select Anchored Object > Options. Enter the specification shown in **Figure 8.12**. Click OK.

   The photo repositions beneath the teaser text on the left edge of the postcard.

3. Create an Object style based on the frame's current position and formatting. Name it **Photo** and apply it to the frame.

4. Insert the Text cursor in front of the last anchor icon. Press the Backspace key to delete the previous paragraph return. Continue to press the Backspace key until the anchor icon moves up to the same line as the others. Be careful not to delete any text, anchor icons, or tag markers.

   The **breed_photo** placeholder is complete.

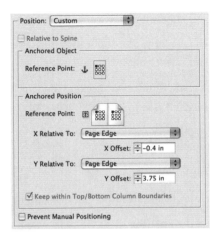

Figure 8.12 These specifications move the photo from its inline position to the left edge of the postcard.

NOTE   *Moving the icons into one line doesn't affect the performance of the anchored object one way or the other. We do it mainly to ensure the label paginates correctly when the data flows to multiple postcards.*

Lesson 8-8: Creating Additional Placeholders

To complete the postcard, the `breed_size` and `location` placeholders need to be converted to anchored frames with sub-structures.

1. Select the mailing label and press Cmd-Y/Ctrl-Y to switch to Story Editor.

2. Select the opening `breed_size` tag marker. Choose Untag Text from the Tags panel menu or the Structure panel menu.

    The `breed_size` tag markers disappear.

3. Use the Backspace and Delete keys to delete the unnecessary paragraph returns, moving the `size` placeholder up to a position at the end of the last anchor icon.

4. Select the `size` placeholder. Press Cmd-X/Ctrl-X to cut it.

5. Press Cmd-Y/Ctrl-Y to switch to Layout view. Select Object > Anchored Object > Insert. Enter the specifications shown in **Figure 8.13**. Click OK.

    ■ The new anchored frame appears above the mailing label.

    ■ The Text cursor is inserted automatically.

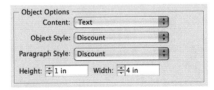

Figure 8.13 Within the dialog you can specify Object and Paragraph styles so the new anchored frame appears at the desired location, already formatted.

6. Using the Selection tool, select the frame and apply the breed_size tag to it.

7. Using the Text tool, insert the cursor in the frame and type **20%**. Press the Tab key to insert one tab character.

8. Type **OFF your next purchase of**. Type a space, press Cmd-V/Ctrl-V to paste the size placeholder, and type another space. Type **dog biscuits!** to complete the discount offer.

- The text formats as you type it in the frame.

- The **breed_size** placeholder is complete.

The location placeholder is the last anchored frame that needs to be created.

9. Switch to Story Editor. Select the opening location tag marker. Click the Untag button in the Tags panel.

The location tag markers disappear.

Let's move the city, state, and ZIP placeholders for the location element into the same line.

10. Delete the paragraph returns that separate each element. Insert a comma and one space between the city and state placeholders. Insert a space between the state and ZIP elements.

- The city, state, and ZIP elements are on the same line.

- The placeholders making up the return address occupy three lines.

11. Select the three lines containing the store address placeholders. Press Cmd-X/Ctrl-X to cut the placeholders.

12. Use the Backspace and Delete keys to delete any remaining paragraph returns, the cursor should be inserted at the end of the last anchor icon. Switch to Layout view.

*NOTE Object styles can include a reference to one Paragraph style. If all text contained in a frame is formatted the same way, this option can save a lot of effort during formatting. InDesign provides a sophisticated feature called Apply Next Style that, in certain circumstances, offers unlimited formatting possibilities, especially well-suited to advertisers and direct marketers (see sidebar **Next Style, Please!**).*

Next Style, Please!

Object styles allow you to apply a single Paragraph style to a frame. On first blush, assigning one Paragraph style to the contents of an entire text frame doesn't sound very appealing. It's true, you can use nested styles to squeeze a little customization out of one style, but what happens when you press the Return/Enter key? Answer: The same style is applied automatically to the next paragraph—unless you use InDesign's Next Style feature.

You may already know that the Next Style feature provides the means for automatically applying different styles as you type each time you press the Return/Enter key. For example, you could set up a sequence of styles to start by typing text formatted with the style called Headline. When you press the Return/Enter key, InDesign can automatically switch to another style called Abstract. Press Enter/Return again, and the style switches to First Paragraph. And then it switches to Body Text.

The feature is called Next Style and it's been around since the invention of Paragraph styles themselves. But what you may not know is that InDesign increases its usability by adding an option called Apply Next Style, which enables you, when activated, to perform the same manner of sequential formatting to a range of paragraphs, selected manually, or to the entire text frame, anchored or unanchored (**Figure 8.14**).

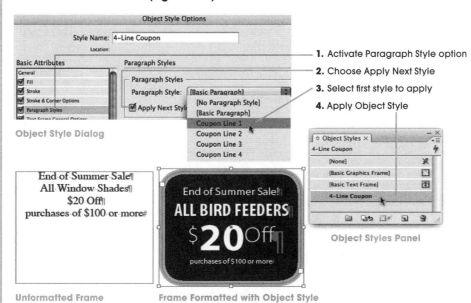

Figure 8.14 Turning the basic unformatted coupon text frame (left) into the finished advertisement (right) is as simple as 1, 2, 3…4.

Combine Apply Next Style with Nested styles and you'll find this one-two punch unbeatable in most XML workflows. To learn more about Apply Next Style, check out InDesign's online help or the books *Real World Adobe InDesign CS3* and *InDesign CS3 for Macintosh and Windows Visual Quickstart Guide,* both from Peachpit Press.

13. Select Object > Anchored Object > Insert. Enter the specifications shown in **Figure 8.15**. Click OK.

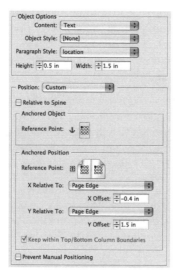

Figure 8.15 These specifications create the **location** placeholder at the top of the postcard.

14. Apply the location tag to the new anchored frame. Insert the Text cursor into the frame and press Cmd-V/Ctrl-V to paste the return address placeholders.

- The three lines of the return address appear.

- The text is automatically formatted

- The frame repositions to the upper left edge of the postcard beneath the logo.

15. Create a new Object style. Name it **location**. Apply it to the frame.

The location placeholder is complete.

You're almost finished. There are a couple of tasks left to do. First, every dynamic structure must feature an extra paragraph return at the end of the layout to ensure the pagination works properly during cloning. Without it, the first line of page 2 will merge into the last line of page 1 and so on throughout the document.

16. Select the mailing label and switch to Story Editor. Observe the layout. If there isn't a final paragraph return, insert the cursor at the end of all the anchor icons and press Return/Enter to insert one (**Figure 8.16**).

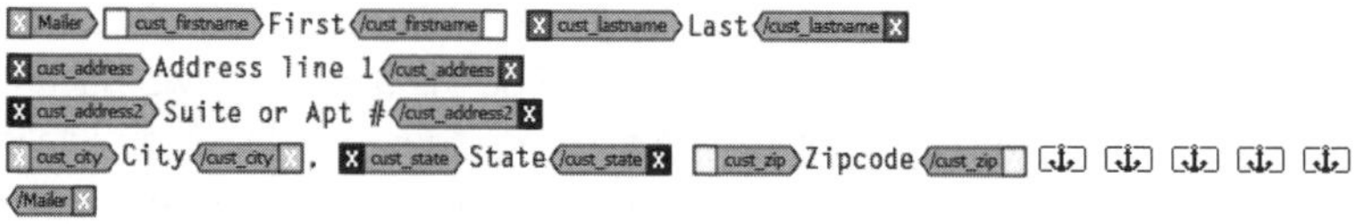

X Mailer ☐ cust_firstname ☐ First ⟨cust_firstname ☐ X cust_lastname⟩ Last ⟨cust_lastname X⟩
X cust_address⟩ Address line 1 ⟨cust_address X⟩
X cust_address2⟩ Suite or Apt # ⟨cust_address2 X⟩
X cust_city⟩ City ⟨cust_city X⟩ , X cust_state⟩ State ⟨cust_state X⟩ ☐ cust_zip⟩ Zipcode ⟨cust_zip ☐ ⎘ ⎘ ⎘ ⎘ ⎘
⟨Mailer X⟩

Figure 8.16 The finished mailing label occupies the first four lines of the placeholder and all the anchor icons appear after the closing tag for **cust_zip**.

*NOTE   The last line should contain no text, no spaces, no tags, and no formatting.
We usually apply the Basic Paragraph style, or the style that's applied to the first line of
the master placeholder.*

Lesson 8-9: Map Tags to Styles

Although many of the Paragraph styles have been applied to the text via the Object styles, you still must map tags to styles ensures the postcard data paginates correctly.

1.   Select Map Tags to Styles from the Tags panel or the Structure pane.

2.   Map the Tags to Styles as shown in **Table 8.2**. Click OK.

Table 8.2 Tag Mapping

TAG	STYLE
cust_address	Customer Address
cust_address2	Customer Address
cust_city	Customer Address
cust_firstname	Customer
location	location
pet_name	Dog Name
size	Discount Text

*NOTE   You may have noticed that we are not mapping every element to a corresponding
style. Because several items share a single paragraph, only one element within the paragraph
needs to be mapped. If this makes you nervous, feel free to map all elements to their appropriate styles. Either way, the end result will be the same.*

3.   Save the file as **my_Postcard.indt**. Close the file.

Congratulations! You've just completed your first XML direct mail piece. Use this power wisely and only for good.

Lesson 8-10: Testing the Postcard

You've made the XML and you've made the postcard, the only thing left to do is test it to see if it works.

1.   Open **my_Postcard.indt**.

2.   Select dataroot in the Structure pane.

3. Import **my_Petshop.xml**. Select the following checkboxes in the XML Import Options dialog and click OK:

- Clone repeating text elements

- Only import elements that match existing structure

- Do not import contents of whitespace-only elements

4. Drag the dataroot icon from the Structure pane to the mailing label.

The frame changes color and displays the overset (+) symbol.

*NOTE   In some cases, dragging the **root** element to the text frame will insert blank lines into the structure. Sometimes this extra space appears at the end of the data, sometimes at the beginning. If your first postcard becomes blank you may have a few empty lines before your first mailing label. Select the frame and switch to Story Editor. Go ahead and delete any empty lines. The rest of the document should be fine.*

5. Load the overset and create a new page using the PF-Postcard Front master page. Autoflow the overset into the master text frame on page 2.

Cross your fingers and your socks-*less* toes. If everything goes smoothly, in a minute or two, you should see 200 custom postcards in the Pages panel. Each card displays names and addresses for a different dog and their owner, a photo of their dog's breed, a teaser, a discount for a specific size of dog biscuit, and the location of the store where they can redeem the coupon. And the best thing is that combined with the right system, each of the postcards can be printed—on high-gloss coated stock at press quality—today and dropped in the mail tomorrow!

This claim is not science fiction. For an XML workshop, we created this very postcard on a Monday morning, emailed it to a local printer, and passed it out to attendees on a Wednesday.

Review

This project brings together in one place all the tricks contained in the last several chapters. You were able to create a complex XML workflow that resulted in the creation of 200 customized postcards almost instantly. In this chapter you learned:

- How to build nested XML sub-structures

- How to create variable-text driven layouts

- How to flow complex XML data into multiple anchored objects

This is as far as we can take you in creating dynamic layouts using XML data. You now have all the skills and tools necessary to create almost any kind of structured document. In the remaining chapters, we examine how XML can be used to repurpose *existing* documents for other print applications as well as for the Web.

Exporting XML

Chapter Objectives

In this chapter, you will learn how to:

- Structure content for exporting
- Export content to XML
- Export content to HTML/XHTML
- Work with content structure to create fully formatted Web pages

In the previous chapters we've taught you almost everything we know about importing XML to create a variety of dynamic documents, from business identities to variable-data marketing pieces. It's time to turn our attention the other side of the divide and explore InDesign's robust capabilities for exporting document content to XML as well as other useful formats.

Until the debut of the Internet, production cycles were like a one-way street with every resource devoted to the singular purpose of putting ink on paper. Once that purpose was fulfilled, the publication and its content were relegated to some library shelf if lucky, or to the bottom of a bird cage if not. Today, the once cast-off text and graphics are being tapped by corporations everywhere as new revenue streams or premium content for subscription services. Take a look on the Web and it seems that every business, corporate entity, and even individual has a Web presence of some sort. Content that lived for a day, a week, or a month in the past now can live forever in the vast halls and cubbyholes of the Internet.

The biggest challenge has not been figuring out what to do with the content as much as simply getting it from one place to the other quickly and inexpensively—a task that is a lot harder than it sounds. Let's take a look at the export file formats InDesign supports. The formats can be divided into two basic categories: comprehensive and text-only.

Comprehensive Export Formats

The comprehensive export formats deal with both the text *and* graphics within a layout. All these formats preserve the look of the InDesign document and offer varying levels of accessibility and *re*usability. PDF and EPS are the heavy-duty favorites in this category. We use them for everything. But although they are great at preserving the look and feel of the original print document, they are not designed to be reusable or adaptable to other purposes. Basically, what you see is what you get.

The InDesign Interchange format, or INX, is designed to help users move the content of a file from one version of InDesign to another, such as from CS3 to CS2. The interesting aspect of the INX is that at its heart it is basically a text-based XML file—a testament to the power and flexibility of the format. There's nothing preventing someone from using it on the Web, though we know of no applications of INX for repurposing outside of InDesign at this time.

JPEG is a raster format that freezes a document in time like a snap shot, converting everything into pixels—pretty but otherwise useless for repurposing. Finally, SVG is a vector-based format, built using XML, that preserves the content of each page of a document in a graphical way that's accessible using a browser. It has the capability of allowing you to zoom in and out of the resulting graphic right in the browser without the loss of quality—truly amazing to see. Unfortunately, uneven support by browsers has caused this format to whither on the vine. Because the Web needs a vector format, we hope it survives, but the jury's still out. Like INX, there are no applications of SVG for repurposing content that we know of.

Text-only Export Formats

The text-only formats—including Adobe Tagged Text, InCopy Story and Document, Rich Text Format, and Text Only—are available whenever you insert the cursor into a text frame. As indicated by their names these formats work only on the text content of your document, ignoring all pictures and other graphics. And there's one more limitation: The text-only formats can only export from one story at a time, drastically limiting their usefulness. Although we have used these formats to move a story out of InDesign from time to time, they would not be very handy in moving large amounts of text or multiple stories at one time.

Copy and Paste

In a moment of repurposing desperation, you may find yourself resorting to a tried-and-true method for moving content from one application to another: copy and paste. But don't fall for that siren's call; you'll just create more work and grief for yourself than it's worth. Few programs support InDesign's vast capabilities for working with and formatting text and graphics. As a result, using copy and paste to move text and graphics from an InDesign document to another program, such as Adobe Dreamweaver, leaves a lot to be desired. Graphics usually don't cross over at all, and text ends up basically unusable—losing both its formatting and structure (**Figure 9.1**). Luckily, there are better ways.

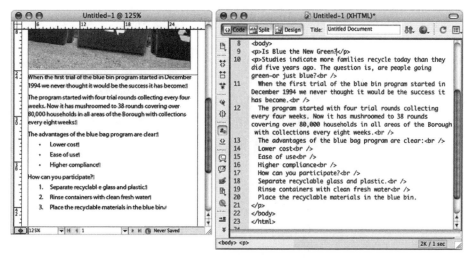

Figure 9.1 Text copied from InDesign to a Web-design program, such as Dreamweaver, loses basic structure—in this case, swapping true paragraph returns for HTML line breaks (**
**).

NOTE   *Download all applicable files for Chapter 9 from www.peachpit.com/indesignxmlguide and copy them to a folder on your hard drive (approximately 11 MB).*

Lesson 9-1: Cross-media Export: The Wrong Way

Over the last few years designers have been looking desperately for a method to create usable Web content from print-based documents quickly and easily. If you've been among those hoping some Adobe engineer would hear your plaintive cry, your prayers have been answered—mostly. Cross-media Export—one of the new features added to the InDesign CS3—on the surface seems to be everything that we wanted. But looks can be deceiving.

NOTE   *Although users of CS2 or earlier versions of InDesign cannot perform the following steps, read through the lesson anyway to learn more about this new feature and to get a better understanding of how to create a usable HTML file from InDesign.*

1. Open **TextExport.indt**. Observe the layout (**Figure 9.2**).

2. Show the Structure pane.

The document contains several text frames, both linked and unlinked, a free-floating graphic, and two items on the master page. Note how the paragraphs display bullets and numbering created using the InDesign's built-in feature. Notice further that the file exhibits no XML tags, elements, or structure whatsoever. In other words, it's typical of most InDesign layouts users have to repurpose for the Web on a regular basis.

NOTE *It's important to emphasize that the bullets and numbering you see in the layout are not actual characters inserted within the text. We created them using InDesign's Bullets and Numbering feature.*

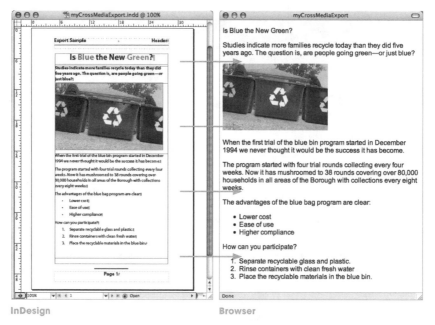

InDesign   Browser

Figure 9.2 The goal of repurposing is to recreate print-based documents (left) for the Internet without losing text, formatting, or graphical elements.

3. Select File > Cross-media Export > XHTML/Dreamweaver.

The Save As dialog appears.

4. Open the Chapter 9 files folder within the dialog, if it is not displayed. Name the file **myCrossMediaExport.html**. Click Save.

The XHTML Export Options dialog appears.

5. Enter the specifications shown in **Figure 9.3**. Click OK.

You can get a complete description of the options in the InDesign Help file.

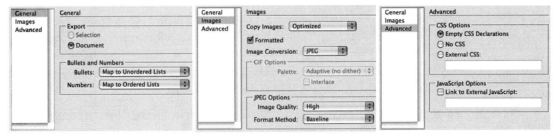

Figure 9.3 Use these specifications to create the sample HTML file.

6. Display the resulting HTML file in your favorite browser.

InDesign successfully exports the document to an HTML file—including the headline, body text, and the image. It arranges the text in the proper order and, best of all, even preserves the bullets and the numbering (**Figure 9.4**). Unfortunately, it's not perfect. On the downside, the picture was repositioned to the bottom of the window, the font color and other text formatting are gone, and the header and footer are no where to be seen.

```
<p class="body">The advantages of the blue bag program are clear:</p>
<ul>
    <li class="bullets">Lower cost</li>
    <li class="bullets">Ease of use</li>
    <li class="bullets">Higher compliance</li>
</ul>
<p class="body">How can you participate?</p>
<ol>
    <li class="numbers">Separate recyclable glass and plastic.</li>
    <li class="numbers">Rinse containers with clean fresh water</li>
    <li class="numbers">Place the recyclable materials in the blue bin.</li>
</ol>
</div>
```

Figure 9.4 Cross-media Export creates code that preserves much of the text formatting, including bullets and numbering.

If this is your first introduction to Cross-media Export you may be feeling disappointment or ecstasy, or—like the boy who asked for a pony for his birthday but got a puppy instead—a little bit of both. Looking only at the browser, it's kind of hard to determine whether this is a success or failure. That's why in **Figure 9.5** we included the HTML code generated by InDesign.

On the surface the code looks great. The text is properly delineated with <p></p> (paragraph) tags; it also uses <ul></ul> (unordered list) and <ol></ol> (ordered list) elements to recreate the bullets and numbering. And there's one more aspect you should notice.

Did you see that each `<p>` element also includes a `class` attribute, such as `heading-1`, `body`, and so on? The construction `<p class="body">` is the HTML equivalent to applying a Paragraph style in InDesign. This coding has, in effect, recreated all the styling from the original document. Wow. Cross-media Export seems to be the answer to all our prayers. If it was, we could end this chapter here and go home. But a closer look at the code reveals two basic problems with this feature.

First, Cross-media Export ignores formatting not applied using Character or Paragraph styles. If you prefer to apply formatting manually in InDesign you're not going to like Cross-media export. If you want to see your bold, italics, and other character-based formats on the Web page, you will have to start using the styles panels for everything.

Second, the singular reliance on the `<p>` tag and *class* attributes for formatting everything limits your overall creativity and ignores other valuable tags, like `<h1>-<h6>`. If you need to move content to the Web, Cross-media Export is definitely better than any of the other methods we've considered so far. For some, it will be all you'll ever need. But for those who need more flexibility and control, we have a better alternative—one that works in both CS2 *and* CS3. And—you probably already guessed—it has something to do with XML. You're so smart.

7. Close the Untitled InDesign document.

The DIV Difference

If you analyze the HTML code created in Lesson 9-1, you may have noticed some elements that you don't recognize (Figure 9.5). One of the advantages of using Cross-media Export is its ability to create `<div></div>` tag structures for you automatically. The `<div>` tag stands for *division* and is used mainly as a structural element, or container, in Web page design. In this case, Cross-media Export wraps a `<div></div>` around any InDesign page element that was contained within a frame. This means the photo, body text, and headline each received this treatment.

```
<div id="mytextexport2">
    <div class="story">
```

Figure 9.5 Cross-media Export automatically adds `<div></div>` tags to the HTML code to help recreate the document structure.

Whoa! If you look carefully at the InDesign template, you can plainly see that the body text is contained in *two* frames. So, you may be wondering: Why is there only one `<div>` tag for this content? The reason is simple: InDesign considers *linked* frames as *one* story and hence one `<div>`—it doesn't matter if the story uses one or a hundred frames. In **Chapter 10** we explore how `<div>` elements work with CSS to format your Web content.

Lesson 9-2: Exporting Content to XML

No other format is as flexible and *reusable* as XML—it preserves the identity, or meaning, of the content like no other format. As you see in each of the previous sample projects, names, titles, prices, and so on are all clearly labeled by XML tag names. These labels and tag names travel with the content throughout the XML work-flow and, best of all, they are preserved within the document forever (or at least unless they are manually removed).

This is great for the small numbers of documents currently being created using XML. But in reality, the vast majority of print-based InDesign documents don't (and never will) start with an XML structure. So, before you can export content to XML, you have to learn how to add structure to documents that don't have one.

1. Open **XMLExport.indt**.

2. Show the Structure pane, Tags panel, tag markers, and tagged frames. Observe the panels and the layout.

Other than the Root element (which is currently not applied to anything), this document contains no XML structure or elements whatsoever. The process of adding an XML structure starts with the elements, or tag names. As we show in **Chapter 2**, tags can be created from scratch or imported from an existing XML file, DTD or another InDesign/InCopy document.

3. Create the following tags:

   - headline
   - bodytext
   - bullet
   - number
   - image

4. Using the Text tool, select and apply the tag headline to the text: **Is Blue the New Green?**.

   The text frame changes color, and the text is enclosed by tag brackets indicating that the tag has been applied.

Stop. Look carefully at the layout. The heading and the frame that contains it display the telltale signs of XML structure. The text displays tag brackets that match the color of the headline element, and the frame displays the color of the Story element. Wait, what Story element?

In Lesson 4-9 in **Chapter 4** we learn that InDesign tags text frames automatically whenever any part of its content is tagged. There's nothing particularly wrong with this new **Story** tag per se, although we prefer to name elements ourselves. However, in some cases, the XML elements used may need to conform to a specific DTD or Schema or workflow already in place. In **Chapter 10**, we describe the use of workflows that take advantage of standardized structures and elements. **Chapter 12** describes the use of DTDs, such as DocBook and others.

5. Press Cmd-Shift-A/Ctrl-Shift-A to deselect all text. Double-click on the Story tag in the Tags panel. Rename it content.

6. Select Tagging Preset Options from the Tags panel menu.

The Tagging Preset Options dialog appears (**Figure 9.6**).

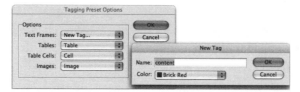

Figure 9.6 When InDesign automatically tags containers, it takes it cue from the settings in this dialog.

7. Select content from the Text Frames pull-down menu. Click OK.

By setting this preset, we're instructing InDesign to use the **content** tag on any new text frame.

8. Apply the bodytext tag to the paragraph that starts "Studies indicate…"

- The paragraph displays tag brackets that match the **content** tag.

- The text frame containing this paragraph as well as the linked frame below it change color to match the color of the **content** tag.

9. Apply the bodytext tag to the remaining paragraphs that are not bulleted or numbered.

NOTE *The power of XML is its ability to identify the individual components of a layout. Therefore, each paragraph should be tagged separately.*

10. Apply the bullet tag to each bulleted paragraph.

11. Apply the number tag to each numbered paragraph.

12. Apply the image tag to the frame containing the photo.

13. Rename the Root element Flyer.

All the text, picture, and frame elements on the page are tagged.

14. Save the file as **myFirstXML.indd** in the Chapter 9 folder.

Observe the names and order of the elements in the Structure pane (**Figure 9.7**). Note how the `headline` and the `bodytext` are contained in two separate `content` elements, and the image element appears at the bottom of the structure. There's really nothing wrong or illegal about it, but the structure would be more usable and flexible in a different configuration.

Figure 9.7 The XML structure exhibits elements that are unnecessary and out-of-sequence as a result of its construction.

15. Close the file.

Lesson 9-3: Optimizing Layouts for XML

As you can see from the Structure pane, the XML is jumbled up because of the way the text and graphic elements were laid out in the original document. When a document is intended strictly for print, there's no right or wrong way to construct it. Our basic rule is: if it *looks* good it *is* good. Design purists may take offense to this principle, but it works. And, truthfully, does the customer or printing press really care whether a story was laid out with three text frames instead of one or two?

However, for projects that must be reused or repurposed, good *looks* must take a back seat to good *structure*. You must give thought to how a document is constructed before you build it so that the process of converting it for the Web or other uses goes smoothly and with as little manual intervention as possible. For example, making a few small changes to our sample document produces a remarkable difference in the outcome.

1. Open **XMLExport.indt**. Observe the document construction.

The problem with this layout is that it uses separate frames for the headline, text, and photo, making it hard to automatically create a single structure when XML is added. In this case, the fix is an easy one: Simply combine all the text into a one frame and insert the photo as an inline graphic. The end result is a document that *looks* the same as before but responds in wholly different fashion to the XML structure.

2. Using the Selection tool, click the Outport of the headline text frame. A Text icon appears. Click the Text icon on the body text frame to link the two together (**Figure 9.8**).

The three frames now constitute one continuous text flow.

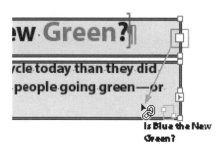

Figure 9.8 Linking the two frames creates a single text flow and streamlines the structure.

3. Leave the frame containing the headline but delete the two remaining text frames.

The headline frame displays an overset (+) symbol.

4. Select the picture frame. Press Cmd-X/Ctrl-X to cut it.

5. Drag the bottom handle of the headline frame down to the bottom margin to display all the text again.

For the picture to appear properly in the HTML it must be inserted in its own empty paragraph.

6. Insert the Text cursor at the end of the bolded paragraph and insert one paragraph return. Select Type > Show Hidden Characters.

7. Locate the ¶ (paragraph symbol) in the blank line and double-click on it to select it. Apply Auto leading to the new paragraph. Click once on the line to insert the cursor and press Cmd-V/Ctrl-V to paste the picture frame.

The picture appears in the new paragraph as an inline graphic. By applying Auto leading, the paragraph spacing will adjust fluidly to accommodate any size image. The layout has now been completely optimized. Let's save the file before proceeding.

8. Save the file as an InDesign template. Name the file **myXMLExport.indt**. Close the file.

9. Open **myXMLExport.indt** to create a new untitled document. Create and apply the tags to this layout as in **Lesson 9-2**. Observe the results in the Structure pane (**Figure 9.9**).

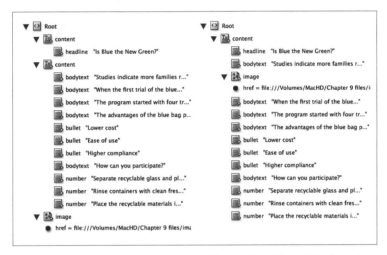

Figure 9.9 The two structures compared side-by-side. Although the layouts appear basically identical, you can see how your efforts have improved the resulting XML.

The structure resulting from this layout was a vast improvement over what you achieved in Lesson 9-2 and highlights the importance of proper construction. Headlines should be linked to their stories, whenever possible, and graphics should be inserted inline or in anchored frames.

10. Press Cmd-E/Ctrl-E or select File > Export.

The Export dialog appears.

11. Select XML from the "Save as type" pull-down menu. Navigate to the Chapter 9 folder and save the file as **myXMLExport1.xml**.

The Export XML dialog appears.

12. In the Images tab, enter the specifications shown in **Figure 9.10** to export the image to a Web-compatible format. Click Export. (For a detailed explanation of these options see **Chapter 2**.)

The exported XML appears in the program you selected in step 10.

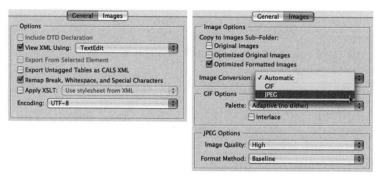

Figure 9.10 Use these settings to create the XML content.

NOTE   *We use this XML to create a Web page in **Chapter 11**.*

13. Close the file. Do not save the changes.

Lesson 9-4: Automating XML Tagging

Creating and applying an XML structure by hand as in Lessons 9-2 and 9-3 may be an acceptable procedure for one-page documents like this, but it's hardly a realistic option for newspaper, magazine, or other long-document publishers. Luckily, InDesign offers a feature to automate just such a workflow.

Scenario: You work for an environmental organization that publishes a monthly print-based newsletter. Once printed, the articles are repurposed to create content for your Web site.

1. Open **Newsletter01.indt**. Open and observe the Structure pane.

This newsletter is a typical print-based document created with no XML structure or underpinnings, but with a strong and consistent use of Paragraph and Character styles throughout. InDesign's Map Styles to Tags feature was designed to automatically apply XML structure to documents by using its text formatting as a guide.

2. Select Load Tags from the Tags panel menu. Select the file **Newsletter_tags.xml** and click Open.

The Tags panel fills with tag names, many of which match the Paragraph and Character styles in use.

Optimize in Advance

As we explain in Lesson 9-3, optimizing your layout with an XML workflow in mind creates better code structure. So, with that in mind we optimized the layout in **Newsletter01.indt** for you. To see the differences between an optimized layout and a more typical print design, open the file **badNewsletter.indt** in the Chapter 9 folder and compare the two files (**Figure 9.11**).

Typical Layout   Optimized Layout

Figure 9.11 As you can see by comparing the two layouts, an optimized design relies more on single and linked frames for text content. Pictures are placed inline instead of free floating.

A typical print-only layout uses more individual frames for text. Pictures and graphics are simply dropped onto the page where they're needed. As in Lesson 9-3, we optimized the layout by using single text frames for the individual departments and inserting pictures inline. The result is XML code that is better organized and more usable in the long run.

A good suggestion is to keep your eyes open and stay flexible as you develop your workflow. Your XML template may change several times as you discover what works and what doesn't. Even several years down the line, don't be adverse to adding a tag here and there or completely rebuilding your template.

3. Select Map Styles to Tags from the Tags panel or the Structure pane menu.

The Map Styles to Tags Options dialog appears.

NOTE   *Don't confuse Map Styles to Tags with its first cousin Map Tags to Styles. They're easy to mix up but they do completely different jobs.*

Tagging Philosophy 101

There are at least two branches of thought regarding automated style mapping. The one-to-one camp believes you should create one XML tag for each Paragraph and Character style in the file. This plan preserves the content's granularity throughout the workflow. This is great for content that will be reused for a similar purpose.

The many-to-one camp believes that the subtle style variations required for print documents creates undue complexity in content destined for the Web or content management systems (CMS). For these workflows you may find it advantageous to map multiple styles to a single XML tag. For example, you would map the Paragraph styles Body, Body-first, Body-news, and Body-tips to one XML tag named body.

Both are perfectly acceptable techniques depending on the needs of your workflow. But if you're not sure which way you should go, always opt for the one-to-one philosophy, which preserves your data as close to its original state as possible. It may add a little extra work, but you'll never regret the results.

4. Click the Map By Name button. Click OK.

- Many of the Paragraph or Character Styles will map to identically named Tags.

- Text frames change color to match the associated tags.

- Tag markers appear on the paragraphs that received an XML element.

NOTE When we work with both Paragraph and Character styles mapping them to the correct tags can get confusing. A trick we use to keep them straight is to capitalize the names for Paragraph styles and use all lowercase for Character style names. Otherwise, keep your eyes peeled for the Character and Paragraph icons beside each style name.

When the dialog disappears you'll notice that almost all the text and frames within the newsletter now display XML structure. The few exceptions are: free-standing graphics or photos (CS2), inline graphics or photos (all versions), items generated from the master page, and incidental text that isn't either part of the editorial content or formatted using a Paragraph or Character style that's mapped to a tag. Overall it's a good start, but it isn't perfect.

Extra Space? No, Thank You

The command Map Styles to Tags has a disturbing trait. Although the capability of tagging vast amounts of content automatically is wonderful, it comes with a price. Study your tagged content carefully; you may need to switch to Story Editor to get the full impact.

In **Chapter 4** we stress that tags should not contain the paragraph returns, tabs, or other spacing not explicitly required by the data itself. Yet, in this layout InDesign broke Designer's XML Rule #5. In **Figure 9.12** you can clearly see that the XML brackets in the layout are including the paragraph returns. Egads!

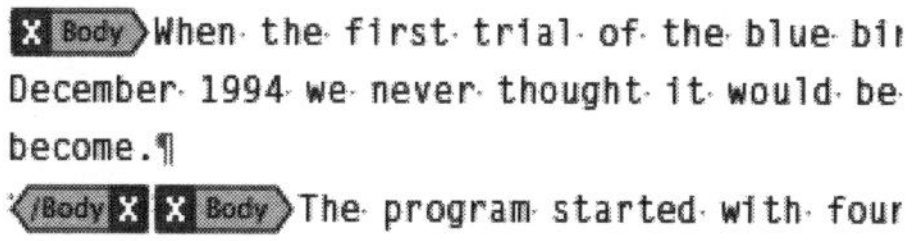

X Body When the first trial of the blue bir
December 1994 we never thought it would be
become.¶
/Body X X Body The program started with four

Figure 9.12 Including paragraph returns within the code brackets may make the XML incompatible with some applications.

An Adobe engineer explained to us that this function was a topic of discussion when the XML features were first added to the program. Obviously, the adherents of "including the spacing" won the argument. But knowing who won doesn't matter now—what's important is that you are aware that the content tagged and exported from InDesign to XML this way will automatically include the paragraph returns and spacing within the tagged elements.

For certain applications you may need to restructure the XML before you can use it. The Find/Replace command in Dreamweaver makes an excellent tool for fixing problems with spacing.

5. Using the Selection tool, click on each of the text frames. Observe the Tag panel as each frame is selected.

Notice how all the text frames are tagged with the **Story** element. As Lesson 9-2 reminds you, InDesign automatically tags a text frame whenever XML is applied to its contents. **Story** is the default name InDesign uses if you don't assign your own in the Tagging Preset Options.

This wasn't a problem in Lesson 9-2 because the layout had only one text frame. The newsletter, like many publications, can be composed of dozens of frames, each of which contains wildly varying content. For example, one frame contains calendar information, another gardening tips, and yet another environmental news. The problem is that InDesign offers only one choice for tagging text frames.

To accommodate the need for differentiating the editorial content, you'll have to create some additional tags and then apply them to the frames manually.

6. Create a tag named News. Apply the tag to the main text frame on page 1 containing the text: Is Blue the New Green.

The **News** tag replaces the **Story** tag assigned to the frame.

You will see that we've already created tags for the other frame categories in the document.

7. Apply the existing tags to the following frames:

TAG NAME	FRAME CONTENTS
Events	events
Toptips	toptips
Greenthumb	green thumb
TOC	inside
Issue_ID	Volume#, Issue #, Month
Image	To all anchored images

8. Double-click the Root element in the Tags panel. Rename the element GreenStartNews.

9. Add the following attribute to the GreenStartNews element: Name: Issue. Value: January.

All text and objects on pages 1 and 2 are now tagged.

10. Save the file as **myNewsletter01.indd** in the Chapter 9 files folder.

11. Select File > Export (or Export XML from the Structure pane menu)

The Export dialog appears.

12. Select XML from the Save as Type pull-down menu. Name the XML file **myNewsletter01.xml**. Click Save.

The XML Export Options dialog appears.

NOTE *The resulting XML file will be used in **Chapter 11** to create a Web page.*

13. Use the same export settings as in Figure 9.10. Click Export.

The exported XML appears in the program specified in Figure 9.10.

14. Save any changes and close the file.

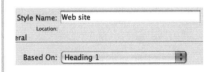
Lesson 9-5: Using XML Templates

The sample project in Lesson 9-4 is a monthly newsletter for an environmental group. The content is tagged and exported each month and uploaded to their server to create content for their Web site. Such a routine procedure demands some sort of automation to increase the efficiency of the workflow. In such cases we recommend an XML template to speed up the tagging process.

InDesign templates are files created in advance that usually include page elements, styles, all the common boilerplate that can make the job of creating a document easier or faster, or both. An XML template is similar in that it contained elements that are *pre*-tagged within a layout, especially text frames that wouldn't be tagged automatically, or correctly, by the Map Styles to Tags command.

1. Open **XMLNewsletterTemp.indt**. Observe the layout (**Figure 9.14**).

Figure 9.14 Pre-tagging the structure streamlines the effort needed to prepare the document content for exporting.

This is the basic template for the newsletter sans content and structure. You will prepare the newsletter template for the XML workflow by creating XML tags, tagging frames, and setting up the Tagging Preset Options.

2. Load all tags from **myNewsletter01.indd**, which was created in the previous lesson.

Note how all the Paragraph and Character styles match the corresponding XML tag names. In turn, the styles used on text and objects not intended for export are not mapped.

3. Select Map Styles to Tags from the Tags panel menu. Click the Map By Name button. Click OK.

Styles are automatically mapped to correspondingly named tags.

4. Select Tagging Preset Options from the Tags panel menu.

The Tagging Preset Options dialog appears.

5. Select News from the Text Frames pull-down menu. In CS3, the Images pull-down menu is already mapped to the Image tag. There is no such option in CS2, so users of that version will still have some manual tagging to do. Click OK.

By assigning these tagging presets, you're instructing InDesign to automatically tag any *un*tagged text frames with the **News** tag.

6. Apply the following tags to the existing content frames:

TAG NAME	FRAME CONTENTS
Events	events
Toptips	toptips
Greenthumb	green thumb
TOC	inside
Issue_ID	Volume#, Issue #, Month
Image	To all anchored images

NOTE *Each department features two frames; one contains a colorful header and the other holds the content. The tag should be assigned only to the content frame.*

While these frames currently have no content in them, tagging them in advance beats InDesign to the punch. When the newsletter is finished, and you're ready to map styles to tags, these frames will already be tagged properly for their specific content. InDesign will tag all the rest with News as specified in steps 4 and 5.

NOTE *Although these frames are included in the template, one or more of these departments may not used in every issue. No problem. Just delete any empty department frames from the newsletter before you export the XML.*

7. Select the Root element in the Structure pane. Click on GreenStartNews in the Tags panel to retag it.

8. Save the file as an InDesign template. Name the file **myXMLNewsletterTemp. indt**. Close the file.

The template is finished and ready to be used in an actual workflow. The styles and XML tags are in place and ready to be applied. To use this file, simply open it and start adding content. When the newsletter's finished, select Map Styles to Tags, and InDesign does most of the work after that. To show you how it works we created a sample newsletter using the template.

9. Open **Newsletter02.indt**. Observe the layout.

Here is the February issue of the environmental group's newsletter, created using the XML template. See how the frames are still showing the tags applied in step 6? Let's prepare the content for use on the group's Web site.

10. Select Map Styles to Tags from the Tags panel menu. Click the Map By Name button. Click OK.

- The layout displays XML-colored tags and frames.

- The Structure pane fills with the newly tagged elements.

11. Observe the content to see if it's properly tagged. Observe the Structure pane. Look for any elements that don't exhibit XML tags or ones that shouldn't have tags in the first place.

Text frames created for the remaining editorial content mapped automatically to the News tag, as defined in step 5. Note how the department frames retained the tags assigned in step 6.

12. Correct any missing or misapplied tags. Select File > Export.

13. Select XML from the Save as Type pull-down menu. Name the file **myNewsletter02.xml**. Click Save.

The XML Export Dialog appears.

Untagged Content Incognita

In every workflow there will probably be some content that travels through the entire production process *untagged*. There are two types of untagged content: structured and unstructured. The newsletter in Lesson 9-5 has both types.

If you have any at all, *unstructured* untagged content is the best kind to have. These are bits of text and graphics sprinkled throughout the layout—such as page numbers, headers, and footers—that are not within the editorial content. These elements are ignored when you export and *don't* end up in the XML. On the other hand, *structured* untagged content poses potential problems.

An example of structured untagged content can be seen on page 1. In the frame that contains the volume number, issue number and month, you can see two bullet characters. These bullets are individually untagged but they reside within the frame that is tagged Issue_ID, which means they are automatically part of the XML structure. When the tagged text is exported to XML, the bullets **(Figure 9.15)** will be too!

What trouble will untagged unstructured content cause? Your guess is as good as ours. It really depends on your code's final destination. Some XML applications will simply ignore any untagged elements, whereas others may crash. A possible solution could be to create a tag for every element regardless of its purpose or to create a catch-all tag such as <ignore> that can be applied to unneeded text and graphics.

For all we know, nothing bad at all will happen. But we thought you should be forewarned.

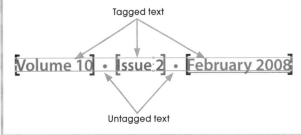

Tagged text

Volume 10 • Issue 2 • February 2008

Untagged text

Figure 9.15 Untagged text within your structure will end up in your XML code like these bullets. What's happens next depends on your XML application.

14. Use the same export settings as in Figure 9.10. Click Export.

NOTE   *We'll use this XML to create a Web page in **Chapter 11**.*

15. Save any changes and close the file.

Lesson 9-6: Exporting Content to HTML/XHTML

Our all-time favorite XML trick doesn't create XML at all—it creates HTML. The reason it's our favorite is simple: There are hundreds of possible applications for the XML you create from InDesign, but the vast majority of it will be used to create Web content. The problem is that XML can't be accessed directly by most browsers. Depending on the browser, XML appears as raw code, or as just a bunch of unformatted gibberish.

Chapters 10 and **11** teach you how to create and format Web pages using the XML you've already exported. But for many, this is just too much work or simply beyond their technical prowess. If you've been looking in vain for InDesign's "export as HTML" button, this is the lesson for you.

"But there is no export-as-HTML button," you say.

You're right, for the most part. But we don't need one as long as we have the ability to export to XML! As **Chapter 1** explains: HTML and XML are both plain-text languages that are intended for different purposes. HTML is designed for display; XML is designed for data. HTML has a fixed number of code elements; XML makes its *own*.

Were you paying attention just then? XML can make *any* kind of element and name it in *any* way you like. So, what's stopping you from simply naming your XML elements after the codes in HTML? The answer: *nothing*.

1. Open **myXMLExport.indt** created in Lesson 9-3.

You tagged the content in this file and exported it as XML earlier in the chapter. Now we'll show you how the same file can be used to create perfect HTML code.

2. Show the Structure pane, Tags panel, tag markers and tagged frames. Observe the panels and the layout.

There are no tag names or apparent structure.

If you are planning on using this technique, it helps to have a basic understanding of HTML code elements and proper structure. There are only 100 or so code elements in HTML that you have to learn, so it's easy to pick up the basics in a weekend or two (although learning how to get the most out of your code will take longer). Creating a workable HTML file will require a handful of tags to format the text and a few more to structure the code.

3. Create the following tags:

   - h1

   - img

   - li

   - p

   - strong

   These tags are code elements used by HTML to format and structure text.

4. Select Tagging Preset Options from the Tags panel menu.

   The Tagging Preset Option dialog appears.

5. In the Text Frames pull-down menu select New Tag (**Figure 9.16**).

   The New Tag dialog appears.

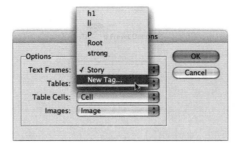

Figure 9.16 The Tagging Preset Options dialog allows you to create and apply tags in one step.

6. Name the new tag div. Click OK.

7. In the Images pull-down menu (CS3 only) select img.

8. Click OK.

   NOTE *This Tagging Preset feature tags free-standing image frames but not inline ones as in the layout. You will need to create this tag and apply it manually.*

9. Click OK to close the Tagging Preset Options dialog.

The tags you specified is steps 6 and 7 are structural elements in HTML used to insert frames (**div**) or images (**img**).

10. Select Map Styles to Tags from the Tags panel menu. Map the Paragraph (¶) and Character (A) styles to the following tags and click OK:

STYLE NAME	TAG NAME
¶ Body	p
¶ Bullet	li
¶ Headling 1	h1
¶ Number	li
A Bold	strong

The layout displays XML structure. The Structure panel fills with content (**Figure 9.17**).

Figure 9.17 If you are new to HTML, you really don't understand how cool this is, but you're only a few steps away from creating a Web page.

A close look at the Structure pane shows that the code is missing three basic building blocks needed for a properly structured Web page: an HTML declaration and two tags, one for the Head and the other for the Body section.

11. Double-click on the Root element in the Tags panel. Rename it html.

12. Create two new tags. Name one head and the other body.

13. Select the html element in the Structure pane. Click the New Element button. Select head from the Tag pull-down menu. Click OK.

The head element appears as the last element in the Structure pane.

14. Repeat step 13, adding body as a new element.

15. Select and apply img to the inline photo.

NOTE *We don't know why, but InDesign doesn't automatically tag inline images. If you want them tagged you have to do the work yourself.*

16. In the Structure pane, drag div into the body element (**Figure 9.18**).

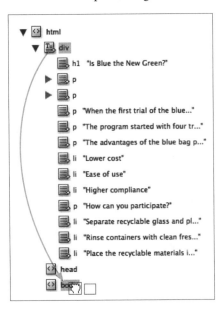

Figure 9.18 By nesting the elements this way you are building an XML structure that will create usable HTML code.

The HTML structure is nearly finished, but there are still a couple of problems that need to be addressed. First, the **img** element is using XML syntax that won't work in HTML.

17. Create an img tag and apply it to the photo.

18. Double-click on the attribute in the img element in the Structure pane.

The Edit Attribute dialog opens.

19. Edit the Name field to say src. Edit the Value field to say images/bluebin_fmt. jpeg. Click OK.

NOTE *When you select Optimized or Optimized Formatted Images in the Export XML dialog, InDesign exports the image and appends the characters **_fmt** to the original filename as well as the appropriate format extension (**.gif** or **.jpeg**). CS2 may append the extension .jpg to the file name, instead of .jpeg. In step 17, you should enter the extension appropriate for your version. You may have to test the procedure once to see how the files are exported.*

The last modification concerns the sentences with bullets and numbering. For the element to work properly, the li codes must be nested in a parent element: ul for bullets and ol for numbers.

20. Create two new tags. Name one ul, the other ol.

21. Switch to Story Editor. Select all three lines of text that are bulleted, including the opening and closing li tags and apply the ul tag (**Figure 9.19**).

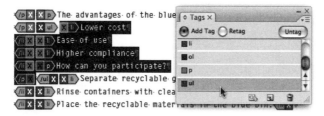

Figure 9.19 To create bullets properly in HTML, the **li** element must be nested in the **ul** tag.

22. Select all three numbered lines, including the opening and closing li tags and apply the ol tag to the selection. Switch back to Layout view.

23. Export to XML. Name the document **myHTMLExport.html**. Click Save.

The XML Export Options Dialog appears.

24. Enter the specifications shown in **Figure 9.20**. Click OK.

A Web page appears in your selected browser containing all the text, the photo, and the bulleted and numbered paragraphs.

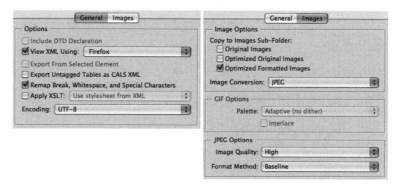

Figure 9.20 Use these settings to create the HTML code.

NOTE *The Remap Break and Whitespace and Special Characters is a new feature in InDesign CS3, which helps to eliminate the weird characters that can plague HTML and XML exported by CS2 users.*

In some browsers, you may notice some strange characters hanging around at the ends of the paragraphs in the exported code (mostly in CS2). These are the invisible and thoroughly annoying codes we first described back in the sidebar "How Plain Is Plain Enough?" in **Chapter 3**. The best way to get rid of them is to open the HTML file in TextEdit or Notepad and save it as plain text.

Also, you may have trouble editing this file in Dreamweaver or other HTML editor as long as the `<?xml ?>` declaration appears in the first line of your code.

25. Open **myHTMLExport.html** in a text or HTML editor. Delete the entire line: `<?xml version="1.0" encoding="UTF-8" standalone="yes" ?>`.

26. Type: `<!DOCTYPE html PUBLIC "-//W3C//DTD XHTML 1.0 Strict//EN" "http://www.w3.org/TR/xhtml1/DTD/xhtml1-strict.dtd">` and save the file.

Although the process requires a little manual intervention, this is a pretty good start. With a little knowledge of HTML and some imagination, you could create Web designs with a high level of complexity.

Lesson 9-7: Advanced HTML/XHTML Export

Let's take a quick look at how you can use the technique you learn in Lesson 9-6 to achieve some advanced HTML capabilities. For one thing, you may have noticed that there's something dramatically missing from the code you created. Web designers are probably asking, "Where's all the styling information?"

In Lesson 9-1 you learn that Cross-media Export can create the HTML structure *and* retain the print-based paragraph styling. It does it by adding a `class` attribute to the `<p>` code element. But Cross-media Export is limited because it relies totally on `<p class>` elements for everything.

Our XML/HTML trick is better because it allows you to use any tag name you want. But it's flawed too, in that it doesn't give you a way to preserve specific Paragraph or Character styles. What we really need is a way to get the XML export to do the same thing as the Cross-media feature. And that's exactly what this lesson is about to show you.

1. Open **AdvancedXMLExport.indt**. Observe the layout and the Structure pane. Option-click/Alt-click on the triangle in front of the `html` element to reveal all the elements in the structure.

You should notice that the HTML-based tags have already been created and mapped to the content. Note how all the paragraphs have been tagged by the **p** code, headings by **h1**, **h2**, or **h3** and frames by **div** or **img** (except CS2 users). The newsletter is ready to export to HTML, but if you did so at this moment you would lose all the styling information that helps to differentiate the text in the various sections of the newsletter.

Here's one possible solution, but it's only for those with plenty of time on their hands:

2. Select the first p element in the Structure pane, which is mapped to the Urban Newspaper Drive event. Click the "Add an attribute" button in the Structure pane.

3. Type class in the Name field. Type event in the value field. Click OK.

You have just modified this element in a way so it will export as **<p class="event">**. Although this works as a way to create the styles you need, there's no way to automate the process without scripts or other programming. So, it's not a method you'll like to contemplate for a 100-page newspaper or magazine. Instead, we'd like to suggest a trick that's quick and easy, and employs our favorite code-editing tool: Find/Replace.

No Shortcuts Allowed

Stop! All you enterprising amateur XML coders out there may have had the brilliant idea to use p class="bodycal" as the actual tag name, but don't even waste your time. Spaces, equal signs (=) and quotes (") are not allowed in tag names. Drat!

---

4. Create a new tag. Name it pclass-bodycal- (don't forget the final hyphen).

Have you figured out what the plan is yet? That's right: You're creating XML tags customized for each Paragraph style. After they're exported to HTML, we'll use Find/Replace to reconstruct the tags correctly. For example, **<pclass-bodycal->** will be rebuilt as **<p class="bodycal">** and so on.

5. Create the following tags for the remaining Paragraph styles:

- pclass-bodynews-
- pclass-bodyfirst-
- pclass-bodytips-
- pclass-event-
- pclass-eventdate-
- pclass-tocitem-

Character styles can also be handled this way, but the HTML construction is slightly different and looks like this: **<span class="blue">**.

6. Create the following tags for the Character styles (don't forget the hyphens):

   - spanclass-blue-
   - spanclass-bold-
   - spanclass-boldblue-
   - spanclass-green-
   - spanclass-pgnumber-

7. Select Map Styles to Tags. Map the Paragraph (¶) and Character (A) styles to the corresponding tags and click OK:

STYLE NAME	TAG NAME
¶ Body	p
¶ Body-cal	pclass-bodycal-
¶ Body-news	pclass-bodynews-
¶ Body-first	pclass-bodyfirst-
¶ Body-tips	pclass-bodytips-
¶ Event	pclass-event-
¶ Eventdate	pclass-eventdate-
¶ Heading1	h1
¶ Heading2	h2
¶ Heading3	h3
¶ TOC Item	pclass-tocitem-
A blue	spanclass-blue-
A bold	spanclass-bold-
A bold blue	spanclass-boldblue-
A green	spanclass-green-
A page number	spanclass-pgnumber-

The modified tags replace the original structure.

NOTE   *Don't forget to apply the **img** tag to the two images in the newsletter.*

By themselves, the <p> and <h1-6> codes—like InDesign's Paragraph and Character styles—can format text and perform a little structural duty on the side. But the real power of Web design resides in the <div> element. Similar to text and graphic frames in InDesign, the <div> element is used by Web designers to wrap, hold, and position page content in the desired location on the screen. A <div> element can stand alone, nest within, or wrap around other **‹div›** and HTML elements. Add CSS to the mixture and you have a thing of beauty.

The **‹div›** elements can be formatted by adding either an **id** or **class** attribute. Both types of attributes can apply font *and* position specifications, but the **id** attribute is designated as a "unique identifier" and is restricted to only one use per page. This makes the **id** attribute a great way to format mastheads, banners, headers, footers, and other elements that usually appear only once. On the other hand, the **class** attribute can be used as many times as you want. With a careful use of **id** and **class** attributes, you can reproduce the three-column design of the print-based newsletter in the browser.

8. Select the first div element in the Structure pane. Click the "Add an attribute" button.

This text frame contains only calendar information. It will be formatted to align to the left edge of the screen.

9. Type id in the Name field. Type events in the Value field. Click OK.

10. Select the div element in the Structure pane that contains the text "Sign Up…" Click the "Add an attribute" button.

This text frame contains the table of contents information for the newsletter, which was generated automatically by InDesign. Normally, we would just toss it away and build our own Web navigation from scratch, but the TOC lends itself to the process and potentially could save us time. For example, we could insert anchors within the respective stories and link to them from the TOC entries with hyperlinks. But it won't do us any good as a navbar at the bottom of the page. If we assign an **id** attribute to this frame, we can repositioned it on the screen later using CSS, as **Chapter 10** demonstrates.

11. Type id in the Name field. Type toc in the Value field. Click OK.

12. Select the div element in the Structure pane that contains the text "Buy local…" Click the "Add an attribute" button.

This text frame contains only environmental lifestyle tips. It will be formatted to align to the right edge of the screen and below the **toc** element.

13. Type id in the Name field. Type toptips in the Value field. Click OK.

14. Select the div element that contains the text "Winter Plant Care…" Click the "Add an attribute" button.

This text frame contains only plant-care and gardening information. It will be formatted to appear below the calendar information on the left edge of the screen.

15. Type id in the Name field. Type greenthumb in the Value field. Click OK.

The remaining four **div** elements are all news containers. This content will appear in the center of the screen between the left and right columns. But with eight **div** elements competing for screen real estate, precautions should be taken to make sure all the content behaves properly in the browser. Good Web design practice recommends that the **div** elements in each column be wrapped within parent **div** tags that can be formatted to create the three-column effect.

16. Add three div elements to the body element in the Structure pane. Add id attributes to each using the values: left, main, and right.

17. Drag the div elements for events and greenthumb into the new div left. Drag toc and toptips into div right. Drag the remaining di elements into div main.

The three **div** elements holding your content are in place, one more **div** is needed to wrap up the whole thing up in a neat package.

18. Add a div element to body. Name it wrapper. Drag left, main, and right into the wrapper element (**Figure 9.21**).

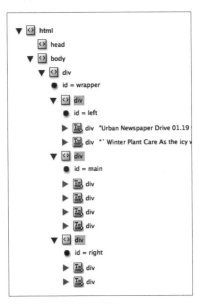

Figure 9.21 Nesting **div** elements like this ensures they will behave in the browser.

Before you can export the content, you have to reconstruct the two img references to be compatible to HTML as in **Lesson 9-6**. It also wouldn't hurt to add width and height attributes to the elements to make sure the images don't appear in the layout at a size that would break your carefully structured code.

Optimized Images May Not Be Optimum

If you select the Optimized Original or Optimized Formatted Images option in the Export XML dialog (**Figure 9.22**), InDesign automatically exports tagged images from your layout at their current dimensions but at a Web resolution of 72 ppi. Although this feature speeds up the process of getting your content to the Web, the exported images may not be acceptable for your desired application.

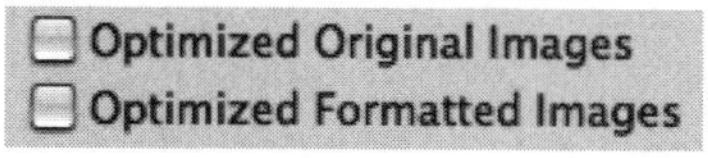

☐ **Optimized Original Images**
☐ **Optimized Formatted Images**

Figure 9.22 This option in the Export XML dialog automates the paper-to-Web translation for images, but you may not like the result.

For example, in the print-based version of the newsletter the width of the photo of the blue bins matches the text column at a width of 3.7 inches. But that translates to only 264 pixels in your browser. On the other hand, in the Web version the text is being displayed in a column-width of 475 pixels. That means if you use the picture as exported, it'll be 211 pixels narrower.

Depending on your workflow, this may not be a big deal. The ability of moving large amounts of print-based content to the Web quickly and easily may well outweigh such minor design glitches.

NOTE It's best to use a program like Photoshop or Fireworks to determine the appropriate dimensions of an image destined for a Web page.

19. In the Structure pane, double-click the attribute for the blue bins photo. Change the Name field to `src`. Change the Value field to `images/bluebin_fmt.jpeg`. Click OK.

NOTE The Windows version of InDesignCS2 may export the images with the extension.jpg, instead of .jpeg. In step 19, use the extension appropriate to your platform.

20. Add an attribute to the blue bins `img`. Name: `width`. Value: `254`.

21. Add an attribute to the blue bins `img`. Name: `height`. Value: `156`.

22. In the Structure pane, double-click the attribute for the plant photo. Change the Name field to `src`. Change the Value field to `images/plants_fmt.jpeg`. Click OK.

NOTE In CS2 you may need to enter **jpg** instead of **jpeg**.

23. Add an attribute to the plants `img`. Name: `width`. Value: `120`.

24. Add an attribute to the plants `img`. Name: `height`. Value: `84`.

The structure is complete and ready for exporting.

25. Save the document as **myAdvancedHTMLExport.indd**.

26. Select File > Export. Select XML in the Save as Type field. Name the file **myAdvancedHTML.html**. Click Save.

27. Enter the specifications shown in Figure 9.20. Click OK

A Web page appears in your selected browser containing all the content from the newsletter. If you're new to Web design, you're probably wondering, "Where's that three-column design we were talking about?"

By itself, *raw* HTML code doesn't really format very much of the look of your Web page. For example, there's no 3-column text tag in HTML. All the things we consider "design" actually come from the attributes that are assigned to each code element after the fact, either manually or via a cascading style sheet (CSS). To produce the magic you're looking for, we need to insert a reference to a style sheet we created specifically for this newsletter. The link to the style sheet can be added using any text editor or Web design program or directly from inside InDesign.

28. In the Tags panel, create a new tag. Name it link.

29. In the Structure pane, select the head element. Click the "Add an element" button. Select link from the Tag pull-down menu. Click OK.

The **link** element appears as a child of **head**.

30. Add an attribute to the link element. Type href in the Name field. Type news-style.css in the Value field. Click OK.

31. Add an attribute to the link element. Type rel in the Name field. Type stylesheet in the Value field. Click OK.

32. Add an attribute to the link element. Type type in the Name field. Type text/css in the Value field. Click OK.

The style sheet link is complete (**Figure 9.23**).

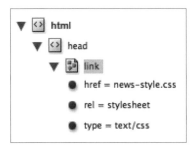

Figure 9.23 Adding all the formatting through an external style sheet allows you to control the look of multiple Web pages all from one set of styles.

33. Repeat steps 22 and 23 to export the edited structure. Name the file **myAdvancedHTML2.html**.

Like magic, the new file appears in the browser, including the graphical newsletter banner (prepared separately) and both photos (**Figure 9.24**). But there's still one thing left to do. You should notice that the text in the browser is all jumbled up and may display some odd characters. The reason the text is messed up is simple; back in step 7 you mapped the InDesign Paragraph and Character styles to *custom* XML tags that we were planning to swap for class attributes later. Well, the time has come!

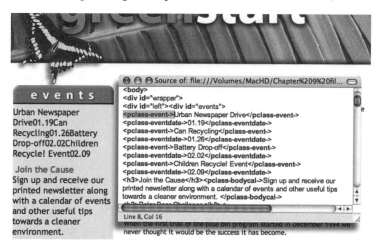

Figure 9.24 The structure seems to be in place, but the formatting has been messed up by the custom tag names we created in step 7.

34. Load **myAdvancedHTML2.html** in TextEdit/Notepad or your favorite text or HTML editor.

35. Replace the first line of the file—`<?xml version="version 1.0" encoding="UTF-16" standalone="yes"?>`—with `<!DOCType HTML>`.

The next step is to simplify all the closing tags to either `</p>` or `</span>`. In TextEdit or Notepad you will have to find and replace every tag individually. Programs with more robust Find/Replace features, like Dreamweaver, should be able to do the job in one or two operations by using wildcards or pattern searches.

36. Find the custom *closing* tag `</pclass-bodycal->`. Replace all with `</p>`.

37. Repeat step 36 for all the custom *closing* paragraph tags created in step 7.

38. Find the custom *closing* tag `</spanclass-blue->`. Replace all with `</span>`.

39. Repeat step 38 for all the custom *closing* character tags created in step 7.

Once you replace the closing tags the hard part's over. Replacing the custom *opening* tags will be an easy, three-step process.

40. Find: `<pclass-` (don't forget the hyphen). Replace all with: `<p class="` (don't forget the double quote).

41. Find: `<spanclass-` (don't forget the hyphen). Replace all with: `<span class="` (don't forget the double quote).

42. Find: `->` (hyphen, right-angle bracket). Replace it with: `">` (double quote, right-angle bracket).

All the custom tags have been replaced with HTML-compatible ones.

43. Save the changes to **myAdvancedHTML2.html**. Load the file into your browser again or, if it's still on the screen, simply refresh the display (**Figure 9.25**).

That's it! By tagging and structuring the content before you exported it to our *hybrid* HTML, you were able to create a complex Web page using your newsletter content and an existing CSS file. In **Chapter 10**, we examine how to produce this kind of magic with CSS.

Figure 9.25 Not bad for a program that can't export HTML!

Review

Chapter 9 has taken us down a long but rewarding road. It shows you that XML can be used as more than just a way to import data for making business cards, atlases, and catalogs. One of the most exciting possibilities is XML's capability to create fully formatted Web content. In fact, by preparing XML templates and standard structures and elements, it's possible to get the process of making instant Web content down to a few clicks of the mouse. Overall, you learned:

- How to structure content for exporting

- How to export content to XML

- How to export content to HTML/XHTML

- How to work with content structure to create fully formatted Web pages

10

XML, HTML & CSS

Chapter Objectives

In this chapter, you will learn:

- What CSS is and why you should care

- How to use CSS to format XML

- How to use CSS to format and structure HTML

You've structured your InDesign document and exported it to XML or HTML. Now what? The answer to this question could take another 300 pages, so we'll try to restrict the topic to a brief tour of cascading style sheets (CSS). Considering that there are already dozens of wonderful books on the subject, we certainly don't intend on giving you a comprehensive tutorial in just a few pages. At the end of the chapter we recommend several books for further CSS research and understanding. Consider this chapter a short primer on the wonders of CSS and how it relates to the content exported from InDesign.

NOTE Download all applicable files for Chapter 10 from www.peachpit.com/indesignxmlguide and copy them to a folder on your hard drive (approximately 3 MB). All the HTML and CSS used within this chapter can be created and edited by any plain-text or HTML editor. We prefer to use Dreamweaver CS3.

Lesson 10-1: Formatting HTML

To get a full understanding of what CSS is, what it can do, and why you should care, we have to go back to basics. The reason is simple: CSS was created in the first place to address some of the weaknesses in HTML.

By itself, HTML doesn't do anything. It must work hand in hand with a browser to create the Web page display. The browser interprets the HTML code and then puts all the elements in the right order and position on the screen—hopefully. HTML was never intended to be used as a vehicle for graphic design; it was supposed to be an engine for text display and that's all. All the extended features we use today, like Javascript, VisualBasic, and CSS, have been cobbled onto the basic underpinnings of HTML to make it do things its founders probably never dreamed of.

1. Launch your favorite browser. Load **HTMLSample.html** from the Chapter 10 folder. Observe the text in the window.

The screen displays three bold headings, four paragraphs of text, and six bulleted lines.

2. Activate the browser's command to view the source code. Observe the code (**Figure 10.1**).

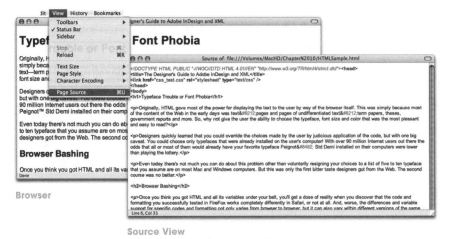

Figure 10.1 The browser (left) interprets the HTML code (right) and displays the results on the screen. Some browsers do a better job than others.

See the eleven different code elements in use: <html>, <head>, <title>, <link>, <body>, <h1>, <h2>, <h3>, <p>, <ul>, and <li>. Can you see how the browser is ignoring what look like paragraph breaks in the code? Only the lines that begin with codes like <h1> or <p> are displayed as paragraphs in the browser.

3. Insert the cursor at the beginning of the line that starts: "For designers who are…" Type `<p>`. Save the file.

*NOTE If your browser's source view doesn't allow you to edit the code, you will have to load **HTMLSample.html** into an HTML or text editor to make the changes.*

4. Refresh the browser display. Observe the changes.

The browser now displays the edited line as a new paragraph.

Did you notice that we didn't close the **<p>** element? You can get away with leaving the **<p>** element, or tag, open in regular HTML, but in XHTML all elements must follow the stricter XML tagging rules. Unfortunately, you'll probably never find out your code violates the rules from a browser, most are pretty slack (some call it forgiving). It's only when you try to use the code in a compliant application that you may get some grief.

5. Add another `<p>` tag at the beginning of the lines that start "Designers wade into…" and "We learned very quickly…" Save the file.

All the paragraphs are delineated by **<p>** tags.

6. Save the file as **myHTMLSample.html**.

7. Insert your cursor after the first `<p>` tag in the ninth line. Type `<font face="Arial" pointsize="12" color="red">`. Save the file. Switch to the browser and load **myHTMLSample.html**.

All the text following the inserted markup code displays as red 12-pt. Arial because we never closed the **<font>** tag. While the unclosed **<p>** tag didn't cause a single problem, here's a case where broken code can come back to bite you. Technically, the browser should ignore the **<font>** command completely until we close the tag properly, but it doesn't. Doesn't anybody follow the rules anymore?

8. Insert the cursor in front of the closing tag for the paragraph edited in step 5. Type `</font>`. Save the file.

The closing tags should now appear like this: **</font></p>**.

9. Refresh the browser display. Observe the changes.

Only the first paragraph appears as red 12-pt. Arial.

10. Repeat steps 7 and 8 for each of the `<p>` tagged paragraphs. Save the file and refresh the display.

The edited paragraphs are formatted as red 12-pt. Arial. The headings remain normal.

11. Close **myHTMLSample.html**.

In this lesson we hope you learned three things. One, line breaks and other spacing in the source code are ignored by the browser. Two, formatting text this way is tedious at best. Three, you never want to format text like this again!

Lesson 10-2: Styling HTML with CSS

CSS offers a better way to format and structure everything in HTML. If you are still hand coding each line of text as in Lesson 10-1, shame on you. This brief demonstration will offer you a miraculous alternative.

1. Open **HTMLSample.html** in your favorite HTML editor. Observe the code itself.

    ■ The text is tagged with HTML codes.

    ■ There are no formatting commands.

    NOTE *In Lesson 10-1, step 5 you added* **<p>** *tags to the untagged paragraph and saved the file. If these tags are not present go ahead and add them now.*

    Note the code in line 3: `<link href="html_style.css" rel="stylesheet" type="text/css" />`. This is a link to a cascading style sheet.

2. Open **html_style.css** in your HTML editor.

    The style sheet contains the code elements featured in **HTMLSample.html** but no styling information.

3. Insert the cursor in the notation for the p code after the { (brace). Type `color: red; font-family: arial; font-size: 12pt;`. Save and close the file (**Figure 10.2**).

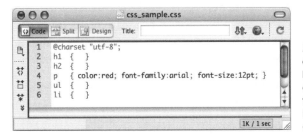

Figure 10.2 CSS rules are written in their own language and syntax, and act like an intermediary for the HTML code telling the browser how to display the content.

NOTE *As in most HTML code, spacing is not important, but punctuation is. Don't miss any of the : (colons) or ; (semicolons).*

4. Load **HTMLSample.html** in your browser.

    All text tagged by **<p>** codes displays as red 12-pt. Arial.

Did you notice the miracle? You formatted the individual paragraphs without even touching them. This is the basic power of CSS and you should now have a hint about why it's so popular. As you will see in the next few lessons, CSS also has the capability to format raw XML and complex XHTML files, like the ones we created in **Chapter 9**.

Lesson 10-3: Styling Raw XML with CSS

"Wait," you protest. "You said XML doesn't store styling information!"

Yep, we did say that. And it's true. But we're not putting the styling information in the XML. It's in the CSS file!

1. Open **myXMLExport1.xml** created in **Chapter 9**, Lesson 9-3 in your HTML or XML editor. Observe the code. Note the code elements used in the file.

    The file is plain XML with no visible styling information.

2. Select File > Save As. Save the file into the Chapter 10 folder.

3. Load **myXMLExport1.xml** in Firefox or Internet Explorer or any other XML-compatible browser. As of this writing, Safari can't display raw XML code.

    The browser displays the complete XML code, including the tags, attributes, and processing instructions.

4. Open **raw_style.css**. Observe the style sheet.

    The style sheet contains the tag names and styling instructions for your XML file.

NOTE The tag names listed in this CSS file should match exactly those in your XML file. If you notice any discrepancy, edit the names in the CSS to match the XML file before you proceed to the next step.

5. Insert your cursor in front of the opening `<Root>` element in **myXMLExport1.xml**. Type `<?xml-stylesheet type="text/css" href="raw_style.css "?>` and save the file.

NOTE This syntax is needed to link an external style sheet to an XML file.

6. Refresh the browser display (**Figure 10.3**).

    The browser should now display the formatted text.

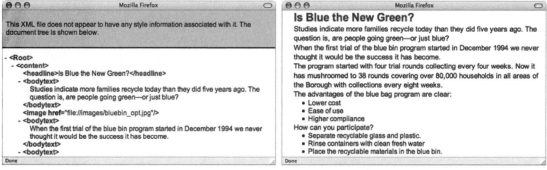

Plain XML   CSS-Formatted XML

Figure 10.3 XML-compatible browsers will display both the raw (left) and formatted XML (right).

Formatting XML with CSS is like a stupid pet trick: It's cute but pretty much useless. The problem lies in the fact that some browsers don't fully support either CSS or XML, or they do a bad job of it. Web designers have to battle browser incompatibility all of the time, and we certainly don't want to invite trouble. Besides, there's no reason to use the raw XML when it's so easy to convert it to HTML or XHTML. Whereas this chapter focuses on CSS, **Chapter 11** shows you how XSL Transformations (XSLT) can turn raw XML into almost anything you need.

Lesson 10-4: Advanced CSS Styling

To understand the power of CSS you'd have to take InDesign's Paragraph, Character, and Object styles, roll them into one feature, and then put it on a steady diet of steroids! CSS can do everything InDesign's styling commands can do and more. CSS takes the basic formatting of text and objects and adds to it the ability to position them anywhere on the screen or even make them invisible, apply interactivity, create borders, load background graphics and colors—and, if that's not enough, it can apply all of these options contextually depending on where the text or object is placed in the layout. Get InDesign to do all this, and you're finally scratching the surface of what CSS can deliver.

One of the ways CSS performs its magic is by taking over the basic way HTML code elements work. HTML code is a hodge-podge of elements that perform different and sometimes conflicting tasks. For example, some elements perform functions that structure the Web page, such as <head>, <body>, and <div>. Others are intended only for formatting, such as <strong>, <em>, and <font>. Yet, there are the exceptions that do both, namely <h1> through <h6> and <p>. All these HTML elements have their default functions hardwired into them.

Type <p> and you create a new paragraph. Type <h1> and it inserts a line break and formats the type to be large and bold. In both examples, the structure and the styling happen automatically. When a code element creates its own space like this it's called a *block* element.

Type <strong> or <em> and the subsequent text becomes bold or italic respectively, but no space is inserted, no new paragraph breaks are created. When the code doesn't generate its own space, it's called an *inline* element. It's important to be knowledgeable of the default settings for every HTML element, regardless of whether you end up using them. If the settings work for you, all the better. But if the default interferes with what you want to do, don't fret. CSS can throw all the rules away! With a few lines of code it can step in and rewire any HTML element to make it do whatever you want it to do.

1. In your HTML editor, open **AdvancedCSS.html** from the Chapter 10 folder.

2. Save the file as **myAdvancedCSS.html**. Observe the code.

This file is exactly like the one created in Lesson 9-7. Note the use of standard HTML elements throughout the code, especially the **‹div›** tag. As we explain in **Chapter 9**, **‹div›** is used mostly as a container, one that can hold text and graphics as well as other **‹div›** elements. Using **‹div›** this way allows CSS to control not just how the contents are formatted, but also how they are displayed, including width, height, and position on the screen.

3. Load **myAdvancedCSS.html** in your browser.

The code displays as a single column of plain text the full width of the screen. Note that the first line of text beginning "Urban Newspaper Drive…" is from the Events section of the newsletter. As long as the text in this section is taking up the entire width of the screen, there's no room for two additional columns of text. We can make the space available by trimming the text down to a more manageable width. As in Lesson 10.1, we'll use an external CSS file.

4. In the HTML editor, insert your cursor into the blank fifth line of code, which appears within the ‹head›‹/head› tags. Type ‹link href="Advanced_style.css" rel="stylesheet" type="text/css" /› and save the file.

NOTE *Did you notice that the syntax of this CSS link is different from the one used in the XML file in Lesson 10.3? Use this syntax for HTML files.*

5. Open **Advanced_style.css** in an HTML editor. Observe the code.

To save time we have already added all the element names for you, but left the styling section blank. If you study the HTML file closely you'll see that the Events text is stored in a **‹div›** element. As already noted, CSS can control the width of HTML elements. Let's set the width to 190 pixels; this will give us plenty room for the other two columns.

6. In **Advanced_style.css**, add the highlighted code to the following element: **div** { width:190px; }

7. Save the file. Refresh the browser display. Observe the changes. Scroll down to the bottom of the page if necessary to see the effect.

NOTE *As you proceed through the lesson you will be working on the CSS file in your code editor and switching back-and-forth to your browser to view the results of your changes on the HTML file.*

The text is now displayed in a column 190 pixels wide—all of it. That's not exactly what we had in mind. But the reason it happened is simple: Formatting the **‹div›** tag in step 6 affects all **‹div›** elements within the entire document. Instead, the command needs to target the specific element you want to change. This is accomplished in CSS by assigning a **class** or an **id** attribute to an element. Luckily, these **‹div›** elements were all assigned **id** attributes in Lesson 9-7. Specifically, the Events text shares its side of the screen with the Green Thumb section and both are contained within the element `<div id="left">`. To fix the styling command from step 6, make the following change:

8. Add the highlighted code to the existing element: `div#left { width:190px; }` and save the file.

9. Refresh the browser display and observe the changes.

As you scroll down the screen you will see that now only the text in the `#left` section (Events and Green Thumb) is displayed at the width of 190 pixels, and there's room for the remaining two columns. Let's move the content of column two into place.

10. Add the highlighted code to the following elements:
`div#left { width:190px; float:left; }`
`div#main { width:475px; margin-left:210px; }`

11. Save the file. Refresh the browser and observe the changes.

The text contained in `<div id="main">` appears in the space to the right of the Events column.

Two columns down, one more to go.

12. Add the highlighted code to the following element:
`div#right { width:190px; top:20px; left:745px; position:absolute; }`

13. Save the file. Refresh the browser and observe the changes.

The text contained in `<div id="right">` appears in the space to the right of the News column.

Now that we have the basic three-column structure ready, we'll show you some of the power of CSS to format text. By default, text in the browser usually displays as Times or Times New Roman. This behavior can be changed with a simple command.

14. Add the highlighted code to the following elements: `body { font-family: Verdana; }`

15. Save the file. Refresh the browser and observe the changes.

All the text in the browser is now formatted as Verdana.

Next to `<html>`, the `<body>` element is the second most powerful HTML tag available to the Web designer. Why? It's because the `<body>` element is the parent of all the visible content on your page. Although it's used mainly as a structural element, that doesn't stop CSS from using it to apply formatting to text. By applying the `font-family` command here, it automatically applies the formatting to all elements contained within, unless overridden by another code element. In fact, this ability to use one element to apply formatting to another or to a whole range of elements at one time is the very definition of the "cascading" part of CSS. But be careful, the real trick is knowing what type of formatting to apply and to which element. Let's see how cascading works.

16. Add the highlighted code to the following elements:

```
p { font-size:11pt; }
#left p { color:#009900; }
#right  p { color:#000099; }
```

17. Save the file. Refresh the browser and observes the changes.

- All text formatted by the **<p>** code displays at 11 points.

- The paragraph text in **<div id="left">** appears green, 11 points.

- The paragraph text in **<div id="right">** appears blue, 11 points.

By adding **#left** or **#right** in front of the **p** code in step 16, the styling targets only the content that appears within that structural element. In other words, we didn't have to format any of <p> codes manually because they actually format themselves based on where they appear in the code. Wow. And, if anyone's starting to think that CSS formatting is a lot of work, remember that all the styling has been accomplished without making a single change to the actual HTML file!

NOTE *Although it's good practice, any time you get tired of typing all this code, feel free to take a short-cut and copy and paste the entire contents from **AdvancedStyleFinal.css** into this file.*

Let's put some final touches to the page. The following code will add graphics, colors, and more to your structure.

18. Add the highlighted code below to the existing elements:

```
body { font-family:Verdana; padding-top:230px; background-image:url(images/
newsbanner.jpg); background-repeat:no-repeat; }
#left p { color:#009900; margin-left:5; margin-right:5; }
#right p { color:#000099; margin-left:5; margin-right:5; }
#events {
    background-image: url(images/eventshead.jpg);
    background-repeat: no-repeat;
    background-position: 0px 0px;
    background-color: #D5FFD5;
    margin-top: 0px;
    padding-top: 40px;
    padding-bottom: 20px;    }
#greenthumb {
    background-image: url(images/Greenthumbead.jpg);
    background-repeat: no-repeat;
    background-position: 0px 0px;
```

```
        background-color: #D5FFD5;
        padding-top: 40px; padding-bottom: 10px;
        margin-top: 15px;             }
#toc {
        background-color: #FFFFCC;
        background-image: url(images/TOChead.jpg);
        background-repeat: no-repeat;
        background-position: 0px 0px;
        padding-top: 35px; padding-bottom: 20px; }
#toptips {
        background-color: #DFF9FF;
        background-image: url(images/Toptipshead.jpg);
        background-repeat: no-repeat;
        background-position: 0px 0px;
        padding-top: 35px; padding-bottom: 20px;
        margin-top: 15px; }
```

NOTE *Did you notice how each CSS rule ends with a ; (semicolon) and how each set of rules is contained within a set of { } (braces)? Keep your eyes peeled for missing or errant punctuation. Leave one off, and the rule is ignored by the browser.*

19. Save the file. Refresh the browser and observe the changes (**Figure 10.4**).

CSS-Formatted HTML

CSS in Dreamweaver

Figure 10.4 Once the style sheet is completed, you can use it to format all of your online newsletters.

The online newsletter is taking shape. The commands inserted in step 18 have added background colors, column headers, a banner graphic, and more to the Web page. But the text is looking kind of boring. Other than a few heading formats thrown in here or there, the paragraph text is all formatted identically. That's because, for the moment, all paragraphs are displaying the style applied to the ‹p› element in general. InDesign used Paragraph and Character styles, like Body-cal, TOC-Item and bodyblue to create a unique look for each section. To replicate this type of custom formatting, CSS uses class=".." attributes. The class attribute is very flexible in that it can be applied to either an object (‹div class="boldblue"›), an entire element (‹p class= "bodynews"›‹/p›), or to a specific range of text (‹span class="boldblue"›‹/span›).

20. Add the highlighted code below to the existing elements:

```
.bodycal, .bodytips, .tocitem { margin-left:5px; margin-right:5px; }
.boldblue { font-weight: bold; color: #2C5980; font-size: 110%; }
.event { font-weight: bold; color: #0DB14A; text-align: center; }
.eventdate {
    font-weight: bold;
    text-align: center;
    border-bottom-width: 3px;
    border-bottom-style: dotted;
    border-bottom-color: #0DB14A;
    margin-right: 40px;
    margin-left: 40px;
    padding-bottom: 5px; }
.pgnumber { color: #FFFFCC; }
```

21. Save the file. Refresh the browser and observe the changes.

In less than 100 lines of CSS code, you have created all the styles you need to format the online newsletter. This file is ready to be used in your print-to-Web workflow. Let's put it all together.

22. Load **AdvancedCSS_2.html** from the Chapter 10 folder in your browser.

23. Activate the browser's command to view the source code. Observe the code.

This is hybrid XML/HTML code we exported from **Newsletter2.indt** in **Chapter 9**. It features the same styles, tags, and structure as the newsletter we used to create the CSS in this lesson and we used the same process to create the final HTML you're looking at. Therefore, the CSS you just finished should be able to format this file the same way.

24. Load **AdvancedCSS_2.html** into the HTML editor. Insert your cursor into the blank line 5. Type ‹link href="Advanced_style.css" rel="stylesheet" type="text/css" /› and save the file.

25. Refresh the browser and observe the changes (**Figure 10.5**).

The February Newsletter appears in your browser fully formatted.

Congratulations! You just completed your primary education in CSS.

Figure 10.5 With one CSS file you can format unlimited numbers of Web pages.

Review

CSS can be used to format raw XML, but its real power is unleashed with properly structured HTML. This chapter has shown you some of the possibilities. It's now up to you to put it all to work.

In this chapter you learned:

- What CSS is and why you should care

- How to use CSS to format XML

- How to use CSS to format and structure HTML

We recommend the following books to learn more about the power of CSS:

TITLE	AUTHOR(S)	PUBLISHER	ISBN	PRICE
Bulletproof Web Design: Improving flexibility and protecting against worst-case scenarios with XHTML and CSS (2nd Edition)	Dan Cederholm	New Riders Press	978-0321509024	$39.99
CSS Web Site Design Hands-on Training	Eric Meyer	Peachpit Press	978-0321293916	$49.99
CSS: The Missing Manual	David McFarland	Pogue Press	978-0596526870	$39.99
Transcending CSS: The Fine Art of Web Design	Andy Clarke	New Riders Press	978-0321410979	$49.99

11

Ajax and XSLT

Chapter Objectives

In this chapter you will learn how to use:

- Ajax and InDesign XML to create interactive Web pages

- XSL to style InDesign XML for the Web

- An XSLT to import XML in InDesign (and why)

- An XSLT to export XML from InDesign (and why)

This chapter continues the theme from **Chapter 10** concerning applications that can take advantage of the XML exported from InDesign. We take a quick look at two techniques that offer very powerful formatting and structural capabilities for your XML output, namely Ajax and Extensible Stylesheet Language Transformations (XSLT). The reason is simple: You're busy and you have no time, so instead of spending time fooling around in the Structure pane with element order and nesting—as in **Chapter 9**—use Ajax or XSLT to create finished documents quickly and easily.

If you haven't heard of Ajax you're not alone. Although it's been around since 2005, support for it has only recently been added to Dreamweaver CS3 in the form of Adobe's Spry framework. *Ajax* stands for Asynchronous Javascript and XML. Basically, it's a new way to deal with old technologies that allows you to create interactive Web sites and applications and, as you can decipher from the name, it uses Javascript and XML to work its magic. Then what's so new?

Ajax applications can work without reloading the entire page the way ASP, PHP, and CF pages usually do. Data fills, or updates, the page on the fly in real time. And, because it uses proven technologies, you can be sure that the effects will work in most browsers. It also has an added advantage that it doesn't require any special server topology, third-party plug-ins, or players. In other words, if the browser supports Javascript and XML, it already supports Ajax.

But Ajax requires lots of coding, which limits its use and adoption by the broader community of designers and Web developers. Adobe's Spry framework is an attempt to break down the barriers to Ajax implementation. It provides a growing library of pre-built Ajax-based widgets that you can access and implement directly from Dreamweaver CS3, using drag and drop elements and applications with a minimum of actual coding. In Lesson 11-1, we experiment with one Spry application using sample XML from **Chapter 8**. For a full list of the available Spry widgets, samples and demos check out http://labs.adobe.com/technologies/spry/.

On the other hand, XSLT is an old stand-by method for repurposing XML. It's been around almost as long as XML itself and enables you to style, reformat, and restructure existing XML files or to use the contents to create wholly new files. For example, an XSLT can create plain text, HTML, or even other XML files. But the main reason we're taking a closer look at the technology is because InDesign CS3 offers, for the first time, the ability to apply an XSLT while you're importing or exporting the XML. We explore a few scenarios for using an XSLT at the beginning or end of an XML-based workflow to get the most out of your content. Let's get started.

NOTE Download all applicable files for Chapter 11 from www.peachpit.com/indesignxmlguide and copy them to a folder on your hard drive (approximately 10 MB).

Lesson 11-1: Creating Instant Web Pages with Ajax

Ajax works best with data-heavy applications such as catalogs, pricelists, and directories, although you can use it to create any type of page or page structure from an XML file. The way it works is by treating every XML file as if it's a database full of content that can be tapped to create the Web page you want using text and/or graphics. Although many prefer to create the code by hand using a variety of text- or HTML-editors, we like to use Dreamweaver CS3.

*NOTE Previous versions of Dreamweaver do not have the built-in Spry components, but the code can still be created by hand. If you do not have Dreamweaver CS3, take advantage of the completed Web page **books-n-more-END.html** included in this chapter's sample files.*

1. Launch Dreamweaver CS3. Create a new Web site using the Chapter 11 folder as the root folder. Open **books-n-more-START.html** from the Chapter 11 folder and observe the structure. Save the file as **mybooks-n-more-START.html**.

NOTE *Best practices for Web design say you should never work on a Web page in Dreamweaver without first creating and opening a Website structure first.*

As you can see, the HTML layout has already been started. The **div** area on the left will be used for a search window; the area on the right will be used for the product detail display. In fact, you should see a Spry Accordion widget on the right side already in place. This element is one of the pre-built widgets of Adobe's Spry Framework added to Dreamweaver CS3. As you will see, the widgets offer, even beginning Web designers, advanced Javascript programming capabilities in drag and drop elements. To add a Spry Accordion yourself, just insert your cursor into your Web page and click the specific button in the Insert panel.

2. In the Insert toolbar, select the Spry tab. Click the Spry XML Data Set button in the toolbar (**Figure 11.1**).

   The Spry XML Data Set dialog appears.

Figure 11.1 Frequent users of Dreamweaver will notice the addition of some new components, like the Spry category on the Insert bar.

Dreamweaver treats an XML file no differently than any other database connection. This dialog establishes how the connection is made and what data will be available to the Web page and Ajax.

3. Enter **ds1** in the Data Set name field. Click the Browse button. Select **Books.xml** from the Chapter 11 folder. Click Open.

4. Click the Get schema button.

   The Row element window displays the structure of the XML data.

Note the tree structure of the XML schema and how it branches at the parent elements such as < >BK and < >Book. The plus (+) symbol on < >Book indicates that the element contains more than one record.

5. In the Row element window, click on the < >Book element to select it.

   The Data Set columns displays the name and Data Type for each XML element contained in < >Book.

6. Click the Preview button.

The Spry preview of XML Data Set dialog appears, showing the first 20 rows of data in the XML file.

7. Click OK twice to return to the Dreamweaver interface.

8. Insert your cursor in the empty div.toc element on the left. Click the Spry Table button in the Insert bar. Enter the settings as shown in **Figure 11.2** and click OK.

A dialog appears asking you to add a Spry region.

9. Click OK to add the Spry region.

The Spry table appears within the **div** container, displaying {**productname**} and {**producttype**} data placeholders.

NOTE   *A Spry region is a code element that connects the table to the XML-based data.*

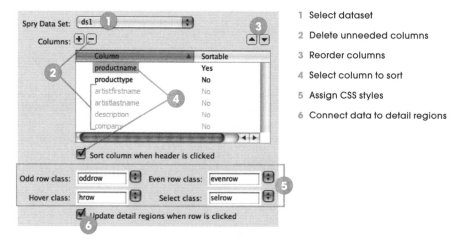

1 Select dataset
2 Delete unneeded columns
3 Reorder columns
4 Select column to sort
5 Assign CSS styles
6 Connect data to detail regions

Figure 11.2 Use these settings to create the Spry-based table. Note how we changed the order of the elements **productname** and **producttype**.

10. Use the <table> Tag Selector at the bottom of the document window to select the Spry table and set the **CellPad**, **CellSpace**, and **Border** fields to **0** (zero) in the Property Inspector.

11. Insert the cursor in the table cell containing the Productname column header, hold the Shift key, and click on the cell containing the {productname} placeholder.

The first column of the table has been selected.

12. Select pname from the Format pull-down menu in the Property Inspector to apply the style to the column in the Spry table. Rename the column header **Product Title**.

The text in the column aligns to the left.

13. Apply the ptype style to the Producttype column in the Spry table. Rename the column head to **Product Type**.

14. Select File > Preview in Browser.

- A browser window opens displaying the Web page.

- The Spry table shows a scrollable list of book titles.

- Note how the rows in the Spry table display alternating fills in the browser but not in Dreamweaver.

Javascripts in the Spry table have made a data connection to the XML file to fill the list with products. Now we show you how to put a detail section into the upper Spry Accordion on the right side of the Web page.

15. In Dreamweaver, insert the cursor in the top panel of the Spry Accordion element. Show the Bindings panel and select the productname content source. Click the Insert button.

The **{ds1::productname}** placeholder appears in the panel.

16. Insert the cursor at the end of the placeholder. In the Properties inspector, select Heading 1 from the Format pull-down menu. Type - (hyphen).

17. Insert the producttype content source from the Bindings panel. While the {ds1::producttype} placeholder is selected, select ptype from the Style pull-down menu.

18. Insert the cursor at the end of the placeholder, press Return/Enter to insert a paragraph return.

19. Insert the artistfirstname content source, a space, and the artistlastname content source in line 2. Format the line with Heading 2 and press Return/Enter to insert a paragraph return.

20. Insert the desciption content source in line 3. Format the line with Paragraph.

In step 17 you selected the content source that will determine what data record will appear on your page. Now we need to create landing spots for the rest of the data, which Spry refers to as **detailregion**. We will use one of the Accordion panels for the product description, and the other panel will be set up for the product-ordering information.

21. Click the `<div.AccordionPanelContent>` Tag Selector at the bottom of the document window. Press Cmd-T/Ctrl-T to access the Quick Tag Editor. Insert the cursor between the " (double-quote) and the > (closing bracket). Insert a space and type **spry:detailregion="ds1"**. Press Return/Enter to close the Quick Tag Editor (**Figure 11.3**).

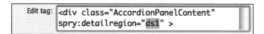
Edit tag: `<div class="AccordionPanelContent" spry:detailregion="ds1" >`

Figure 11.3 The Quick Tag editor provides an easy way to edit essential code components.

22. Save the file. Preview the changes in your browser.

When you click on a book title in the Spry table, the detail region displays the specific data for that item. Notice how the CSS and Javascript behaviors work together to provide a complete interactive experience. Let's add the ordering information to the lower Accordion panel.

23. In Dreamweaver, hover your mouse pointer over the black-shaded row containing the words *Ordering Information*, and an eye icon will appear. Click the eye to reveal the lower content area.

The content panel opens, revealing a table we previously inserted for the project.

24. Insert the cursor in the top row of the table. Insert the `productname` content source from the Bindings panel. Format the line as Heading 2.

25. Insert the `productid` content source in the cell to right of the text: Product #. Format it as Heading 3.

26. Insert the `company` content source in the cell to right of the text: Publisher:. Format it as Heading 3.

27. Insert the cursor in the cell to right of the text: List Price. Type $ (dollar sign) and insert the `price` content source. Format it as Heading 3.

28. Click the `<div.AccordionPanelContent>` tag selector. Press Cmd-T/Ctrl-T to access the Quick Tag Editor. Insert the cursor between the " (double-quote) and the > (closing bracket). Insert a space and type **spry:detailregion="ds1"**. Press Return/Enter to close the Quick Tag Editor.

29. Save the file. Preview the changes in your browser (**Figure 11.4**).

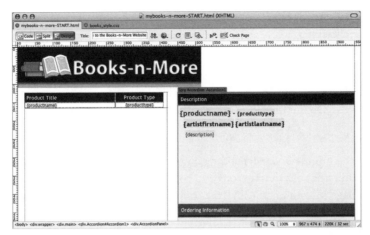

Figure 11.4
The completed elements create an interactive link between the book list and the detail view on the Web page.

Congratulations! You just created your first Ajax application using Dreamweaver's Spry framework tools. To get a full appreciation of the power and flexibility of this technology, check out Dreamweaver CS3's online Help file and the Adobe Labs Web site: http://labs.adobe.com.

Lesson 11-2: Using XSLT on Import

In Lesson 7-9, you learn how to modify an existing XML file to use the data for a different purpose: a pricelist. Although editing the code is easy, it takes time and effort away from the main task of creating the catalog itself. In this lesson, we demonstrate how an XSLT can be used to achieve the same goal without ever touching the original file.

NOTE *This and the other lessons using XSLTs can only be performed by InDesign CS3.*

1. Open **Import-XSLT.indt**.

2. Show the Structure pane, tag markers, and tagged frames.

The document is a template for the book catalog with structures in place for the both the book listings and the pricelist. Note how the pricelist layout uses a parent element named `BKP` and child elements named `Blist`, `format`, `title`, `lastname`, `firstname`, `released`, `sku`, and `srp`. Note how `lastname` appears before the `firstname`. In all these aspects the template differs from the sample in **Chapter 7**.

3. Select the `BK` element in the Structure pane. Import **Books.xml** from the Chapter 11 folder.

   The Import into Selected Element checkbox should be selected by default.

4. Select only the following checkboxes in the XML Import Options dialog and click OK:

    ■ Clone repeating text elements

    ■ Only import elements that match existing structure

    ■ Do not import contents of whitespace-only elements

    ■ Delete elements, frames, and content that does not match imported XML

After a minute or so, depending on the speed of your computer, the layout for book listings fills with descriptions and cover images. No data fills the pricelist placeholder on page 3—and none will, if we continue to use this XML file as is. The reasons should be obvious: An XML file that's compatible to the listings placeholders could not possibly work in the pricelist structure because of the differences in the names and order of the elements. You could duplicate the XML and edit the XML as we did in **Chapter 7**. Or you could use an XSLT to do all the work without even opening the XML file.

5. Select the BKP element in the Structure pane. Import **Books.xml**.

6. Select only the following checkboxes in the XML Import Options dialog:

    ■ Apply XSLT

    ■ Clone repeating text elements

    ■ Only import elements that match existing structure

    ■ Do not import contents of whitespace-only elements

    ■ Delete elements, frames, and content that does not match imported XML

7. Select Choose/Browse from the XSLT pull-down menu (**Figure 11.5**). Open **Pricelist-Import.xslt**.

NOTE *During the import process step 7 activates, a dialog may appear warning about an error, such as "International sorting unavailable..." Ignore the message and click OK to continue importing. We know the dialog appears because we inserted a sort command in the XSLT, but no one could tell us what it means. (It's especially odd seeing how the data is actually sorted in the end result.)*

8. Click OK to import the XML.

    ■ The pricelist fills with descriptions for the books.

    ■ The list is sorted by author.

    ■ The names are listed last name first.

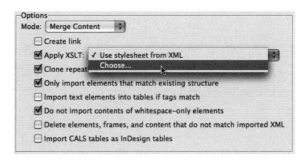

Figure 11.5 An XSLT can be used during import to reformat or restructure an existing XML file to make it compatible even in a workflow for which it was not designed.

NOTE   *Unlike InDesign's XML default workflow, an XSLT is not limited by having to match a file's existing structure and elements. It literally makes up its own rules.*

Will the wonders of XML never cease to amaze us? With the intervention of a simple XSLT you have converted XML designed for one purpose so that it could be used by a completely different structure. To help you understand how this magic came to pass, we dissect the XSLT below.

Deconstruction of Pricelist-Import.xslt

```
<?xml version="1.0" encoding="UTF-8"?>
<!-- The following element defines the version and namespaces for the XSLT
being used. -->
<xsl:stylesheet version="2.0"
xmlns:xsl= "http://www.w3.org/1999/XSL/Transform"
xmlns:xs= "http://www.w3.org/2001/XMLSchema" xmlns:fn="http://www.
w3.org/2005/xpath-functions" xmlns:xdt="http://www.w3.org/2005/xpath-
datatypes">
<!-- The following element defines what type of file will be created from
the XML. -->
<xsl:output method="xml" version="1.0" encoding="UTF-8" indent="yes"/>
<!-- The next element tells InDesign, or the processing application, to
transform the XML starting at the root element. -->
<xsl:template match="/">
<!-- This element creates a new root for the XML data that matches the
structure of the pricelist placeholder. -->
<BKP>
<!-- The next two lines establish the path from which the data will be
accessed and how it will be sorted. The "for-each" statement creates a loop
that repeats the process until all the data contained in the specified
element(s) is (are) transformed. -->
<xsl:for-each select="BK/Book">
        <xsl:sort select="artistlastname"/>
```

```
<!-- The next line creates the parent element Blist. -->
<Blist>
<!–The next three lines create a new child data element called "format" and
fills it with data from the original element "producttype". -->
<format>
                <xsl:value-of select="producttype"/>
</format>
<!-- The following lines create the rest of the data elements for the
book listing and fills them with the appropriate data. Notice that several
elements have not been recreated. By ignoring them in the XSLT the elements
will not appear in the resulting XML at all. -->
<title> <xsl:value-of select="productname"/> </title>
<lastname> <xsl:value-of select="artistlastname"/> </lastname>
<firstname> <xsl:value-of select="artistfirstname"/> </firstname>
<released> <xsl:value-of select="year"/> </released>
<sku> <xsl:value-of select="productid"/> </sku>
<srp> <xsl:value-of select="price"/> </srp>
</Blist>
<!-- The next elements close the loop, the root, the template and the
stylesheet. -->
        </xsl:for-each>
</BKP>
</xsl:template>
</xsl:stylesheet>
```

NOTE *To learn more about XSLT and how to use it, check out the XML reading list at the end of* **Chapter 1**.

In this example, the XSLT renamed the tags from the original XML file and switched the order of the author's first and last names so they could be displayed and formatted as a pricelist in our product catalog. But there's almost no limit to what you can do with well-written XSLT. Some possibilities include:

- Reordering the data elements to create alternate listings focused on price or author rather than title and format.

- Sorting the products by title, author, format, or price.

- Grouping products by author or price, instead of by format.

Lesson 11-3: Using XSLT on Export

Chapter 9 explores several ways to repurpose the content of your InDesign documents to use on the Web or elsewhere. Lesson 9-7 shows how you can get the most out of your print-based documents when exporting the content to the Web. But is all that mucking around in the Structure pane necessary? No, not really. With the right XSLT, you can take the content of almost any document from print to the Web with a few clicks of the mouse.

1. Open **Export-XSLT.indt**.

   The document contains four sections: a product listing and a pricelist for both books and audiobooks.

2. Show the Structure pane, tag markers, and tagged frames.

   The Structure pane shows four sections: BK, BK2, AB, AB2.

Using an XSLT you will export the contents of the book listings to create a Web page display.

3. Select File > Export. Navigate to the Chapter 11 folder. Select XML from the Save as Type pull-down menu and name the file **Booklist.html**. Click Save.

   The Export XML dialog appears.

NOTE *Oddly enough, although you've chosen to export XML, the dialog allows you to add any extension to the filename you desire.*

4. Select the following checkboxes and click OK:

   ■ View XML Using: (*Select your favorite browser here*)

   ■ Remap Break, Whitespace and Special Characters

   ■ Apply XSLT

5. Select Choose/Browse from the XSLT pull-down menu.
   Open **HTML-Export.xslt**.

6. Select the appropriate encoding for your workflow (UTF-8, UTF-16, or Shift-JI5) and click OK to export the XML.

   ■ The browser appears, displaying a three-column table of book titles and author names.

   ■ The list does not display any of the audiobooks.

7. Activate the browser's command for viewing the HTML source code.

The XSLT created this HTML document from scratch using the content and structure of the InDesign catalog. Let's see how it happened.

8. Open **HTML-Export.xslt** in TextEdit/Notepad or your favorite HTML or XML editor. Observe the code elements and structure.

Do you recognize some of the code described in **Pricelist-Import.xslt**? Can you see the basic structural elements of an HTML file, such as the tags for `<head>`, `<body>`, and `<table>`? Do you see how the XSLT command `<xsl:value-of select="producttype"/>` is designed to retrieve the data tagged **producttype** from InDesign and insert it into a table cell `<td>...</td>`? Someone good at writing code can generate almost any type of output from an existing XML file. Let's see how easy it is to modify an XSLT.

9. Copy the code `<th><font color="white">Author</font></th>`. Insert a paragraph return at the end of the line. Paste the code in the blank line.

10. Change `Author` to `Price`.

11. Copy the code `<td><xsl:value-of select="artistlastname"/></td>`. Insert a paragraph return at the end of the line. Paste the duplicate code in the blank line.

12. Change `"artistlastname"` to `"price"` (Watch your case and spelling!). Save the file.

13. Export the catalog content from InDesign to **Booklist.html** as in steps 3 and 4.

    ▪ The browser appears displaying a four-column table.

    ▪ The new column contains the price data.

NOTE *Do you notice that **HTML-Export.xslt** is still selected in the Apply XSLT pull-down menu?*

Basically copying and pasting two lines of code and making some simple text changes in the XSLT easily modifies the resulting display in the browser. Let's see how easy it is to display the data in a different manner.

14. Insert the cursor at the end of `<xsl:for-each select="Inventory/BK/Book">`. Insert a paragraph return.

15. Type `<xsl:sort select="artistlastname" />` and save the file.

16. Export the catalog content from InDesign to **Booklist.html** as in steps 3 and 4.

    The table data is now sorted in alphabetical order based on author last name.

All this is great but there's more than one section in the catalog. Has anyone noticed that we're missing the data from the audiobook section? The HTML displays only book data because of the line in the XSLT that says `<xsl:for-each select="Inventory/BK/Book">`. Because the path statement targets only the **BK/Book** branch of the XML structure, only book data is retrieved. Let's see how the XSLT can get the browser to display all the data.

17. Select all the code from `<xsl:for-each select="Inventory/BK/Book">` to `</xsl:for-each>` in the code (eight lines total). Press Cmd-C/Ctrl-C to copy.

18. Insert the cursor at the end of the line `</xsl:for-each>`. Insert a paragraph return and paste the code into the blank line.

19. In the new code, change `"Inventory/BK/Book"` to `"Inventory/AB/Audiobook"`. Save the file.

20. Export the catalog content from InDesign to **Booklist.html** as in steps 3 and 4.

    The table data now contains book and audiobook data sorted by format and author last name.

Congratulations! You've just scratched the surface of the endless possibilities XSLT offers to your XML workflow.

Keep It Down with XHTML

Throughout the book we make a point to identify any crucial rules that apply to XML or an XML workflow, especially when the violation of such a rule can break the code. In most cases when you're dealing with XML it's painfully obvious when you break the rules: The screen goes blank or displays an error message. At other times, the error isn't be discovered until it's too late.

You may have noticed that in some places we're kind of sloppy how we name our XML elements. For example, we've used mixed-case characters in various tag names, such as **‹BK›**, **‹Book›** and **‹book›**. Because XML allows you to name the elements any way you want, normally this is not a big deal. But you should also be aware that certain workflows require tags be constructed in specific ways, and XHTML is one of those cases.

XHTML is a close cousin of HTML. In fact, it's almost an identical twin except for a handful of differences. For one thing, XHTML tag construction must follow the stricter XML naming rules, *not* the looser HTML ones. And, according to the rules, all tag names used in XHTML must be lowercase, so that they're written like this: **‹html›**, **‹head›**, **‹body›**, **‹h1›**, **‹p›**, and so on.

The problem is that browsers (where XHTML is mostly used) are all very forgiving when it comes to following rules. If you use uppercase or capitalized tags when creating XHTML, you probably won't discover the problem in a browser. In fact, we can't cite a single instance where the *case* of our tags has causes a glitch in any application. But just because something bad hasn't happened yet, doesn't mean it never will.

So, when an XHTML application finally lowers the boom, you can't say we didn't warn you, "Keep those tag names down!" (Lowercase, that is.)

Lesson 11-4: Advanced XSLT

We promised to show you how to create an online newsletter with the XML you exported in **Chapter 9**, and we always keep our promises.

1. Open **January.xml** in TextEdit/Notepad or your favorite HTML or XML editor. Observe the code.

This file should be a duplicate of the one you exported in Lesson 9-5. If you diagrammed its basic parent/child structure, it would look like this (the + indicates more than one element in the file):

```
<GreenStartNews>
    <Events>
    <Toptips>
    <news>+
    <TOC>
    <Issue-id>
    <Greenthumb>
```

2. Load **January.xml** in an XML-compatible browser.

   The raw, unformatted code displays in the browser.

We've created an XSLT that will generate a complete Web page using the XML content exported from the newsletter. The only thing you have to do is to tag the text, frames, and any images with the appropriate elements as shown in Lesson 9-5 and then apply the XSLT. The XSLT can be attached directly to the XML itself using a link reference or applied while InDesign exports the XML. To link the XSLT to the XML file do this:

3. Load **January.xml** in an HTML or XML editor. Insert the cursor at the end of the line `<?xml version="1.0" encoding="UTF-8" standalone="yes"?>` and insert a paragraph return.

4. Type `<?xml-stylesheet type="text/xsl" href="NewsletterFormat.xslt"?>`. Save the file as **myJanuary.xml**.

NOTE *Although this file is saved as *.xml it will still display properly in the browser, because of the transformations performed by the XSLT an .HTM or .HTML extension on the file is not a requirement.*

5. Load **myJanuary.xml** in any browser.

Most current browsers should display a completely formatted Web page. When XML is linked to an external XSLT file—as it is in this example—the transformation takes place entirely in the browser. The XML file is not changed and no permanent HTML file is created. However, that is not the case when the XSLT is applied during the process of exporting XML from InDesign.

6. Open **JanuaryIssue.indt**.

A fully tagged, print-version of the newsletter appears.

It's important to point out that this file is based on the XML template created in Lesson 9-5 and that the text structure was created automatically by mapping tags to styles. Other than applying a few tags to specific text frames by hand to create an XML template, no other adjustments were made to contents of the Structure pane. The power and allure of XSLT is that it doesn't need much help to create its magic.

7. Select File > Export. Select XML from the Save as Type pull-down menu. Name the file **JanNews.html**. Click Save.

The Export XML dialog appears.

8. Enter the settings as shown in **Figure 11.6**. Select **NewsletterFormat.xslt** from the XSLT pull-down menu and click Export.

The browser appears displaying the finished online newsletter.

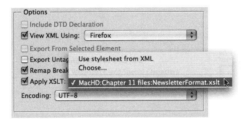

Figure 11.6 Use these settings to export fully transformed XML.

9. Activate the browser's view source command.

Unlike the example created in step 4, the result here is not an XML file linked to an XSLT. Instead, InDesign CS3 has used the XSLT to transform the XML data into a fully realized HTML file. With few or no changes, this same XSLT can be used for every issue of the newsletter going forward to create instant content for your company's Web site. Don't believe us? Try it for yourself:

10. Open **FebruaryIssue.indt**. Repeat steps 7 and 8 to export the content to XML. Name the file **FebNews.html**.

The content of the February issue is recreated in HTML.

One XSLT, two newsletters. Now, if only the print-version of the newsletter could be as easy to create.

Strange Cargo

In the **Chapter 3** sidebar "How Plain Is Plain Enough?" we describe invisible characters that infest XML exported from InDesign. Except for a single line of code we inserted in the XSLT, these strange characters would be plainly visible in the HTML output in this lesson. Don't believe us? Try this: Open **NewsletterFormat.xslt** and locate the code `<meta content="text/html;charset=utf-8" />` and delete it. Export the newsletter content again as in steps 7 and 8. The result will be a newsletter full of weirdness (**Figure 11.7**). You can eliminate the characters by opening and saving such files as plain text described in the sidebar referenced above, or simply leave the line of code in the XSLT! We vote for method #2. In fact, jot the code down and make sure you add it to your own XSLT files before you export XML from InDesign. In any situations where these characters still appear in a browser, remember you can always open the file in TextEdit or Notepad and save them as plain text, as the aforementioned sidebar describes.

> through the entire summer. Weâ€™ve got lots of tasks to accomplish before September, so the callâ€™s going out for as many volunteers as we can get. If last yearâ€™s any example,

Figure 11.7 A former typesetter identified these characters as typesetter mark-up for special characters, paragraph breaks, tabs, and other spacing.

Review

As you can plainly see from **Chapter 11**, InDesign's XML export features open up a world of possibilities for repurposing your print-based content to a host of new Web and data applications, limited only by your imagination.

In this chapter you learned:

- How to use Ajax and InDesign XML to create interactive Web pages

- How to use XSL to style InDesign XML for the Web

- How and why to use an XSLT to import XML in InDesign

- How and why to use an XSLT to export XML from InDesign

12

What's up, DocBook (and Other DTDs)

Chapter Objectives

In this chapter you will learn:

- What standards-based XML is

- What DocBook and other DTDs are

- How to create valid XML structures in InDesign

At the end of the 19th century when Thomas Edison and others were electrifying the world for the first time, there were no standards restricting the design and manufacturing of electrical devices. Everything was custom made, from generators to motors, from outlets to switches. In many neighborhoods the air overhead was a rat's nest of crisscrossing wires from competing electric companies. Even the light bulbs of the day were custom made and could not be used in a competitor's equipment.

This situation eventually changed as consumers and government regulation forced the electric companies to conform their products to a limited number of formats. Standardization increased competition, lowered the cost of electrification, and made possible the modern world we now enjoy. Standards surround us on a daily basis; they're everywhere. Even the simple nuts, bolts, nails, and screws that hold together everything you own—from your house to your car to your computer (Mac or Windows)—are manufactured to exacting standards which, if not met, cause the product to be rejected.

Likewise there is a need for standards-based XML within the communities of publishers, manufacturers, and even government agencies. One reason is simply to make it easier to move the content of books and manuals from print to the Web. Other reasons include accessibility technologies that connect book content to Braille devices and document readers for those individuals with limited vision or other disabilities. The problem is in the nature of XML itself: If XML can literally be *anything* you want it to be, how do you share it with other individuals, companies, or applications?

One way would be to create an eXtensible Stylesheet Language Transformation (XSLT) to translate XML from one format to another. It's a method that's used every day around the world, but it takes time and expertise not commonly available in every company. Instead, why not just build similar or compatible XML in the first place by using a standard structure and set of elements?

There are two basic methods for building standard XML: Document Type Definitions (DTD) and Schemas. They both allow you specify, in advance, the allowable elements and structure of a standards-compliant XML file. Written in a different language with its own structure and syntax, DTDs have been around longer and have widespread acceptance in most industries. Developed specifically for XML, Schemas on the other hand bring some new tricks to the game. For example, in addition to name and order, Schemas can also specify the *type* and *format* of the data contained in XML elements.

Unlike a DTD, a Schema can specify that an element, say `<startdate>`, must contain date or time data and that the information must appear in the following format: `<startdate>03-01-2008</startdate>`. If you enter the date any other way, the element is just as broken as it would be if you spelled the tag name incorrectly or inserted it out of order. As you might guess, this capability has made Schemas more popular in XML applications that deal with numeric data.

Although the industry trend is heavily favoring Schemas, the DTD still reigns supreme for text-centric applications such as book publishing and technical manuals—and in InDesign itself. Currently InDesign has built-in support only for DTD-based structures. We hope the support extends to Schemas in the next version of InDesign, but for the purpose of this chapter we focus exclusively on how to work with DTDs.

NOTE *Download all applicable files for Chapter 12 from www.peachpit.com/indesignxmlguide and copy them to a folder on your hard drive (approximately 1 MB).*

Lesson 12-1: Interpreting DTD Rules

The first step in building or formatting a DTD-compliant structure is figuring out what elements are allowed in the document and what order they can occupy. Unfortunately, we know of no shortcuts for creating valid structures from scratch; you just have to learn how to read and interpret DTD rules (or hire someone who does).

1. Open **docbook.dtd** in your favorite HTML or XML editor. Observe the code.

NOTE *Because of the structure of the DTD, you'll want to use an HTML or XML editor for the lesson. TextEdit and Notepad won't be able to handle the task this time.*

What you're looking at is an older, simplified version of the DocBook DTD that has been compiled into a single file. The current version of the DocBook DTD (v4.5) actually consists of more than a dozen separate interlinked files. It's intended for use on the Internet and requires a live connection to the Web for validation. If your computer's not online while you are working with the full version of the DTD, InDesign will not be able to validate your structure at all. The specifications for version 5 of DocBook were published in September 2007 and were in beta testing at the time of this publication.

The DocBook DTD is designed for publishers of books and technical manuals. The DTD defines a common set of elements and structures that are allowed in compliant XML. It has been around for years and has evolved to be able to support the needs of the diverse publishing industry. You might wonder how a single set of rules could possibly anticipate and accommodate the disparate needs of multiple publishers, but at over 4,000 lines of code, DocBook somehow finds a balance between order and flexibility.

For the purposes of this lesson we are using this single-file version simply to illustrate the proper way to read and interpret DTD rules. InDesign's built-in validation feature can help you build and test simple structures, but we highly recommend that you purchase an XML editor that provides strong validation capabilities to work with complex DTDs like DocBook. (In **Chapter 2**, we describe two great candidates, Altova XMLSpy and SyncRo <oXygen/>.) The current version of the DTD can be found in the DocBook folder of the Chapter 12 resource folder or downloaded from www.docbook.org.

2. Activate the program's Find command. Type **!ELEMENT book** into the "Find what" field. Click Find.

The **book** element is highlighted in the code.

```
<!ELEMENT book (((title | titleabbrev | subtitle)*, info?), (glossary |
bibliography | index | toc | dedication | preface | chapter | appendix |
article | colophon | part | reference)+)>
```

The code printed in the paragraph above is the complete <book> element rule from the DTD. As you already know, all XML files must have a root element and the first task of the DTD is to name the elements allowed within the structure. Although more than 350 *legal* elements are declared by the DocBook DTD, only a handful of them can be used as a document root. One way to know that an element is a root candidate is when it can contain other parent elements.

For example, one of the highest-level elements in the DocBook DTD is called <set>. This element can hold one or more <book> elements, but no other element may contain a <set> (except another set). The <book> element is second highest in the DTD for the same reason.

Sometimes it helps to diagram a rule to understand what it says. Refer back to "Reading DTD" in **Chapter 1**, if necessary, to help you parse out the structure of the book element. Here's our best attempt:

```
element-name ( ( (elements listed here may appear zero or multiple times in
any order)*, mandatory-position/optional-element?), (these elements must follow
after items in previous list but within may appear one or more times in any
order in their own list, for book to be valid at least one element from this
list must be used)+)
```

Two keys things to remember when you read any DTD: The , (comma) indicates that both the element and its position are *mandatory*, whereas the | (pipe) indicates that both the element and its position are *optional*. The * asterisk means that zero or more elements can be used. The + (plus) means one or more elements can be used. To help illustrate what constructions are legal and illegal, we offer some sample structures in **Table 12.1**. By parsing the DTD rule for the <book> element, can you figure out why each of these samples either make or break the grade?

Table 12.1 *Sample XML Structures*

COMPLIANT (LEGAL) STRUCTURES	NON-COMPLIANT (ILLEGAL) STRUCTURES
<book><title>..</title> <part>..</part></book>	<book><part>..</part> <title>..</title></book>
<book><toc>..</toc> <chapter>..</chapter> <chapter>..</chapter></book>	<book><info>..</info> <title>..</title></book>
<book><article>..</article> <index>..</index><book/>	<book> <book>..</book></book>

DTD structure troubleshooting tips:

- Are you using legal elements?

- Are your elements in the correct/allowable order?

- Are your elements nested properly?

- Are you using the correct/allowable number of elements?

Lesson 12-2: Creating DocBook-compatible Structures

There are several ways to create a DTD-compliant structure. One method is to create the structure first and add the content later.

NOTE *During this lesson you will switch between your HTML or XML editor and InDesign.*

1. Launch InDesign. Create a new letter-sized document.

2. Select Load DTD from the Tags panel or Structure pane menu.

3. Select **docbook.dtd** and click Open.

- The Tags panel fills with all the DocBook-legal tag names.

- A DOCTYPE title element appears in the Structure pane.

InDesign automatically selects the first element within the DTD to use as the root. Although many DTDs list the root element first, this is not the case with DocBook. In fact, DocBook offers several elements that can be used as the root, depending on whether the publication is being created all in one file, chapter by chapter, or using some other method of organization. To create a structure based on the element **book**, do this:

4. Select DTD Options from the Structure pane or Tags panel menu.

The DTD Options dialog appears.

5. Select book from the "Validate from" pull-down menu. Click OK.

The DOCTYPE element now displays a target root element of **book**.

A compliant structure starts with the root element.

6. Select Root in the Structure pane. Click book in the Tags panel.

The Root element is renamed **book**.

According to the **book** element observed in Lesson 12-1, there are only 16 *legal* child elements that can be inserted in the root of **book**. Furthermore, the elements **title**, **titleabbrev**, and **subtitle** have precedence over the other 13 and must appear in the structure before any of the other elements, if used at all. Because every book has a title, the **title** element is a good place to start.

7. Select New Element from the Structure pane. Choose title from the Tag pull-down menu. Click OK.

The **title** element appears as a child of **book**.

The **subtitle** element is a peer of **title**. To add it correctly, do it this way:

8. Select the book element in the Structure pane. Select New Element from the Structure pane menu. Choose subtitle from the Tag pull-down menu. Click OK.

The **subtitle** element appears as a second child of **book** and below the position of **title**.

Most books list the author's name along with the title, but **author** is not listed in the rule as a legal child of **book**. To find out how you can add **author** correctly will take some detective work.

9. Switch to your HTML or XML editor. Search for Element author in the DTD.

The DTD displays the following rule:

```
<!ELEMENT author ((personname, (personblurb | affiliation | email | address | contrib)*) | (orgname, (orgdiv | affiliation | email | address | contrib)*))>
```

This rule defines how the author's name must be structured, but it doesn't tell us in which of the 16 child **book** elements **author** may appear.

10. Search for author in the DTD. Select the dialog's "match whole word" checkbox. Keep searching until you find all the elements in which author may appear.

Amazingly, you'll find that **author** is a legal child element of over 60 other elements, including: **title**, **titleabbrev, subtitle**, and **info**. Instead of creating 60 unique author-type elements to perform 60 different jobs, the DTD uses the same element 60 different ways.

This means you don't have to create a tag that says <titleauthor>, you simply insert <author> within the <title> element, such as <title> <author>..</author> </title>. By using one element in this way, you create a unique meaning for it *in context*. In other words, by inserting the <author> element within <title> it's like saying that the person identified is the *author* of the *title*.

Being able to use existing elements in multiple ways reduces the total number of elements you need to create any needed structure. This flexibility is the reason why the DocBook DTD can meet the needs of multiple book publishers.

Let's add an **author** element to the book, using **info** as its parent.

11. In InDesign, select the book element in the Structure pane. Add info as a new element.

12. Select the info element in the Structure pane. Add author.

The **author** element appears as a child of **info**.

According to the **author** rule, you can't insert a name here. Let's look at one possible construction.

13. Select author. Add personname.

14. Select personname and add firstname.

- The **firstname** element appears as a child of **personname**.

- Note how the **personname** element is still selected within the Structure pane.

15. Add surname (**Figure 12.1**).

- The **surname** element appears as a child of **personname** and below **firstname**.

- The **author** element is complete.

Figure 12.1 It takes a little detective work to figure out how to put together compatible elements.

16. Click the "Validate structure using current DTD" button in the upper left of the Structure pane. Observe the error message that appears at the bottom of the Structure pane.

When you click the Validate button, the Structure pane splits into two separate sections. The top contains the structure, and the bottom shows the validation errors. The dividing line between the two sections can be dragged up or down to display more of one section other the other.

The error message currently displayed indicates that a required element is missing (**Figure 12.2**). This message may be somewhat confusing to those new to DTD grammar. Didn't the **book** rule say that none of the elements was mandatory? Yes, but the + (plus) sign at the end of the second element group indicates that at least *one* of the following elements must appear in its structure for it to be valid: **glossary**, **bibliography**, **index**, **toc**, **dedication**, **preface**, **chapter**, **appendix**, **article**, **colophon**, **part**, or **reference**. Take your pick. Our choice is **chapter**. The **chapter** element is added as a peer, or sibling, of **title**, **subtitle**, and **info**.

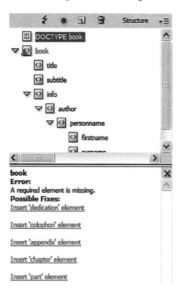

Figure 12.2 InDesign tries its best to suggest fixes for the validation error, but a good XML editor is vital for creating compliant structures.

17. Select book and in the Structure pane add chapter as a new element.

Until you understand how to build compliant structures you'll spend a lot of time in the DTD.

18. Switch to your HTML/XML editor and search for Element chapter.

The **chapter** element is vastly more complex than the others you have used so far. To start with, it lists almost 80 legal content elements and more than a dozen sub-element content models. Luckily, InDesign can help us decipher the DTD rule, as well as fix problems that we encounter.

19. In InDesign, click the "Validate structure using current DTD" button. Observe the error message in the Structure pane.

According to the error message, the structure is missing a required element. Do you see the list of possible fixes following the error message?

20. Find `Insert 'para' element` in the list of possible fixes and click it.

The **para** element appears as a child element of **chapter** in the Structure pane.

21. Re-validate the structure.

The message "No known errors" appears in the Structure pane.

22. Save the file as an InDesign template. Name it **myDocBookStructure.indt**.

Congratulations! Although you're far from finished, you've successfully started a compliant DocBook structure. It's a simple matter now to use this structure for a new publication.

23. Drag the book element from the Structure pane to page 1 of your document.

A text frame appears on the page tagged for the **book** element.

24. Switch to Story Editor (**Figure 12.3**).

Story Editor displays a row of XML tag markers matching the structure of the **book** element.

Figure 12.3 By adding elements to the Structure pane you can easily assemble the DTD-compliant elements.

25. Insert the cursor between the title tag markers. Type **The Designer's Guide to Adobe InDesign and XML**.

26. Insert the cursor between the subtitle tag markers. Type **Harness The Power of XML to Automate your Print and Web Workflows**.

And that's all there is to it.

Lesson 12-3: Using Pre-Built DTD Structures

If you're going to be working with DTDs on a regular basis, building the structures from scratch ends up being a giant black hole sucking up all your free time. One method of saving you from all this tedium is to create the compliant structures in advance and simply import them as you need them. To show you how this can be done, we created three DocBook-compliant sub-structures for the **book**, **chapter**, and **glossary** elements and saved them as individual XML files.

1. Create a new, letter-sized document.

2. Load **docbook.dtd**. Select DTD Options from the Structure pane or Tags panel menu. Select book from the "Validate from" pull-down menu. Click OK.

   The DOCTYPE element displays **book** as the validation target.

3. Select Import XML. Select **BookSTART.xml** from the Chapter 12 folder. Click Open. In the XML Import Options dialog, deselect all checkboxes. Click OK.

   - The Structure pane fills with some basic elements for the **book** structure.

   - The Root element changes to **book**.

4. Select the book element in the Structure pane. Import **ChapterSTART.xml** from the Chapter 12 folder. In the XML Import Options dialog, deselect all checkboxes and choose Append Content from the Mode pull-down menu. Click OK.

   A new, completely formed **chapter** node has been added to the **book** structure after **title** and **subtitle**.

   NOTE *As long as all checkboxes are deselected you can use either Merge or Append Content in the dialog—the result is the same.*

To add new chapters to the book, simply import **ChapterSTART.xml** to insert them in the structure. You can use this method to add other elements too.

5. Select the book element in the Structure pane. Import **GlosarySTART.xml** from the Chapter 12 folder. In the XML Import Options dialog deselect all checkboxes and choose Append Content from the Mode pull-down menu. Click OK.

   A new, completely formed **glossary** node has been added at the end of the **book** structure.

6. Click the "Validate structure using current DTD" button.

   The structure is error-free.

Congratulations! You just created the framework for a DocBook-compliant document. The only thing left to do is write the book!

Lesson 12-4: Making Existing Documents DTD Compliant

Creating a compliant structure from scratch is always the best plan, but what can you do for all those unstructured documents sitting on your hard drive? Adding compliant structures to such documents presents some interesting challenges, depending on what DTD you are trying to match. Luckily for us, InDesign has some powerful tools for creating valid structures quickly and easily.

1. Open **SampleBook.indt**.

This document is a small portion of the book *The Brothers Karamazov* by Fyodor Dostoevsky. It was printed in Russia in serial form in the 1870s and translated into English as a single work in 1879 by Constance Garnett, who translated several works of Dostoevsky and other notable Russian authors.

Although DocBook was not developed for structuring novels, this sample offers some interesting challenges to show you how to adapt a particular DTD to an existing document.

The first thing you need to do is to identify the existing organizational framework that might assist you in structuring the content. In the case of this book, it's divided into multiple sections called parts, books, and chapters, which ideally would be structured like this:

```
<book>
    <part>
        <book>
            <chapter>
            <chapter…>
    <part>
        <book>
            <chapter>
            <chapter…>
```

Unfortunately, one glance tells you that DocBook won't support that kind of structure. For example, a **book** element can contain both **part** and **chapter** elements, but it can't contain other **book** elements. Similarly, **part** elements can contain **chapter** elements, but not **book** elements. To build a compliant structure, you have to use a little creativity and adapt to the circumstances. For this document the **set** element holds the secret for a successful structure. Not only can it hold all the elements we already mentioned, it can hold other **set** elements as well!

2. Load **docbook.dtd**. Select DTD Options from the Tags panel menu. Select set from the "Validate from" pull-down menu. Click OK.

   ■ The tags available in the DTD appear in the Tags panel.

   ■ The DOCTYPE declaration in the Structure pane displays the **set** element.

3. Select Map Styles to Tags from the Tags panel or Structure pane menu. Map the Styles as specified in the following list and click OK:

Body Text	para
Book Section Subtitle	subtitle
Book Subtitle	subtitle
Book Title	title
Byline	personname
Chapter Subtitle	subtitle
Chapter Title	title
Part Title	title
Published Date	pubdate

   ■ The main text frame changes color to indicate that it's tagged for the **Story** element.

   ■ The text itself shows tag markers matching the elements within the DTD.

The text within the book is tagged according to the selections you made within the dialog, but you are far from done. Unfortunately, although the Map Styles to Tags feature tagged the individual elements correctly, it drops the ball when it comes to a complex structure like DocBook. The rest of the work has to be done by hand.

The first issue we need to address is the location of the existing content. Because the text was already in place before you applied the XML structure, it appears within a **Story** element, which was created automatically by InDesign. We could retag this element with the **set** tag, but doing so would complicate the structure unnecessarily. So, instead, we're going move the content from the **Story** element to the existing root element.

4. Insert the Text cursor anywhere in the Story frame. Press Cmd-A/Ctrl-A to select all. Press Cmd-X/Ctrl-X to cut the text.

   All the content is removed from the linked text frames.

5. Select the Root element in the Structure pane and retag it as set.

6. Drag the set element from the Structure pane to any of the linked text frames.

   ■ The linked frames are retagged as **set**.

   ■ The **Story** element disappears from the Structure pane.

7. Insert the Text cursor into any of the linked text frames. Press Cmd-V/Ctrl-V to paste all the text.

   The text reappears in the frames, fully tagged and formatted.

The following steps will result in a fully compliant DocBook structure when you're finished, but don't think there's any magic in the order in which the tagging is applied. Feel free to experiment and develop your own techniques. As long as the structure is compliant when you're finished, that's all that matters. Although retagging can be done in the Layout, Structure pane, or Story Editor, you'll find the job hardest and most problematic in the Layout itself—the tag markers are just too difficult to see and identify.

8. Select the first personname in the Structure pane. Select the Add Tag radio button in the Tags panel. Click author in the Tags list.

   The **personname** element is inserted into a new **author** element.

9. Select **Fyodor** and tag it as firstname.

10. Select **Mikhailovich** and tag it as othername.

11. Select **Dostoevsky** and tag it as surname.

12. Select the second personname in the Structure pane. Select the Add Tag radio button in the Tags panel. Click othercredit in the Tags list.

13. Select **Constance** and tag it as firstname.

14. Select **Garnett** and tag it as surname.

15. Select the author, othercredit, and pubdate elements. Select the Add Tag radio button and click info in the Tags list.

    All three elements are inserted into a new **info** element.

16. Select the title, subtitle, and three para elements of Chapter 1. Select the Add Tag radio button and click chapter in the Tags list.

17. Repeat step 11 with all the remaining chapters.

18. Select the title and all the chapter elements for Book I. Select the Add Tag radio button and click book in the Tags list (**Figure 12.4**).

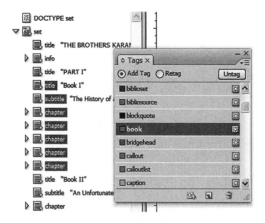

Figure 12.4 There's no magic to creating a compliant structure, just a lot of tedious work in the Structure pane and Tags panel.

19. Repeat step 13 for Book II.

20. Select the Part I title and both book elements. Select the Add Tag radio button and click set in the Tags list.

That's it—the structure is complete. Let's validate it against the DTD.

21. Click the "Validate structure using current DTD" button.

The Structure pane shows no errors. You've created a fully compliant DocBook structure that's ready to be exported to XML.

Review

As you can see from the previous lesson, the hardest part of creating compliant structures is simply interpreting the DTD rules themselves. But the benefits of building standards-based XML can't be underestimated. DTDs have already been created for many industries and workflows to help exchange data and comply with government standards. Before you set off to create your own XML standard, you may want look to what already exists. You may find a DTD that meets your needs perfectly. Check the following link for more information: http://xml.coverpages.org/xmlApplications.html.

In this chapter you learned:

■ What standards-based XML is

■ What DocBook and other DTDs are

■ How to create valid XML structures in InDesign

Index

& (ampersand), 8
braces (braces), 278
• (bullet), 8
: (colons), 272
, (comma), 17, 300
© (copyright symbol), 8
" " (double quotes), 7, 13, 261
= (equal sign), 261
/ (forward slash), 6
> (greater than), 8
< > (left and right angle brackets), 1
< (less than), 8
( ) (parentheses), 17
| (pipe symbol), 17, 300
+ (plus sign)
  multiple element indicator for DTDs, 300, 304
  override symbol, 228
  as overset symbol, 216
  used in schemas, 283
™ (registered trademark), 8
; (semicolons), 272, 278
' ' (single quotes), 7

A

about this book, x-xii
absolute paths, 161–162
Access
  creating nested XML sub-structures in, 219–222
  importing data to InDesign, xi
  making XML files in, 85–88
Add Tag radio button (Tags panel), 59
Adobe Dreamweaver. *See* Dreamweaver
Adobe InCopy. *See* InCopy
Adobe InDesign. *See* InDesign
Adobe Labs Web site, 287

Ajax (Asynchronous Javascript and XML)
  about, 281–282
  creating instant Web pages with, 282–287
  further study for, 287
  using XML with, 281–282
ampersand (&), 8
Anchored Object Options dialog, 165, 166
anchored objects, 141–156. *See also* frames; inline objects
  anchored frames vs. inline graphics, 200
  cloning, 148–151
  converting from inline to, 228–229
  correcting bugs in anchored frames, 146
  dropping parent icon on linked text frames, 146, 324
  flowing text into anchored frames, 158–160
  identifying in Story Editor, 58
  inline anchored objects, 58, 165, 166
  merging layout with data, 142–143
  overview, 141, 156
  as target for tags, 151
  text flow into multisection layout, 144–147
  using Object styles to prevent shifting, 169–170, 324
Apply to entire document? dialog (Word), 76
Assignment Available icon (InCopy), 62
assignments, 62–63

Asynchronous Javascript and XML. *See* Ajax
atlas, 157–178
  anchoring graphics for, 165–168
  creating code references for graphics, 160–163, 164
  fixing graphics reference typos in, 176–177
  flowing text into anchored frames, 158–160
  formatting elements with nested styles, 172–173
  making styles for elements in, 173–174
  mapping tags to Paragraph styles, 174–175
  setting up structured layout for, 163–164
  testing template for, 175
  troubleshooting structure of, 176
attribute types key for DTDs, 18
attributes
  collapsing, 29
  editing, 164
  expanding, 28
  placing values in quotes, 13
  showing in Structure pane, 27
  swapping class, 266–267
  XML syntax for, 7
autoflowing layout, 108–110. *See also* flowing text
automating XML tagging, 246–251

B

background frames, 168
Berners-Lee, Tim, 3
blank lines. *See also* white space
  added with Map Styles to Tags command, 249
  inserted with root elements, 234

F

File menu, 24
FileMaker Pro, 81–85
  creating XML in, 81–83
  entering data into, 83–84
  exporting XML from, 84–85
files. *See also* .TXT files
  .gif, 258
  JPEG, 236, 258
  opening XML in InCopy, 63
  reimporting to correct frame
      creep, 147, 324
  saving in Word as XML, 77–78
  support site for sample, 23
  template, 100
  using multiple XML, 183–185,
      210–211
Find/Replace command
  creating sub-structures with,
      221–222
  finding and replacing tags,
      195–197
  reconstructing exported XML
      tags with, 261, 267–268
floating frames, 130–131, 138–139
flowing text
  applying tags to anchored frames
      before, 226, 324
  in business card layout, 108–110
  into anchored frames, 158–160
  recipes into cookbook layout,
      144–147
  to text frame of direct mail
      postcards, 214–217
_fmt filename appendage, 258
formatting. *See also* CSS; XSLT
  adding via external style
      sheets, 266
  cookbook structure, 151–153
  errors using, 153–154
  HTML with tags, 270–271
  images when exporting, 265
  preserving tagged element's
      paragraph, 123–125
  template's Paragraph styles, 209

XML content with styles, 49
forward slash (/), 6
frames
  checking icons for specific
      anchored, 227
  converting placeholders to
      anchored, 229–230, 232–233
  creating placeholders in
      anchored, 224–226
  deleting empty, 191–193
  dropping parent icon on linked
      text, 146, 324
  fixing incorrectly tagged
      text, 122
  floating, 130–131, 138–139
  flowing text into anchored,
      158–160
  optimizing XML layouts,
      243–246
  reapplying Object styles to
      position anchored, 217
  reimporting files to correct
      frame creep, 147, 324
  removing tags from linked, 42
  setting up nesting structures for
      anchored, 221–222
  tagged anchored, 142
  using master text, 147, 148, 163
  working with background, 168
free-floating objects, 168
further study
  Ajax, 287
  books on XML, 21
  CSS books, 280
  XSLT, 290

G

.gif files, 258
GML (Generalized Markup
      Language), 2–3
grammar of DTDs, 16–18
graphics
  anchoring inline, 165–168
  applying tags to, 40
  background frames for, 168

creating XML code references for
      imported, 160–163, 164
CSS code for adding, 277–278
identifying graphic elements,
      45–46
importing into XML structure,
      164
solving problems in reference
      typos to, 176–177
untagging, 41–42

H

hard returns
  Mac and PC keys for, 149
  XML and, 68, 118, 121, 324
HTML (Hypertext Markup
      Language)
  about, 2, 3
  adding styles via external style
      sheets, 266
  CSS for formatting and
      structuring, 274–280
  dealing with graphics in, 160,
      161
  defined, 9
  disadvantages of copying and
      pasting XML to, 237
  distinguishing tags for XML
      and, 14
  editing in Dreamweaver, 269
  exporting XML content to,
      255–268
  formatting with tags, 270–271
  inserting <div> tags in exported
      XML, 240, 262–263
  punctuation in, 272
  reconstructing exported XML
      tags with Find/Replace, 261,
      267–268
  sample of, 4
  structuring exported XML with
      declarations and tags for,
      257–258
  styling with CSS, 272
  supported in Dreamweaver, 89

Know the Rules and Don't Break Them!

XML works great as long as you follow the *rules*. Make a small mistake in print or Web design and you often don't notice until the project has been finished and is "in the can." But an XML workflow is different. Make a single mistake, even a simple one, and the whole thing crashes. We've already discovered the hard way what will break your code and your project and compiled a simple list of 15 XML rules for designers. You'll find them sprinkled throughout the book, but here they are together to make them easier to remember and follow!

Designer's XML Rule #1 XML only allows elements to be used once in each layout.

Designer's XML Rule #2 Use a root element when you want to flow multiple records.

Designer's XML Rule #3 Tag names created in InDesign must match exactly those from the XML file. No exceptions.

Designer's XML Rule #4 Always insert a hard return after the last element of any dynamic, structured layout.

Designer's XML Rule #5 Do not tag spaces, tabs, and hard returns unless you want the XML to replace them.

Designer's XML Rule #6 For some reason InDesign won't clone the formatting on some tagged elements. For example, the first line of card two may pick up the formatting from the last line of card one. To keep this from happening and to preserve the desired formatting, always map the tags to the styles.

Designer's XML Rule #7 Select Merge Content to replace all existing placeholder text. Select Append Content to insert additional records.

Designer's XML Rule #8 You can drop an XML parent icon on any linked text frame in a multipage structured document. Note: An anchored frame is *not* linked to the structured flow. Therefore you can't use it to flow additional records.

Designer's XML Rule #9 Re-import the same XML file with the identical settings to correct frame creep (CS2 only).

Designer's XML Rule #10 Text to be cloned must be outside of any tagged placeholder element. Remember, items within the tags—such as the placeholder text—are completely replaced by the imported XML content.

Designer's XML Rule #11 If the structure is faulty in any way, the cloning and formatting process will fail, partially or entirely.

Designer's XML Rule #12 Format all anchored objects with Object styles to prevent shifting and to ensure consistent positioning during cloning.

Designer's XML Rule #13 A master place-holder must contain all elements desired in the final document structure.

Designer's XML Rule #14 A tag must be applied to an anchored frame before content can flow into it.

Designer's XML Rule #15 Don't format text you want to remain untagged using Paragraph or Character styles mapped to XML tags or even ones based on styles that are mapped.

We hope this list is helpful. If you discover some *rules* of your own, let us know and we'll add them to the list. Good Luck!